BRITAIN AND THE PROBLEM OF INTERNATIONAL DISARMAMENT

In the aftermath of the Great War, multilateral disarmament was placed at the top of the international agenda by the Treaty of Versailles and the Covenant of the League of Nations. This study analyses the naval, air and land disarmament policies of successive British governments from 1919 to 1934, articulating their dilemma either to fulfil their obligations or to avoid them. Drawing from a vast array of sources such as public record documents, official archives, personal papers, memoirs and autobiographies of key political figures, Dr Carolyn Kitching presents an exhaustive research on the repeated attempts of British government officials to evade the obligations assumed in 1919.

Daring and controversial, the present study challenges the hitherto accepted view that Britain occupied the high moral ground by drastically reducing its armaments and argues that, during this period, British disarmament policy was reactive and generally failed to provide the leadership that this extremely sensitive time in international politics demanded. The author provides a very balanced and thoroughly examined view of British policy in a global context, evaluating its relationship with other European governments and highlighting the contribution of the League of Nations in the context of postwar international politics. Her clear focus and informed conclusions provide valuable insights which have direct application to the present debate on disarmament and arms control.

This work will appeal to both international and military historians and political scientists concerned with foreign policy and the problems of conflict prevention and resolution.

Dr Carolyn J. Kitching is a Lecturer in International Relations at the University of Teesside. Her specialist fields are disarmament and the United Nations.

ROUTLEDGE STUDIES IN MODERN EUROPEAN HISTORY

BRITAIN AND THE PROBLEM OF INTERNATIONAL DISARMAMENT

1919–34

Carolyn J. Kitching

London and New York

First published 1999
by Routledge
11 New Fetter Lane, London EC4P 4EE

Simultaneously published in the USA and Canada
by Routledge
29 West 35th Street, New York, NY 10001
© 1999 Carolyn J. Kitching

Typeset in Garamond by Routledge
Printed and bound in Great Britain by TJ International Ltd, Padstow, Cornwall

British Library Cataloguing in Publication Data
A catalogue record for this book is available from the British Library

Library of Congress Cataloging in Publication Data
Kitching, Carolyn, 1947–
Britain and the problem of international disarmament, 1919–34 / Carolyn
Kitching.
p. cm. – (Routledge studies in modern European history; 3)
Includes bibliographical references and index.
1. Disarmament–History. 2. Great Britain–Military policy. 3. Great
Britain–Foreign relations–1910–1936. I. Title. II. Series.
JZ5625.K58 1999
327.1'74'0941–dc21
98–23385
CIP

ISBN 0–415–18199–2

IN MEMORY OF DR DICK RICHARDSON

CONTENTS

ACKNOWLEDGEMENTS

I gratefully acknowledge the assistance of individuals and institutions who facilitated my research and helped in the production of this study. In particular I am indebted to the following who gave permission to read or quote from the unpublished private papers listed in the bibliography: the University of Birmingham Library, the British Museum, the Brotherton Library, University of Leeds, Cambridge University Library, the Churchill Archive Centre, Cambridge University, Mr Richard Leach, for access to biographical notes on his grandfather, William, The House of Lords' Record Office, Middlesbrough Central Library, the Public Record Office and Salop County Record Office.

Special thanks are reserved for the late Dr Dick Richardson, University of Teesside, for his patient supervision and guidance, Professor David Dilks, University of Hull, for his encouragement and support and Dr David Whittaker, University of Teesside, for his gallant proof-reading.

Last, but by no means least, I am indebted to my husband and sons, without whose patience and tolerance the work could never have been completed.

1

INTRODUCTION

Britain's approach to the problem of international disarmament during the period between the two world wars has received very little attention compared with the amount of research carried out on British foreign policy in general. The importance of the subject has, in the main, been overlooked by those who have attempted to explain the breakdown in international relations which resulted in the Second World War. Yet the disarmament question is a significant factor in this breakdown, being closely inter-linked with the search for security and stability which were so notably absent during the period. The present study seeks to redress this imbalance in the historical literature by analysing Britain's attitude towards disarmament in the crucial years 1919–34.

The majority of studies of international disarmament between the two world wars have covered either specific conferences or issues or shorter time periods than that covered in the present study. These include Dick Richardson's study of the 1924–9 Baldwin administration, *The Evolution of British Disarmament Policy in the 1920s* (1989), Brian McKercher's study of the same period, *The Second Baldwin Government and the United States, 1924–1929* (1984) and an analysis entitled *The Washington Conference, 1921–22*, edited by Erik Goldstein and John Maurer (1994). Christopher Hall's *Britain, America and Arms Control, 1921–37* (1987) basically covers the naval disarmament question. As regards older works, John Wheeler-Bennett published two studies covering the disarmament and security questions, *Information on the Reduction of Armaments* (1925) and *Disarmament and Security Since Locarno, 1925–1931* (1932). He also published two books on disarmament *per se*. One, entitled *Information on the Problem of Security (1917–1926)* was co-edited with F.E. Langermann in 1927, while the other, an in-depth study of the World Disarmament Conference of 1932–4, *The Pipe Dream of Peace*, was published in 1935. These studies are all very thorough, but are dated and suffer from Wheeler-Bennett's marked anti-French, pro-German bias. Other studies of the World Disarmament Conference are Dick Richardson's unpublished MA thesis entitled *The Problem of Disarmament in British Diplomacy, 1932–1934* (1969), and John Underwood's unpublished Ph.D. thesis entitled *The Roots and Reality of British Disarmament Policy 1932–34* (1977). More recently, in 1995 and 1993 respectively, there have been articles in edited volumes by Dick Richardson on 'The Geneva Disarmament Conference, 1932–34', and, jointly with the author of the present study, on 'Britain and the World Disarmament Conference'.[1] Another recent work, *The Quest for Stability: Problems of West European Security 1918–1957*, edited by Ahmann, Birke and Howard in 1993, contains important articles by Zara Steiner on 'The League of Nations and the Quest for Security', and Philip Towle on 'British Security and Disarmament Policy in Europe in the 1920s'.[2] A volume edited by Brian McKercher in 1992 entitled *Arms Limitation and Disarmament: Restraints on War, 1899–1939*, also contains articles on specific disarmament conferences and related issues.[3]

There have been significantly fewer studies of British disarmament policy over the full period covered by the present work. Rolland Chaput produced a study in 1935, entitled *Disarmament in British Foreign Policy*, and in 1980 David Shorney wrote a Ph.D. thesis entitled *Britain and Disarmament 1916–1931*, which also examined disarmament policy in relation to foreign policy, as well as looking at the effects of party politics and public opinion on the formulation of disarmament policy. The latter study ended prior to the commencement of the Disarmament Conference. Thus only Chaput covers the whole of the period presently under review and whil he had the irreplaceable benefits of contacts with both observers and policy-makers, he did not have the benefit of access to government records or the private papers of members of the policy-making élite. Moreover, like Wheeler-Bennett's works, it is dated.

Chaput's terms of reference were to encompass 'the attitude and policy of the British government throughout the various negotiations for naval, military and air disarmament' in an attempt to answer the question '[w]hat is the position of Great Britain on disarmament and what role does it play in the scheme of British foreign policy?'[4] In reaching an answer to his question he concluded that:

> the British Government proceeded along the path of disarmament
> so long as this path ran parallel to that of its traditional foreign
> policy. Where these paths diverged, the British Government elected
> to follow the known road to security in preference to the theoretical
> utopia of world brotherhood.[5]

At a very general level, this conclusion mirrors that of the present study. What Chaput was unable to do, however, because of the limited sources upon which he was able to call, was to analyse the intricacies of discussions surrounding the evolution of disarmament policy within the confines of the Cabinet room and the corridors of power within Whitehall. Moreover, the framework of his approach meant he was unable to make effective comparisons between successive governments. Thus, not only is his study dated, it is methodologically and analytically limited. In addition, contrary to Chaput's view that disarmament was successfully integrated into British foreign and security policy during the period under review, it remained very much a separate problem, and as such was handled in very different ways by the individual governments of the period. This often resulted in a confused approach to the problem. As the present study will show, the Conservative-dominated administrations effectively had no disarmament policy at all; or rather, they attempted to ignore a subject which they demonstrably failed to understand. In contrast, the two minority Labour governments at least tried to define a distinct disarmament policy, though their success in its implementation was necessarily hampered by their tenuous hold on power as well as by internal differences of opinion.

Differences of opinion on the question of the term 'disarmament' as well as on methods of its implementation are a theme that runs through the present study. A brief analysis of the theory and practice of disarmament is given in Chapter 2, which serves to demonstrate the basis of successive British governments' failure to understand the concept, and therefore its implementation. Chapter 2 also sets out the background to the problem; how disarmament came to be on the international agenda in the first place, and consequently why Britain was faced with the dilemma of choosing between two equally unwelcome policy alternatives. Basically, ministers came to the conclusion that Britain could either accept her obligation to disarm, by international agreement in accordance with the Peace Treaties of 1919, with the risk of compromising her ability to uphold her Imperial commitments, or she could ignore, or actively avoid, meeting this obligation, with the risk of jeopardising European stability because of its impact on German revisionism and French insecurity. Either way, British security was perceived to be at risk.

The question of differences of opinion is also brought out in Chapter 3, which constitutes a brief examination of the views on disarmament of a representative cross-section of members of the policy-making élite. The importance of the human element in policy formulation and implementation cannot be overlooked, and, as Chapter 3 will demonstrate, many of the individuals concerned looked less than favourably on the prospect of Britain reducing the level of her armaments in line with an international agreement rather than purely in line with her own perceived requirements. This analysis of individual attitudes demonstrates how difficult it was for those few politicians and civil servants who had a real commitment to disarmament to counter the more pronounced anti-disarmament, or simply indifferent, stance of the majority of their colleagues.

The study then goes on, in Chapters 4 to 8, to analyse in detail the attitudes taken by each individual government during the period 1919–34. Within these administrations, the level of government discussion of disarmament varies considerably depending on the length of time for which the administration was in power, as well as its actual commitment to addressing the problem. The Lloyd George coalition, for example, believed it was carrying out a policy of disarmament in that it very rapidly reduced the level of Britain's armed forces immediately after the Great War, and was also responsible for taking a firm stand over the Washington Naval Conference of 1921–2. The Bonar Law/Baldwin administrations of 1923, on the other hand, took no firm steps towards disarmament although one member of the latter, Lord Robert Cecil (later Viscount Cecil of Chelwood), did attempt to push forward a considerable measure of indirect disarmament via the machinery of the League of Nations. This, however, was in a private rather than official capacity. Subsequently, the first Labour government was in power for too short a period and lacked the necessary majority to take significant steps, though its commitment to creating the 'right atmosphere' produced a considerable breakthrough in relations between the Powers over the question of reparations. Baldwin's 1924–9 administration, whilst improving the international perception of security through the Treaties of Locarno, took no significant steps to evolve a comprehensive disarmament policy, and, in fact, the few steps which it did take had a largely negative effect. From 1929–31, the second Labour government again suffered from the lack of a majority but was nevertheless able to make considerable strides towards indirect disarmament and security through the League, and towards a significant measure of naval arms control via the London Conference and Treaty. The chapter relating to the National government between 1931 and 1934 is, of necessity, longer than the others as it covers the intricacies and detail of the final attempt to solve the disarmament dilemma – the World Disarmament Conference of 1932–4. It was at this point that British ministers finally realised they could not escape their dilemma. Decisions had to be taken, and Britain must accept the consequences of those decisions. The study concludes with the collapse of the Disarmament Conference, when the disarmament question was dropped from the international agenda and the question of rearmament took its place.

The importance of the present study is that, for the first time in over sixty years, Britain's approach to the problem of international disarmament is treated as a whole. Admittedly, in order to encompass the time-span involved, it has been necessary to omit some of the more detailed, or less significant, discussions which took place on the subject during the period under review, and to concentrate on the major developments.[6] Questions of chemical warfare and the arms trade, for example, are not covered.[7] But such omissions do not in fact detract from the overall view of British policy during the sixteen-year period covered as, in general, they merely serve to underline the basic approach adopted by successive governments. Again, in order to cover such a long time-span, it has been necessary to concentrate on British sources; it is, after all, the British point of view which the study seeks to analyse. Reference is made to such sources as German, French and United States foreign policy documents in order to gauge reaction to British policy, but in the main the study concentrates on the purely British angle. Within the British government archives at the Public Record Office, a 'tiered' approach has been adopted. Extensive use has been made of Cabinet and Committee of Imperial Defence records, and selected Foreign Office documents, while the private papers of Cabinet ministers and civil servants have been examined in order to contrast the more personal observations of the policy-making élite with the official government records.

The overall thesis put forward is twofold; first that Britain had no positive strategy towards international disarmament during the period under review, unless a policy of merely reacting to moves made by others can be classed as a strategy, and second, that, with one or two notable exceptions, the members of the British policy-making élite did not understand the very concept of international disarmament. On this point the central argument is that British ministers, in public at least, consistently argued that the arms reductions undertaken purely for reasons of economy following the First World War, effectively constituted *unilateral* disarmament, and that no further effort was required. The reality of the situation was far different. The provisions of both the Treaty of Versailles and the Covenant of the League of Nations demanded that *all* Powers reduce the level of their armaments, by international agreement, in order to achieve international stability and security. Britain's unilateral reductions, whilst admittedly stretching her military commitments to their limits, were carried out without reference to the obligations for multilateral disarmament, and were never taken below the level required for her own security. In practice, British ministers were confronted by a dilemma – a choice between equally unwelcome alternatives. If, on the one hand, Britain were to carry out her commitment to reach an *international* agreement she could conceivably be compelled to make force configurations which were not in line with her own perceived requirements. On the other hand, if Britain abrogated her international commitment, she would not only break her moral obligations under the Treaty and the Covenant, but help to provoke German revisionism and promote a situation which would almost certainly lead to increased instability and to the *re*armament of *all* the European Powers.

In practice, Britain's answer to the disarmament dilemma was to avoid being placed in a position of actually having to confront the problem for as long as this strategy remained possible and, when this option was no longer available, to try to ensure that the blame for failure to meet international obligations was placed firmly on the shoulders of others. It can, of course, be argued that a policy of international disarmament was not the correct course for the powers to adopt during the inter-war period; and certainly international tensions and instability did little to contribute to the possibility of a successful agreement. This, however, is not the point at issue. All the signatories of the Treaty of Versailles and the League Covenant were committed to the search for disarmament through international agreement, and therefore its wisdom, or otherwise, is not discussed in the present study. What *is* important is that, given the commitment to reach an international agreement, the Powers, but more especially Britain, appeared to do little to redress the main cause of instability – the problem of Franco-German relations. Again and again the question of Anglo-French security relations arose in Cabinet discussion, and successive governments could hardly fail to recognise that France's insecurity precluded her from making further reductions in the level of her armaments without compensatory security guarantees. Theoretically, of course, Britain had it in her power to alleviate France's insecurity through an alliance or military commitment; and the prospects for negotiating an international disarmament agreement would have been considerably enhanced if Britain had adopted such a course. But governments continually shied away from this possibility, on the grounds that it would merely increase the discrepancy between Britain's military commitments and her ability to uphold them. Such a course would also necessitate changes in Britain's military configuration and (probably) *increases* rather than decreases in men, *matériel* and expenditure. In other words, rather than seeing an enhanced security relationship with France as a possible way out of the dilemma, British ministers perceived it as *part of* the dilemma. In this sense, the dilemma was self-imposed. It is recognised that the possibility of France accepting *any* guarantee which Britain could provide became increasingly remote with the passage of time, as evidence of German rearmament became increasingly impossible to ignore, but even in the early part of the period under review, Britain consistently avoided realistically confronting the security question.[8] Overall, therefore, whilst it may be impossible to predict with complete accuracy what effect an Anglo-French security agreement would have had on the quest for international disarmament, given that the Powers were *committed* to disarmament it appears illogical and short-sighted on the part of the British government to refuse to take possibly the only course which *might* have made that policy viable.

2

THE CONCEPT AND CONTEXT OF DISARMAMENT, 1919–34

The concept of disarmament

Before embarking on a detailed analysis of British disarmament policy in the years 1919–34, it is important to define what exactly is meant, for the purposes of this study, by the term 'disarmament'. It has been used to cover all conditions, from the complete abolition of armaments, to the reduction of levels of armaments, and even to the *increase* in their level where the aim is to achieve a measure of limitation and control. It can thus be seen that the term is open to great misinterpretation, and in order to avoid such misinterpretation a number of political scientists, after the Second World War, began to use the term 'arms control' rather than the traditional 'disarmament' as the generic word for negotiations which sought to limit armaments by international agreement. Control of armaments, it was felt, removed the apparent anomaly of a 'disarmament' agreement which actually led to an *increase* in their level. As far as Hedley Bull, one of the most important of the British political scientists to adopt this phrase, was concerned, the aim was to counter the proponents of 'general and complete disarmament' such as Philip Noel-Baker.[1] The academic debate over 'disarmament' and 'arms control', however, did not really begin until the 1950s and so is not dealt with in the present study.

During the inter-war period the generic term 'disarmament' was used by politicians, diplomats, political scientists, journalists and the public alike to describe the limitation and control of armaments by international agreement, and this is the definition of the term used in the present study. The term was useful in that it could be used to describe all manner of situations and occasions – disarmament conventions, disarmament conferences, qualitative disarmament, quantitative disarmament, naval disarmament, land disarmament, chemical disarmament – it was a simple word to cover what, to the comparatively uninformed, was a simple concept. But once the concept began to be explored in depth, it became markedly less simple, and it is this confusion of interpretation which underpins the present study. Just what *did* disarmament mean to successive British governments during the period 1919 to 1934? Having stated above that there was general agreement that 'disarmament' meant the 'limitation and control of armaments by international agreement', it is important to examine Britain's attitude towards what has been termed the 'myth' of her own disarmament.[2] This is because successive British governments complicated the issue by bringing into the equation the question of arms reductions undertaken as a matter of policy but outside the context of international negotiations – often called *unilateral* disarmament. There is no doubt that unilateral disarmament did exist at that time, but the question of how the concept of unilateral arms reductions undertaken as a matter of policy came into conflict with the idea of disarmament *by international agreement* is an important factor in examining Britain's approach to disarmament at international level.

Another important factor here is that Britain's interpretation of the term itself would change over the years: initially the definition of 'limitation and control by international agreement' appeared to be the accepted norm, although the emphasis in public was always on *reduction*, but towards the end of the period under review the government retreated from that usage. Certainly by November 1933, when it was becoming increasingly obvious that no state was willing to reduce the level of its armaments in view of Germany's expansionist policy, the Ministerial Committee on the Disarmament Conference attempted to justify Britain's unwillingness to advocate reductions in armaments by maintaining that the League of Nations had perhaps been using the term 'disarmament' wrongly: 'a good many misapprehensions might be cleared up if the term "limitation" was used instead of the term "disarmament"'.[3] This statement emphasises not only the confusion over the term itself but the confusion which undoubtedly existed in the minds of British ministers throughout the period 1919–34.

As important as the *meaning* of the term 'disarmament' are the questions of whether or not it is a desirable or even feasible goal, and opinion on these points is as varied as on the term itself. Even amongst those who have no doubts as to the desirability of disarmament, there is disagreement on the means of achieving it, and it is important to examine these arguments before looking at the measures taken towards achieving it during the period under review. Why should nations wish to limit their armaments by international agreement? What possible advantage can be gained from this course of action? To the proponents of disarmament there are a number of reasons why arms levels should be limited, and preferably reduced. Writing in 1926, Philip Noel-Baker declared that:

> It is commonly agreed that the purpose of disarmament is twofold: first, to reduce the economic burden laid upon the peoples of the world by excessive preparation for war; second, to prevent that competition in preparation *from which war results*.[4]

Quoting calculations made by Sir Josiah Stamp on the real economic cost of armaments, Noel-Baker asserted that 'one could . . . state, without much fear of serious error, that the standard of life throughout great industrial powers would be lifted by over 10 per cent by the cancellation of the expenditure on armaments'.[5] The cost was not only to be measured in economic terms, but in terms of the depletion of mineral resources of the world – steel, coal and oil – and in the 'moral sacrifice and spiritual degradation' which the burden of world war had imposed on the generation of European nations which had endured the First World War. To this catalogue of negative effects of armaments, Salvador de Madariaga added the wastage of human potential; not only does the arming, feeding, clothing and paying of those in the armed forces cost huge sums of money, but these men are 'diverted from productive occupations'.[6] The loss is, therefore, doubled; first, there is the financial cost involved in having these men in the armed services, and second, the national economy is reduced by the amount which they could have contributed had they been employed in 'productive occupations'. Madariaga admits that the military profession 'calls forth many a fine quality in man', including courage and self-denial, but military training is not the only way to attain such virtues. 'It is evident', he declared, 'that the virtues usually associated with war and with soldiers can be bred without having to pay for them as expensively in blood, treasury and spirit as the war system makes us do'.[7]

A further charge laid at the door of armaments, and one firmly embedded in Noel-Baker's theory, was that the escalation in the level of armaments – an arms race – is one of the actual *causes* of war. This theory was the prevailing reasoning behind the search for disarmament in the period under review. In the aftermath of the First World War, many leading ministers and politicians came to the conclusion that the arms race itself, the frantic acquisition of armaments by the major Powers, was the chief cause of the war. This belief has been summarised in the oft-quoted words of Sir Edward Grey, British Foreign Secretary in 1914:

> The moral is obvious: it is that great armaments lead inevitably to war. . . . The enormous growth of armaments in Europe, the sense of insecurity and fear caused by them – it was these that made war inevitable.[8]

This belief was widely accepted both in Britain and in the section of American public opinion which followed the teachings of Woodrow Wilson. It appears, after all, to have a simple solution: eliminate arms – and eliminate wars. *Si vis pax, para pacem.* If you want peace, prepare for peace.

This apparently simple philosophy, however, leads to the next question: supposing disarmament to be *desirable*, is it actually feasible? How does one go about achieving disarmament? If the arms race theory is accepted, it would appear to be quite reasonable to expect that all countries who wished for peace would agree, unquestioningly, to get rid of their armaments. There is, however, an alternative explanation of arms race dynamics, which is not that arms races cause wars, but that tensions cause a build-up of arms. The theory is summed up by Hans Morgenthau thus:

> Men do not fight because they have arms. They have arms because they deem it necessary to fight. Take away their arms and they will either fight with their bare fists, or get themselves new arms with which to fight.[9]

This theory emphasises the need for security and stability: only when men cease to feel threatened will they dare to put away their weapons, and making sure that men do not feel threatened would seem to be a much more difficult task than merely taking away their weapons. Salvador de Madariaga offers very much the same explanation of disarmament theory, believing that:

> The trouble with disarmament was (it still is) that the problem of war is tackled upside down and at the wrong end. . . . Nations don't distrust each other because they are armed; they are armed because they distrust each other. And therefore to want disarmament before a minimum of common agreement on fundamentals is as absurd as to want people to go undressed in winter. Let the weather be warm, and people will discard their clothes readily and without committees to tell them how they are to undress.[10]

The differing theories of approach to disarmament were to be a constant problem during the inter-war years: in public the majority of British politicians accepted Grey's arms race theory,[11] whereas in private they were more inclined to the view that security should come before arms reductions – at least as far as *British* security was concerned. As far as the security of *other* states was concerned, however, British governments could agree that Grey's theories had almost universal application!

This theory of arms reductions versus security should be seen as an oversimplification of the disarmament question. Men do not have arms solely 'because they deem it necessary to fight'; they have arms because arms symbolise power, a fact which again Madariaga recognised: 'the problem we all inaccurately and many misleadingly call Disarmament was at its core one of political relations mostly between the big powers'.[12] Thus the very notion of a 'disarmament' conference was absurd as far as Madariaga was concerned because nations go into a disarmament conference in order to maintain, and if possible improve their relative armaments. 'That is why', he maintained, 'a "Disarmament" Conference does not begin to talk sense until it sees itself as an Armaments Conference'.[13] Those who would avoid war by reducing armaments over-simplify the problem:

> A war is the *ultima ratio* in a conflict; a conflict is the outcome of a dispute that has got out of hand; a dispute is the consequence of a problem that has proved insoluble; a problem is born of a question that has not been tackled in time.[14]

The question must therefore be asked, when searching for disarmament *by international agreement*, 'what are the factors *against* such an agreement proving possible?' Rather than assuming that merely by removing, or at least significantly reducing or limiting armaments, wars will be abolished, we should ask what are the reasons *why* the Powers concerned would not agree to reduce or limit their armaments? Does the answer to this question lie in Madariaga's assertion that nations remain armed 'because they distrust each other'? And if so, what steps can be taken to engender trust between nations? As Madariaga again insists, the relations between nations are crucial to obtaining agreement; if relations are good, and trust is strong, then agreement can be reached, otherwise it is an impossible task. He analysed inter-war attempts at achieving disarmament as follows:

> The trouble was . . . that nothing to do with disarmament ever makes sense, since either the general state of the world adds up to dissent or to consensus, and in the first case disarmament is impossible and in the second disarmament would be spontaneous.[15]

But this is perhaps to paint too gloomy a picture of the prospects of achieving disarmament. There have been many successful disarmament agreements, and even during the period under review there were sufficient successes for it to be felt that the pursuit of a general disarmament agreement was not a fool's errand. It could well be argued that there is a middle road between the two apparent extremes of the 'arms races cause wars' versus the 'tensions cause armaments' schools of thought. As Dick Richardson points out '[a]rmaments are both the product *and* the cause of tension; and a disarmament agreement is itself a method of relieving tension by political accommodation'.[16] When international tensions are high, and arms levels are escalating, the successful conclusion of a disarmament agreement can go a long way towards reducing overall tension as well as preventing further arms escalation. The Washington and London Naval Conferences are examples of disarmament agreements reducing tension and creating a more stable international atmosphere – at least for a while. This does not contradict Madariaga's theory of dissent versus consensus; rather it straddles a line between the two: if nations are sufficiently aware of the increase in dissent, they can work towards achieving consensus, even if only in a limited area. If they will go some way towards addressing a question before it becomes a problem, then there is no reason why a limited agreement cannot be reached.

There are, of course, other factors aside from the security and trust questions which prevent the successful conclusion of disarmament negotiations. The most important of these is actual *belief* in disarmament, either in principle or in practice. As mentioned earlier, there are those who see armaments as power and a trained and disciplined fighting force as a symbol of strength, moral as well as military. There is, perhaps, little that can be said to influence the opinions of such people, nor for that matter those with a vested interest in maintaining a high level of armaments, the military-industrial complex, and the military élite whose *raison d'être* would vanish without a war to plan and fight. More capable of persuasion are those who see obstacles to agreement in technical terms: the difficulty of comparing a tank with a submarine, for example. These are obstacles which *can* be overcome if the willingness is there: it is not necessary to draw up an equation which exactly defines how many tanks are equal to one submarine, indeed it is a standard procedure in disarmament terms to compare like with like, not like with unlike. Nor is it a foregone conclusion that military men, by definition, want to wage wars. What *is* necessary is the willingness of governments and individuals to tackle these technical difficulties in a positive manner.

Dick Richardson highlights five main conditions which *must* be present before any disarmament agreement can be reached.[17] First and foremost, there must be a belief in disarmament among the parties involved; they must all *want* the negotiations to succeed. In this respect, during the period under review, the all-important question of *belief* in disarmament amongst members of the British policy-making élite will be discussed in the following chapter. The second prerequisite is strong political leadership; the ability to set an agenda for disarmament and maintain it. As will be seen in Chapters 7 and 8, Britain was able to do this at the London Naval Conference in 1930 but significantly failed to do so at the Geneva Disarmament Conference of 1932–4, even though the chance was there. The third factor required is political will; the ability to overcome the technical and political obstacles which are so often thrown in the path of negotiations. The importance of this factor will be highlighted in Chapters 4, 7 and 6, when the control exerted over the Admiralty by Lloyd George and Ramsay MacDonald at the Washington and London Naval Conferences respectively is compared with the failure of the second Baldwin government to do the same at the Geneva Naval Conference.

A fourth factor necessary to achieve agreement is a sound understanding by participants of the technical side of disarmament. Political leaders must not allow themselves to be blinded by the technical obstacles which are likely to be thrown in their path by military experts with a vested interest in retaining their prestige, armaments and agenda. They must also be aware of genuine alternatives to existing military policies. The fifth and final ingredient is an awareness of the problems and concerns of the other parties involved and the ability, if necessary, to adjust state policy accordingly. Each state will have different perceptions of its own, and others', requirements, and agreement will be harder, if not impossible, to achieve if negotiators can see only their own side of the problem. This particular aspect is highlighted in the period under review by the apparent inability of France and Britain to see each other's point of view over the relative importance of the army and navy to continental and maritime powers respectively.

In summary, the disarmament debate is not as simple as it at first appears; it is certainly not as simple as Sir Edward Grey's assessment would make it. If it were simply a question of removing armaments from the equation, and thus removing wars from the international agenda, it would surely have been done long ago. Arms are more than a means to fight a war; they are a defence against untrustworthy neighbours, a symbol of power and prestige, and, as far as Britain was concerned during the period under review, the only means by which she could police her Empire. The negotiation of successful agreements to reduce or limit the level of armaments is a complex procedure, requiring a number of factors which must come together at the right time, and without which agreement is almost certainly impossible.

Although the present study is concerned specifically with the British approach towards disarmament in the years 1919–34, British disarmament policy during this period cannot be looked at in isolation. It is both necessary and important to look at the international context in which the disarmament problem was set. Why was disarmament on the international agenda in the first place? Why was Britain confronted with a dilemma she would, by definition, have preferred to avoid? The answers lie in the peace settlement of 1919.

Disarmament and the peace treaties

Disarmament was placed firmly on the international agenda when the victorious Allies met in Paris to draw up the terms of the peace with Germany. It is not within the remit of this current study to examine in detail the negotiations which led to the Treaty of Versailles; they have been well documented elsewhere.[18] But a number of aspects must be noted, in particular the vastly different approaches of Britain and France towards the eventual peace terms. France, having been invaded by Germany twice in the previous fifty years, was determined that Germany should be reduced to a level – political, military and financial – from which she could never again rise to challenge France. Britain, on the other hand, did not seek as severe a punishment of Germany. Her major declared aim had been the elimination of the German fleet, since Britain's naval supremacy was seen as essential to her existence. Unlike the

French, the British government did not wish to see Germany herself crushed, merely the 'Prussian militarism' which it held to have been responsible for the war.[19]

In practice the Treaty of Versailles imposed stringent penalties on Germany. Her disarmament was dealt with under Part V, the Disarmament Clauses, the Preamble to which stated:

> in order to render possible the initiation of a general limitation of the armaments of all nations, Germany undertakes to observe the military, naval and air clauses which follow.

Under these clauses Germany was allowed to retain an army of no more than 100,000 men, on a long-term service basis, and was prohibited from possessing 'aggressive weapons' such as tanks, heavy guns over 105 mm, battleships over 10,000 tons, military aircraft, poison gas and submarines. The navy was restricted numerically to six battleships, six light cruisers, twelve destroyers and twelve torpedo boats, with a maximum personnel of 15,000; the general staff was abolished; the military training of civilians prohibited, and strict regulations applied to all military establishments. To enforce the Treaty, Inter-Allied Control Commissions were established with extensive powers of inspection – though they would be withdrawn when the Allied occupation of Germany was ended.

When presented with these terms the Germans asked for clarification of the Preamble, to which the French leader, Clemenceau, on behalf of the Allies, replied that the Allied requirements in regard to German armaments

> were not made solely with the object of rendering it impossible for Germany to renew her policy of military aggression. They are also the first step towards that general reduction and limitation of armaments which they seek to bring about as one of the most fruitful preventives of war and which it will be one of the first duties of the League of Nations to promote.[20]

It was here that the beginnings of confusion and differences of interpretation began. In particular, was Germany's continued long-term disarmament conditional on the Allies fulfilling their own vague and imprecise 'obligations' to disarm? International lawyers and politicians would argue over the precise implications of the Versailles disarmament clauses for many years – without success!

If the Allied 'commitment' to disarm in the Preamble to Part V was vague and non-specific, the Powers in question took on a statutory obligation to disarm in the Covenant of the League of Nations. Under Article 8, members of the League pledged themselves to the reduction of armaments to the lowest point consistent with national safety and the enforcement by common action of international obligations. . . . [21]

The Council was charged with formulating plans for reduction, taking into account the geographical situation and circumstances of each state. But if, from a strictly legal standpoint, it was from Article 8 that the international discussions for disarmament originated, in practice the drive behind the negotiations was the potential threat that Germany might seek to free herself from the Versailles restrictions using the Preamble to Part V as an excuse. As Cecil pointed out, whilst there was a good deal of logic-chopping over the interdependence of Allied and German undertakings in 1919, in reality the discussion was futile, because:

> [w]hatever conclusion might be reached from a careful examination of the wording of the two promises, there never was any serious doubt as a matter of common sense that the Germans would . . . expect their late opponents to disarm as soon as Germany had done so, and if they did not, Germany would certainly regard herself as free to re-arm. [22]

This, in fact, was the most important point; as far as Germany was concerned she had accepted the disarmament clauses of the Treaty on the understanding that the other nations also intended to disarm. She would not, in practice, whatever the precise legal position, accept permanent inferiority. This would become increasingly clear as Germany recovered her economic and political position among the Powers in the 1920s and early 1930s.

Disarmament and international security, 1919–34

Throughout the period 1919–34, the problem of disarmament was inextricably connected with the problem of security; and the problem of security was inextricably connected with the problem of German power. Could the 'new world order' associated with the Treaty of Versailles and League of Nations ensure stability? Could Germany be reconciled to the new international system? Certainly those who framed the League believed they were creating a system which *could* deal with the problem of Germany, or, for that matter, any other state with revisionist intentions. The very concept of collective security – all for one and one for all – was enshrined in the Covenant. Under Article 11 members of the League recognised that peace was indivisible, and under Article 10 undertook to respect and preserve each other's political independence and territorial integrity against external aggression. Articles 12, 13 and 15 committed the signatories to submit their differences to the Permanent Court of International Justice for arbitration and judicial settlement, or for enquiry by the League Council. There was, however, a 'gap' in the Covenant which allowed parties to go to war after three months should a unanimous decision not be forthcoming. The strongest measures available to the League in the event of one of its members resorting to war in violation of its obligations were contained in Article 16, under which members agreed to impose an absolute and immediate economic and diplomatic boycott on the Covenant-breaking state, and to accept the ruling of the Council should it be found necessary to apply military sanctions.

But if, in theory, the basis for a comprehensive system of collective security was laid down by the Covenant, in practice it was found to be severely wanting. There was no definite obligation for members to participate in military measures, no provision for an international force, and a unanimity rule within the Council provided a perfect excuse for those unwilling to fulfil their obligations to refuse to do so. The legal restrictions lacked means of enforcement, and the sanctions provisions under Article 16 were weak and imprecise, again enabling those who so wished, to avoid them.

The situation was compounded by the refusal of the United States to enter the League as a result of the Senate vote on the Treaty of Versailles on 19 March 1920. The security system had been undermined before it had even been implemented. The problem, however, was not simply one of the United States not entering the League. As part of a series of mutual concessions which helped to facilitate agreement at Versailles, the French had given up a claim for an independent Rhineland state (under French control) in return for the demilitarisation of the Rhineland, a fifteen-year Allied occupation and an Anglo-American guarantee of French security. The story of the abortive Anglo-American guarantee to France has been well documented,[23] but its importance cannot be overemphasised. Arguably, the existence of the guarantee might have dissuaded Germany from ever again attempting an invasion of France, and even have ensured the stability on which an international disarmament agreement could have been reached within the terms of Article 8 of the Covenant. Without the guarantee, the French were forced to rely on their own military strength to deter future German aggression. Inevitably, the level of armaments which they felt was consistent with national safety was increased and the margin for negotiating a disarmament agreement correspondingly decreased.

The possibilities of arriving at a disarmament settlement were further decreased by the fact that the disarmament clauses of Versailles relating to Germany were difficult to enforce. Indeed, once the Allied control commissions and occupying troops were withdrawn Germany would be left completely free to verify her own disarmament – a disarmament which was undertaken very much against her will! While, as Henry Kissinger points out, 'In the innocent days before the study of arms control had become an academic subject, no one thought it odd to be asking Germany to verify its own disarmament',[24] André Tardieu, then principal French negotiator at Versailles, perceptively informed Colonel House in 1919 that 'the failure to set up verification machinery would cripple the disarmament clauses of the Treaty'.[25]

It can be argued that the search for disarmament was doomed to fail, given the shaky construction on which it was based. Certainly the absence of water-tight means of ensuring Germany's permanent inferiority, coupled with France's inherent and natural distrust of German intentions, would make the latter reluctant to reduce her armaments beyond a certain point. The question was what level was 'consistent with national safety'. In this respect, the French attitude was no different from that of Britain. As far as France was concerned, the only possible inducement to undertake a radical reduction of armaments throughout the period under review was a firm commitment from Britain; and Britain, as the following analysis will show, consistently took the short-term view that such a commitment was not in Britain's interest. Henry Kissinger sums up the position in respect of France's search for an alliance:

> the only first class power available was Great Britain, whose political leaders did not accept the views of their military advisers. Instead their policy was based on the mistaken belief that France was already too powerful and that the last thing it needed was a British alliance. Great Britain's leaders considered demoralized France to be the potentially dominant power and in need of being balanced, while revisionist Germany was perceived as the aggrieved party in need of conciliation. Both assumptions – that France was militarily dominant and that Germany had been harshly treated – were correct in the short term; but as premises of British policy, they were disastrous in the long term. Statesmen stand or fall on their perceptions of trends. And British postwar leaders failed to perceive the long-range dangers before them.[26]

This may be a rather harsh judgement – the benefit of hindsight enables the observer to see what *should* have been done in the long term – but it is surely one of the duties of statesmen to at least *attempt* to look at the possible long-term consequences of their actions and decisions. Thus, although British statesmen recognised the existence of French insecurity, they failed to understand it or accept it at face value, consistently searching for some other reason for France's refusal to reduce her armaments in relation to Germany – vindictiveness, desire to dominate Europe – anything rather than accept the need to make a commitment to French security. Britain's reluctance to make this commitment is, perhaps, understandable, given the prevailing opinion, both amongst statesmen and the general public, that it was Britain's commitment to France which had dragged her into the war in 1914. However, as this study will show, it was to become increasingly obvious that no agreement could be reached without such a commitment, but, paradoxically, the closer British statesmen came to recognising this fact, the less likely did France's willingness to rely on a British guarantee alone become.[27]

The rejection of the new world order by the United States led France to search for other means to increase her security and, in the absence of a British guarantee, she turned to smaller powers – Czechoslovakia and Poland – in an attempt to replace the old Franco-Russian alliance which had helped to protect her in the past. France, in effect, adopted the 'belt and braces' approach – the new collective security apparently offered by the League alongside the old alliance system. But what was actually needed if international disarmament was to be achieved was a complete re-orientation of policy by all powers world-wide. This was implicit in the new system envisaged by Woodrow Wilson when setting out his Fourteen Points on which the League of Nations was founded. The problem was that the failure of the United States to join the new system led to its inability to operate, without actually removing the commitments made by those Powers who *did* ratify both Treaty and Covenant.

A further problem, as far as Britain was concerned, was that the US withdrawal from the League, together with the isolationism of Bolshevik Russia, propelled Britain – and France for that matter – into an artificially powerful position within the League. Intrinsically, however, Britain's global commitments outstretched her ability to uphold them in the longer term. Certainly with hindsight, it can be seen that Britain was vastly overcommitted, and as her colonies demanded more freedom and independence her days of supremacy, whether as an Imperial or world power, were drawing to an end. The old order had changed – or rather was in the process of change. If Britain had been able to recognise the overcommitment, to see the need to withdraw from her Imperial position, and ultimately the inevitability of her involvement in European affairs, she might – just – have committed herself far more fully to resolving the fundamental question of European instability – the question of Franco-German antagonism. As Madariaga pointed out, 'a problem is born of a question that has not been tackled in time', and during the 1930s the problem of Franco-German relations was allowed to escalate into a conflict. It can be argued that Wilson's idealism asked too much of those involved; his new system demanded that they thought and behaved as part of the same international family – a difficult concept at the best of times – but the United States' withdrawal from the family doomed it to failure. Those who remained, in theory, as part of the same family, continued, in their hearts, to assert their own individuality over family responsibility.

The problem of individuality versus family responsibility was one which was to dominate the attempts of the League to carry out its duties, and the conflict implicit in this problem would lead, within twenty years, to the collapse of the structure so painstakingly assembled at Versailles. Many volumes, great and small, have been written on the origins of the Second World War,[28] and it is certainly outside the scope of the present work to examine these origins in any detail. It is, however, extremely important to recognise that the formulation of Britain's defence, and consequent disarmament, policy took place against a background of unrest and uncertainty within the international community. The peace treaties arguably created more problems than they solved. The question of French insecurity in the face of possible German revisionism was only one manifestation of the potential unrest, for German revisionism, at least initially, was directed towards the east rather than towards France herself. It was, as Ruth Henig points out, 'significant that the new states of Poland, Czechoslovakia and Romania were referred to in Germany as *Saisonsstaaten* – states born to die within a single season',[29] which was scarcely likely to engender feelings of security within these states. Russia, weakened though she was by war and internal revolution, also had an interest in the new East European states, as much of their newly acquired territory had once been hers, whilst to her east, Japan sought to expand into Manchuria and the Chinese mainland.

The situation in Austria was no less unsettled, as many of her inhabitants favoured a closer union with Germany, a move expressly forbidden under the Treaty of Versailles. In Italy there was much resentment that few of the spoils of war to which she felt entitled had actually been realised, and this resentment would have far-reaching consequences as the emerging Fascist Party sought to redress the balance of power. These political uncertainties were compounded in all the nations concerned, by the financial and economic consequences of four years of war, the costs incurred by the victors being around two and a half times those of their opponents.[30] War debts, principally owed to the United States, and taxation combined to cripple national economies and throughout the period compounded the political strains experienced by all governments, both internally and internationally.

This is, of necessity, an extremely brief background to the postwar international situation, but it does demonstrate the sense of instability which permeated international relations during the period under review and undoubtedly hampered the search for a disarmament agreement. Nevertheless, international statesmen *were* committed to such an agreement, difficult though it may appear, and Britain was no exception.

Britain's dilemma

In the aftermath of the 1919 settlement, with the disarmament of Germany and the military supremacy of France over her eastern neighbour, the British policy-making élite were determined not to enter into any further military commitments on the European continent. Many clung to the traditional British aloofness from European affairs. This is hardly surprising. Britain's chief concern was her Empire, and her aim was to return to her former position as a great trading nation. She thus required a large fleet, sufficient armed forces to police her Empire, and stability in Europe, which included an economically strong Germany. But the world was not the same as the pre-1914 world; Britain's freedom to manœuvre was restricted both by increased Imperial responsibilities and by new international obligations. Lloyd George might rail against the obligations of the Treaty of Versailles and the League Covenant, but he was pledged to support them,[31] and none more so than the disarmament provisions. The problem was that the obligation to disarm multilaterally as a matter of *external* policy, impinged upon, and was in potential conflict with, the organisation of armaments as a matter of *internal* policy.

Left to herself Britain was quite happy to reduce her armed forces, both men and *matériel*, in line with her own requirements, that is, sufficient for domestic and Imperial needs. Driven by the twin demands of the Treasury and a public fed on the idea that the arms race had caused the horrors of the war, there was enormous pressure on her, as there was on each of the other victorious Allies, to 'disarm'. But what exactly did successive British governments understand by the term 'disarmament'? As the following chapters will show, Britain consistently maintained that the efforts she made in reducing the level of her armaments, for the purposes of economy and public relations, constituted a large measure of disarmament, albeit of a *unilateral* nature. There is no denying that in the immediate postwar years Britain did, in fact, make enormous reductions, especially considering that the territorial provisions of the peace treaties had greatly increased the size of the Empire. The War Office in particular complained constantly that it was barely capable of carrying out Britain's Imperial obligations with the vastly reduced resources at its disposal. The reductions which she made, however, had nothing to do with the pursuit of multilateral disarmament. At the time, Britain did not, in fact, have a multilateral disarmament policy as such.

In 1919 Britain adopted the 'Ten-Year Rule' which assumed that no new major war would occur within ten years. At the time, this seemed an eminently sensible policy. There was no real threat to British security. Germany was disarmed, Japan remained friendly, the United States had no aggressive intentions against the Empire, the Soviet Union was too weak to pose a problem, and France, despite occasional scares, was not a realistic threat. With the sinking of the German fleet at Scapa Flow Britain's naval supremacy was assured, and as an island power she had little use for a large army; its primary purpose was the policing of the Empire. To reduce Britain's forces substantially then, did not place Britain's security under threat. The point – and it cannot be emphasised too strongly – is that the reductions in Britain's forces in the years immediately following the peace settlement were undertaken on sound military and economic grounds: they had nothing to do with the obligations to disarm under the Treaty of Versailles and League of Nations Covenant.

Certainly there was no 'disarmament by example' on the part of any British government in the period under review, whether in the sense that British arms reductions were intended as a positive contribution to the League of Nations' efforts to secure multilateral disarmament, or in the sense that Britain's arms reductions were unique amongst the Powers. In both respects, the idea of Britain's 'disarmament by example' is a myth – though there is little question that in the early 1930s many British ministers, having portrayed the myth as reality, came to believe in it. In fact, after reaching a low point in 1923, Britain's defence expenditure began to increase. Figures for 1924–9 show defence spending in the region of 14 per cent of government expenditure and 3.2 per cent of national income, figures roughly comparable with those of the other major Powers. In terms of per capita expenditure, however, these figures were far higher than those of any other power: 'some 1.75 times that of France, over twice that of the United States, 2.5 times that of Italy, 3.5 times that of Japan, 5 times that of Germany, and 6 times that of the Soviet Union'.[32]

Although it was not immediately obvious, Britain was faced with a dilemma – a choice between equally unwelcome alternatives – which arose because of the *international* nature of her commitment to disarm. On the one hand, a reduction of armaments by international agreement, in order to comply with the terms imposed on Germany and create international stability, might conflict with the force configuration which the government believed necessary to meet security requirements. It might also involve the outcome feared most – an increased security commitment to France. On the other hand, there were potential advantages in securing an international agreement; for example, further economic savings and, at least in theory, the removal of Germany's excuse to re-arm. A policy of multilateral disarmament would also appeal to the greater proportion of public opinion. Conversely, *failure* to reach an international agreement also posed a dilemma. On the one hand, there were several potential advantages. Britain would be free to organise her forces and the security of the Empire in her own way, and, above all, avoid a further commitment to France. On the other hand, there were also potential disadvantages. These included the breaking of the *moral* obligation to fulfil her part of the Treaty and Covenant and an increase in expenditure in order to match the expansion of the US and Japanese navies and the French air force, and, eventually, the prospect of German re-armament. Thus whichever way they turned, ministers found themselves in a dilemma. The *international* commitment to disarm posed questions – and answers – which successive governments would have preferred not to face. In fact, for most of the period under review, Britain's preferred course of action would have been to *ignore* the disarmament question altogether, in the hope that it might somehow 'go away'. In practice, this was impossible.

3

THE HUMAN ELEMENT

Before going on to an in-depth analysis of the way in which individual British governments tried to solve (or avoid) the disarmament dilemma, it is important to examine the attitudes of the individuals who formed those governments. Whilst any one government may have official policies on a number of issues, the influence of the individuals within that government cannot be overlooked. Individuals help to formulate collective policy, but, more importantly, they must then interpret that policy in their own sphere of interest. This can be done with a greater or lesser degree of enthusiasm, depending on the privately held views of the Minister or official in question. It is obviously impossible to look at every individual member of each administration, but the views of the most prominent on the disarmament question, as well as on the League of Nations and, importantly, the question of French security, will now be considered in some detail. For convenience, the list has been broken down into three categories, Liberal, Conservative and Labour, although in view of the fact that many members of each political persuasion served in both Coalition and National governments, and one changed party allegiance, the influence of each individual clearly varied in relation to the ideological mix of the government in question.

Liberal ministers

The involvement of Lloyd George in the disarmament process began with the part he played in the drawing up of the Treaty of Versailles. Lorna Jaffe, in her book *The Decision to Disarm Germany* (1985), accuses Lloyd George of inconsistency in his views on disarmament, pointing out that during his period as Minister for Munitions, when he revamped Britain's munitions industry and pressed for the introduction of conscription, he appeared to have forgotten his Radical Liberal roots which had previously called for expenditure on arms to be reduced in order to assist social reforms.[1] Lloyd George, however, did *not* forget his Radical roots. In the spring of 1917 it was he who pressed the Imperial War Cabinet to include disarmament among Britain's war aims, and this was not the unilateral disarmament of

Germany, but a general reduction of armaments.[2] In his biography of Lloyd George, Thomas Jones, Deputy Secretary to the Cabinet from 1916–30, states that the British Prime Minister shared the view that disarmament would lead to security and 'support[ed] Wilson's proposal to disarm Germany as a preparation for a general reduction of armaments'.[3] Lloyd George proclaimed, both at the Paris Conference and in the House of Commons, that general disarmament was essential to the success of the League; without it the League would be like other conventions of the past – 'something that would be blown away by the first gust of war'.[4] He took the initiative in producing his 'perception of a post-war settlement'.[5] The Fontainebleau Memorandum 'was designed to impress the French Prime Minister with the virtues of moderation in the terms to be imposed on Germany',[6] and contained, amongst all the more frequently cited examples of moderation, a commitment to the establishment of the League. It also maintained that 'it is idle to endeavour to impose a permanent limitation of armaments upon Germany unless we are prepared similarly to impose a limitation upon ourselves'.[7] It went on:

> it is essential that the leading members of the League of Nations should maintain considerable forces both by land and sea in order to preserve liberty in the world. But if they are to present an [sic] united front to the forces both of reaction and revolution, they must arrive at such an agreement in regard to armaments among themselves as would make it impossible for suspicion to arise between the members of the League of Nations in regard to their intentions towards one another. If the League is to do its work for the world it will only be because the members of the League trust it themselves and because there are no apprehensions, rivalries and jealousies in the matter of armaments between them. . . . Unless we secure this universal limitation we shall achieve neither lasting peace, nor the permanent observance of the limitation of German armaments which we now seek to impose.[8]

There are, of course, questions over the significance of the Fontainebleau Memorandum. It has been said that it 'spoke the language and breathed the spirit of statesmanship',[9] but also that its 'significance was . . . that it provided a manifesto for future appeasement . . . '.[10] If Britain's security was guaranteed, with the elimination of the German fleet, France was offered only the paper pledge of the Anglo-American guarantee. In reality, Lloyd George's motives for producing the Memorandum are rather less than clear: was it to guarantee French security, to prevent a stalemate at the peace negotiations, or to gain the United States' support? As far as disarmament is concerned, on paper it represented a great awareness of the problem; but evidence of attempts to follow through the awareness into commitment is very hard to find. Lloyd George made a few attempts but without real conviction, at least as far as disarmament and the League were concerned. The rhetoric was fine, but his support for the League appeared to stem more from his desire to secure US support during the peace conference, and from the pressure of public opinion, than a commitment to its principles.[11] By December 1920 he was condemning the League as more likely to become a centre of intrigue than a real benefit to the peace of the world:[12] it was 'deceptive and dangerous' and could 'do nothing but pass useless resolutions'.[13] In practice, he never attended any meetings of the League, even when pressed by Cecil and other members of the British Empire Delegation, to take the lead in disarmament proposals. As Cecil observed, Lloyd George proclaimed that the only hope of safety was disarmament, but said nothing to encourage the efforts in that direction then being made at Geneva.[14]

Sir John Simon,[15] a lawyer, and Foreign Secretary in the latter part of this study, held traditional Liberal views on disarmament, although by July 1932 he had, at least in Cecil's opinion, 'for all practical purposes ceased to be a Liberal'.[16] Simon's support for disarmament in general, and the 1932–34 World Disarmament Conference in particular, would seem to be almost meaningless in view of his inability to put forward or push through any policy. Anthony Eden, at that time a relatively junior representative at the Disarmament Conference, bemoaned the fact that, whilst nominally leader of the UK delegation, Simon 'was not suited to drive the Conference. John Simon's brilliant analytical mind hated to take decisions'.[17] Similarly, Simon's biographer, David Dutton, observes that 'Simon's desire to embrace as many alternatives of policy as possible proved most damaging during his years as Foreign Secretary . . .'.[18] Simon would have preferred to leave the whole of the Disarmament Conference to Eden; he was, according to Ramsay MacDonald, much more preoccupied with his own position than with the Geneva situation.[19] He was, in the opinion of one observer at the Conference, 'guided by the principle that, at every cost, John Simon should remain the Foreign Secretary'.[20] It could, of course, be argued that any government minister wants, above all, to remain in office, but at a time of such crucial importance for world peace it is unfortunate that Britain should have been represented by a man whom some contemporaries labelled the 'worst foreign secretary in 50 years'.[21] In his autobiography, Simon deals with the Disarmament Conference in four pages, none of which display any real personal involvement, and revolve around the theme of Britain's unilateral reductions in armaments and consequent lack of influence among nations who 'were not really all striving for the same thing'.[22] Brilliant and analytical as his brain may have been, what was needed at Geneva was a principled but realistic advocate of British policy with a real understanding of the problems of international disarmament. Unfortunately, as Vansittart observed, Simon 'lacked the quality of being ready to go to the stake over an issue in which he believed'.[23] Neither did he inspire confidence in his

European counterparts. Philip Noel-Baker, for example, quotes the views of a French delegate that 'Within a week of Henderson's arrival in Geneva, he had won everybody's confidence and trust; within a week of Simon's arrival, no-one believed a word he said'.[24]

Sir Herbert Samuel,[25] the Liberal leader at the time of the Disarmament Conference, shared his Party's support for all-round disarmament and collective security, and in June 1932 he was appointed a delegate to the conference. He supported the Geneva negotiations with great enthusiasm, being anxious to 'help save the conference from futility'.[26] However, by September 1932 circumstances had led Samuel to believe that the Liberals must leave the government, and he resigned his position as Home Secretary. This not only indicated the weakness of his position within the government during the critical months of early 1932, but any potentially favourable influence which he might have had on the Disarmament Conference or on government policy was lost.

Conservative ministers

Opinions on Stanley Baldwin[27] vary perhaps more than on any other politician of his time; the enigma has been examined, but not understood. He displayed a quiet, administrative approach to government, rather than the flamboyant leadership of Lloyd George or Ramsay MacDonald. Even his colleagues could not agree on the success or failure of his role. Amery declared that he was not interested in politics, and that he saw his job as assuaging industrial strife,[28] and in this area he was arguably successful. Austen Chamberlain saw Baldwin's position as being much strengthened by his handling of the General Strike.[29] But whilst his colleagues praised his qualities of patience, honesty, sincerity and generosity,[30] they were equally critical of his abilities as Prime Minister. Sir Maurice Hankey called him 'a nice fellow, but not the stuff of which British Prime Ministers are made'.[31] Thomas Jones, on the other hand, defended Baldwin on the grounds that 'meditatively he was very active'.[32] Lloyd George once called him 'the most formidable antagonist whom I have ever encountered'.[33]

Baldwin had apparently little interest in foreign affairs in general, or disarmament in particular,[34] having once gone so far as to maintain that disarmament was visionary.[35] As Prime Minister from 1924–9, he left the handling of foreign affairs almost entirely in the hands of his Foreign Secretary, Austen Chamberlain. He had little sympathy for the French, and was reputed to have said to a friend that 'One of the things that comforted me when I gave up office was that I should not have to meet French statesmen any more'.[36] Earl Beatty, the First Sea Lord from 1919–27, believed him to be ignorant of the needs of the Empire and suspicious of the United States.[37] Cecil also notes Baldwin's antipathy towards the United States, cursing them as 'futile and useless' during discussions on disarmament in 1933.[38] Significantly, however, by 1933 Cecil observed that the US delegate to the Disarmament Conference now believed that Baldwin was keener on disarmament than MacDonald.[39] As far as the League was concerned, Cecil regarded him as 'temperamentally' in favour,[40] but Baldwin himself believed that the League faced two obstacles, 'the prejudice of people who think it can do nothing and the support of people who think it can do everything'.[41]

Arthur Balfour[42] was a supporter of the League, but not as a 'super-state'.[43] He saw the weapons of the League as 'delay and publicity' rather than 'fleets and armies',[44] though by 1923 he had come to the conclusion that 'nothing, not the League of Nations or anything else, is going to give us peace . . . '.[45] Although Balfour was excluded by Lloyd George from many of the negotiations at the Paris Peace Conference, including the drafting of the Fontainebleau Memorandum and the Anglo-French guarantee, since he 'wasted a lot of time',[46] he was arguably the most successful Conservative 'disarmer' during the whole period of this study, his skill, diplomacy and personality helping to bring the Washington Naval Conference to a successful conclusion. As far as land armaments were concerned, however, Balfour was of the school which believed that, having drastically reduced her armaments in the immediate postwar period, it was not Britain's business to take a leading part, 'but only a helpful part', in the quest for general disar-mament through the League.[47]

Lord Robert Cecil,[48] the most fervent Conservative disarmer of them all, possessed 'a smile like a Chinese dragon to express a stubborn mind banged, barred and bolted against arguments'.[49] This judgement may, perhaps, have been a little harsh, but Cecil was unswerving in his support for the League in general, and for disarmament in particular. He agreed wholeheartedly with Viscount Grey's contention that 'competition in armaments leads to war', and believed that 'almost every man of eminence in public life' also supported Grey's conclusions.[50] Cecil was responsible for drawing up, almost single-handedly, the proposed Treaty of Mutual Assistance in 1923, and when this was rejected was prepared to support its successor, the Geneva Protocol, which, he maintained, would not of itself produce disarmament, although the security engendered by the Protocol certainly would.[51] Unlike many of his colleagues he recognised the overpowering need which the French had for security; the French were not, he pointed out, afraid for the immediate future, but for what might happen to their children. This fear, he believed, was 'spread over the whole of France. Every man and woman in France has that terror in their mind'.[52]

Cecil worked tirelessly for the League and Disarmament, more often than not in direct conflict with his colleagues, who variously described him as 'a crank'[53] who 'bids fair to kill the League by excess of enthusiasm,'[54] a 'pleasant companion' but 'impractical' whose obsession, since the formation of the League, was to 'disarm peace-loving nations'.[55] Leopold Amery described Cecil's eventual resignation from the Cabinet in 1927 over the failure of the Coolidge Naval Conference as 'a great relief' as 'his innocent faith in the League of Nations [was] a dangerous weakening in our sense of responsibility for world peace and our own security'.[56] He has been described as quick-tempered, self-righteous and stubborn, with a career 'distinguished by reliance on the threat of resignation'.[57] When resignation actually came, Cecil laid the blame squarely on his Cabinet colleagues; he maintained that they were 'not strong enough to resist the Admiralty',[58] and in explaining his resignation to Baldwin he declared that 'on the broad policy of Disarmament the majority of the Cabinet and I are not agreed. To quote a well-known phrase, we "do not mean the same thing"'.[59] Cecil, in fact, felt himself closer to the foreign policy of Ramsay MacDonald than of his own Party; in March 1929 he informed Lord Grey that he could not advise people to vote for the Conservatives,[60] and when MacDonald's Labour government took office, he declared it to be a 'genuine and wholehearted peace ministry'.[61] The admiration was apparently reciprocated, MacDonald having declared that without Cecil the League would not have survived.[62]

Cecil was succeeded as Chancellor of the Duchy of Lancaster in the second Baldwin administration by Lord Cushendun,[63] a die-hard Ulster Unionist. Opinion varies on Cushendun's commitment to the League and to disarmament. Cecil, perhaps naturally, was highly critical of his successor; he maintained that Cushendun hated Geneva, was bored by the whole thing, took no interest in the League and disbelieved in the possibility of disarmament. He had a destructive attitude, and incurred a good deal of resentment against his rudeness and 'patronizing cynicism'.[64] Cecil was not the only one who thought Cushendun less than ideal for his task; Bridgeman declared that Cushendun had been given an 'unpleasant job' at Geneva, as he hated fighting for anything unless he was convinced the Pope was on the other side.[65] He then, however, 'got the Geneva microbe very badly' and lost the 'die-hard spirit', being always ready to make concessions in order to help the League, for which the British Empire suffered.[66] Cushendun himself believed that all proceedings at the League on the subject of disarmament were 'doomed to failure'. A general Treaty of Disarmament was an impossibility, and in the absence of a 'common denominator', the only logical way to achieve agreement was to examine the armaments of each nation in turn, and each in turn would have to justify the level it deemed necessary 'to reach the lowest point consistent with national safety'.[67]

Austen Chamberlain[68] as Chancellor of the Exchequer under Lloyd George, and in the early postwar rush to save money, was not confronted with contentious decisions on multilateral disarmament. But when he was brought into the 1924 Cabinet, as part of Baldwin's rift-healing process, he was given the post of Foreign Secretary, and thus brought face to face with the problem. Chamberlain believed that, whilst the subject of disarmament had occupied perhaps the most prominent place in the discussions of the

League Assembly, 'there [could] be no reduction without security'.[69] He was well aware that the League's first two major attempts at achieving security, the Treaty of Mutual Assistance and the Geneva Protocol, had both been undermined by British governments, and was cautious about making a third attempt 'without the certainty of success'. In this respect, he maintained France's 'refusal to disarm' was not as a result of military fever, but of 'deep-rooted fear, arising from past history, in regard to her future safety'.[70] Chamberlain was thus more inclined to work on the establishment of security, preferring to leave the disarmament question in the hands of Cecil, admitting that he could not give to it the time which it really required.[71] He assured Cecil that he did attach great importance to the limitation and restriction of armaments, but 'attached more importance to other factors in preserving the peace of the world' and did not think that 'the idea of beginning with a great world conference was the most practical form of approach to the problem'.[72] His successful conclusion of the Locarno Treaty promised, in his own view, a much greater possibility of disarmament than any 'great world conference'. Significantly Cecil's own opinion was that Chamberlain became one of the League's most convinced supporters, which was a notable compliment from Cecil![73]

Winston Churchill[74] not only changed Party allegiance, from Liberal to Conservative, but changed positions almost from one end of the spectrum to the other, from Secretary of State for War to Chancellor of the Exchequer. Rather like a chameleon, Churchill took 'his colour from the particular office he happen[ed] to be holding at the time'.[75] He was, as Bridgeman observed, a Big Navyite at the Admiralty, and the reverse as Chancellor.[76] In many respects Churchill was inconsistent; for example, in 1920 he believed that a guarantee to France and Belgium was essential for security,[77] but by 1925 he was arguing against a pact with France until she had made peace with Germany:[78] to remain aloof from France would make her more amenable.[79] Again, on the question of Singapore, he declared himself in favour of the base, as a purely defensive measure and one of the links in inter-Imperial communications,[80] but two months later proposed that Britain should renounce all her 'previously agreed policy for basing a fleet at Singapore' and should 'give up Hong Kong as a Naval station'.[81]

In other respects, Churchill was totally consistent. In 1919, Hankey declared that 'Churchill obviously does not care to be a War Minister without a war in prospect, and finds the task of curtailing expenditure distasteful'.[82] On one occasion, Frances Stevenson remarked that Churchill was giving Lloyd George great trouble because he was 'anxious that the world should not be at peace, and is therefore planning a great war in Russia. . .'.[83] By 1927 Cecil felt that war was still the only thing which interested Churchill.[84] However, it could be argued that, whilst finding the task of curtailing expenditure 'distasteful', he actually carried out the task very well. Bridgeman, as First Lord, for example, recounts the 'dog-fight' which he had with Churchill over the naval estimates.[85] But if reduction in defence expenditure was his job as Chancellor, he was determined that such reduction should not jeopardise British security. For instance, in July 1926 he argued that the services should reduce their estimates because 'he was convinced that the picture of Japan going mad and attacking us had no sure foundation whatsoever'.[86] As regards the League, Churchill was no great supporter. In December 1924, for example, he argued that the new international body was not in a position to preserve peace. Peace could only be attained 'by the maintenance of good understandings between various groups of powers' and whilst this could possibly be achieved under the auspices of the League, he favoured a step-by-step approach to reaching the understandings which would lead to peace.[87] He informed Cecil that both the Geneva Protocol and disarmament seemed very unreal, and that while he was fighting the Admiralty's increased naval construction programme he did not do so for reasons of disarmament.[88] Britain required 'liberty' in the matter of armaments, not the 'handcuffs' of a disarmament convention.[89]

Sir Samuel Hoare,[90] was perhaps less hostile to disarmament than many of his colleagues. He did, however, have very definite views on how disarmament could and could not be achieved. Only a simple, step-by-step approach to the reduction of arms levels would work; any attempt to achieve a result 'by embracing . . . every conceivable question that is connected with it' would prohibit any progress being made.[91] The advent of the aeroplane had added a new dimension to the disarmament problem, which Hoare was quick to appreciate. Thus, whilst the discovery of flying was 'the greatest discovery of the twentieth century', he feared that it might prove to be a 'Frankenstein that will destroy civilisation'.[92] The difficulty was the impossibility of distinguishing between military and civilian aircraft; limiting military aircraft would not solve the problem because civilian aircraft could be converted almost instantly to perform the task of a military machine. 'Civil aeroplanes with no military aeroplanes to meet them, could with impunity deal death and destruction upon the men, women and children of the great cities.'[93]

Overall, Hoare was perhaps sceptical of the possibilities of disarmament rather than hostile towards the concept. Disarmament, he maintained, would not end war; disarmament talks did not 'mitigate international jealously [sic] and suspicion', indeed they tended to 'increase rather than diminish armaments, hasten rather than postpone war'.[94] In his unpublished typescript memoirs, he claimed that '[t]he Two Hague Conferences, the Anglo-German talks and the discussions of the Disarmament Conference at Geneva have probably done more harm than good'.[95] Whilst accepting the link between disarmament and security, he believed that security must come first. It was unreasonable to suppose that signing a Treaty of Mutual Assistance, the Protocol, the Optional Clause and other all-in arbitration treaties which no one wished to carry out, would save Europe.[96] A gradual change in the mentality of nations, and the adoption of every method for the strengthening of the forces of goodwill would create a situation in which, step by step, the reduction of aggressive weapons could be achieved.[97] Even so, Hoare claimed that the first duty of a British statesman was 'to maintain unity at home and to be sure that no action that he takes at Geneva or in the capitals of Europe will be injurious to the unifying forces of the Empire'.[98] '[E]ach country should arrange its armaments in accordance with its necessities', and, when this had been done, inform all friendly states of its proposals, whilst making every effort to eliminate 'causes of difference between States'.[99] Disarmament, therefore, was possible, in Hoare's view, but not by means of an all-embracing international conference.

Leopold Amery,[100] did not believe that disarmament could secure peace, nor that arms races, in general, led to war. Indeed, there might be occasions 'when the strain of competition to avert the danger of war may even hasten it'.[101] 'Wars', he told the House of Commons on 5 July 1933, 'are brought about by causes far deeper than armaments'.[102] Amery maintained that 'the disarmament of the free is the tyrant's opportunity', and if it strengthened the relative position of those who wished to overturn the existing international order, it could be positively dangerous.[103] He did not accept that the Treaty of Versailles contained any contractual obligation or pledge 'as to the date when general disarmament was to begin, or as to the extent to which it was to be carried'.[104]

In common with many Conservatives, Amery put more faith in the Empire than in the League of Nations.

> Some of us may have doubts whether all the nations represented at Geneva will spring to arms in time of danger, but we have no doubts whatever that all the members of our British Commonwealth will spring to arms at once in defence of the British Empire.[105]

He had no faith in any general schemes for disarmament or security, believing that both the Treaty of Mutual Assistance and the Geneva Protocol would have meant Britain putting her fighting forces at the disposal of a League of Nations General Staff.[106] When the collapse of the Disarmament Conference of 1932–4 was becoming apparent for all to see, his exasperation with the 'wild-goose chase after mechanical, reach-me-down schemes of world disarmament and peace', led him to compare himself with the boy who saw through the Emperor's new clothes.

> So far as I was concerned both Disarmament and a League of Nations with power to coerce belonged to the same category of imaginary Imperial robes.[107]

Another of the service ministers who had no faith in the League was W.C.

Bridgeman.[108] The League, he believed, was run by 'international cranks' who attempted to tie free people 'by fetters too rigid to be borne', and accused Cecil of wishing to leave all disputes to the 'tender mercies' of these cranks.[109] He fought long and hard with Churchill over cuts in the naval estimates, which he admitted was a difficult task, as Churchill knew much about Admiralty business whilst he himself was inexperienced. The battle was so intense that the Sea Lords threatened to resign, and Bridgeman recognised that this would make his own position extremely difficult.[110] He believed implicitly in a strong British navy, denouncing the Foreign Office for daring to suggest that there was 'no risk of war for ten years'; how could they, or anyone else predict the next war, he demanded?[111] 'It is amazing', he complained, ' that . . . politicians are ready to be convinced by the glib amateur strategist, and will never listen to the advice of life-experts'.[112] Bridgeman did work very hard to obtain agreement at the Coolidge Naval Conference in 1927, but perhaps more in order to prevent the United States obtaining supremacy than from any desire to reduce the level of naval armaments.

Lord Londonderry, Secretary of State for Air during the 1932–4 World Disarmament Conference, was an inauspicious choice in view of his passionate anti-disarmament stance. When the subject of the prohibition of bombers was put to the Conference, he acknowledged that benefits would no doubt accrue from the abolition of bombing, but it seemed to him to be a 'Utopian picture'. He believed that any convention would be dangerous as it 'would almost certainly be violated directly war broke out'.[113] In 1935, when speaking in the House of Lords about the events of 1932, Londonderry made his most famous speech, during which he declared: 'I had the greatest difficulty, amid the public outcry, in saving the bomber.'[114]

Equally unfortunate were the choices of First Lord of the Admiralty, and Secretary of State for War in the National government, Sir Bolton Eyres-Monsell, and Douglas Hogg, the first Lord Hailsham, respectively. Eyres-Monsell actually attended the 1932–34 Disarmament Conference for a few days, and as he was leaving for London, remarked to a group of British delegates '[t]he sooner your bloody conference is wound up, the better for all concerned'.[115] Of Hailsham, Cecil observed that privately he did not conceal his contempt and disapproval of disarmament.[116] Together, the three Service Ministers of the National government formed a massive hurdle to any constructive attempt to achieve success in the negotiations at Geneva.

The most junior Conservative minister to be involved in the disarmament question was Sir Anthony Eden, who became Under-Secretary to the Foreign Office in September 1931. He was sent to Geneva, as a substitute delegate to the Disarmament Conference, on 2 November 1932, 'without a single syllable of instruction or advice'.[117] Eden 'strongly favoured an arms agreement, in the national as well as the international interest', the alternative being 'nervous tension in the world and costly rearmament'.[118] Armaments, he believed, were 'the expression of political ambition or fear'.[119] Once arrived at Geneva, he worked closely with the Foreign Office adviser, Alexander Cadogan, and the chief military adviser, Major-General Temperley. These three junior delegates recognised long before their political superiors in London, that the disarmament negotiations were, in Cadogan's words 'drifting to disaster'.[120] Between them they drew up a Disarmament Convention which was designed give the initiative back to Britain, and to breathe life back into the proceedings. Eden was, according to the rest of the British delegation, including the 'sailors, soldiers, even airmen', the only one who understood the problem.[121]

Labour ministers

James Ramsay MacDonald[122] held strong views on disarmament, whilst recognising that the question would present any government with a dilemma:

> It is a very serious dilemma, and it is this: On the one hand, you say to a Government, 'Do not spend in armaments'. The Government says, 'We must spend; public opinion compels us to spend; public fear compels us to spend'. That is one side. The other horn is, 'Spend, and you make war inevitable'. It is a horrible dilemma, in which every Government will find itself . . . .[123]

MacDonald had carried his objections to the First World War further than many of his Labour colleagues by resigning in protest at conscription, and was more surprised than most at his subsequent election as Chairman of the Party in early 1923.[124] In 1917, in a study entitled *National Defence: A Study in Militarism*, he declared that 'arms never can provide for national security . . . they only keep nations insecure',[125] and that the contemplation of use of military power to preserve the peace merely played into the hands of the militarists. MacDonald firmly believed that security must come before disarmament; in correspondence with Cecil on the proposed Treaty of Mutual Assistance in 1924 he declared '[m]y own feeling about Disarmament is that we ought to advance the political side a bit further before we can expect any good result from a direct approach to the problem'.[126] In 1927, following the collapse of the Geneva Naval Conference, he remarked in his diary that 'Geneva has revived the Protocol as I knew it would have to do so soon as it would be convinced of the futility of considering armaments apart from security.'[127]

For MacDonald, disarmament was part of his socialist ideology[128] having more to do with peace than any political or economic considerations:

Disarmament is of little value apart from peace. I take a minor interest in it for purposes of economy; from the point of view of peace it is a major issue. But that drives it back on to political conditions which are the sources of war. Armaments only give nations a chance of coming out of a war as victors, reduction in armaments only secure [*sic*] that a war will begin slowly and then develop. The over-riding task of Governments is to secure peace.[129]

MacDonald thus worked towards disarmament from a different angle from the majority of his contemporaries; neither treaty obligations nor economy were the driving force behind MacDonald's search for disarmament. His outlook was apparently based firmly on the Morgenthau theory, and his aim was to remove the perceived need to fight. He was only too aware, however, of the problems of achieving such an idealistic situation; in 1923, whilst in opposition, he remarked to Cecil, 'whilst in my present position I can indulge in absolute ideas, had I to face the actual day to day responsibility I might be compelled to make compromises'.[130]

If the creation of a suitable political atmosphere was MacDonald's ambition, he was in no doubt as to where the chief obstacle lay; France was the peace problem of Europe, her mentality being purely militarist. 'Problem is', he commented in his diary in 1930, 'will France allow Europe to disarm?'[131] French diplomacy was 'crooked' and 'an ever-active influence for evil in Europe';[132] the sole problem for Europe was how to keep France in her place.[133] MacDonald supported the League of Nations, and earned praise from Cecil for his visits and speeches to the Assembly, but he never wholeheartedly believed that the League could achieve disarmament by means of large, general conferences, preferring to use his own personal diplomacy. Whilst MacDonald obviously had many detractors, especially after the fall of the Labour government in August 1931, many of his peers had great admiration for his abilities. Esher, for example, thought him a 'statesman and a humanist', Templewood believed he was wise in starting at the political end; Cecil maintained that he really understood foreign policy, whilst Scott, of the *Manchester Guardian* declared him to be 'the best Foreign Minister we have had in recent times'.[134]

During his second period in office, MacDonald was forced to abandon the idea of being his own Foreign Secretary, and, much against his will, appointed Arthur Henderson to the position. The antagonism between the two was increased following the fall of the second Labour government, Henderson sharing the Labour Party's sense of betrayal and MacDonald being indignant that Henderson remained President-elect of the forthcoming Disarmament Conference.[135] The antagonism between Prime Minister and Foreign Secretary, more pronounced on MacDonald's part, hindered Henderson in many aspects of his work. Henderson was a great believer in disarmament through the League and, having lost a son during the Battle of the Somme, determined in his role of Foreign Secretary to create a situation in which war was unthinkable. An author of the Geneva Protocol, he was a firm adherent of collective security, and was one of the few British statesmen in the inter-war years to understand and appreciate the concerns of the French and the successor states of Eastern Europe. With the death of the German statesman, Gustav Stresemann, in October 1929, he became the leading figure at Geneva and the League, eclipsing even Aristide Briand of France. His personal relations with individual members of foreign governments were always cordial, even warm, and as the leading international statesperson of the time was confirmed as President of the Disarmament Conference.[136] Not without reason, Henderson has often been considered Labour's best Foreign Secretary in the twentieth century.[137] The success of the Disarmament Conference would have been his crowning achievement.

It has been said of Philip Snowden[138] that 'his good faith and . . . devotion to Labour principles were beyond challenge' and that he was trusted by everyone in the Labour Party.[139] As Labour's leading expert on financial affairs (until 1931) he was in favour of arms reductions as a means of reducing expenditure, and in the first Labour administration fought a tenacious battle with the Admiralty over the naval estimates, which 'ended . . . in a draw'; a compromise was reached on cruiser requirements, whilst Snowden 'gained a point by securing a stoppage on the fortifying of Singapore'.[140] In contrast, he made few ventures into the area of multilateral disarmament, although he did protest very strongly to Baldwin in May 1932 that the Cabinet's decision to defend the use of chemical weapons would 'make a very bad impression on public opinion in this country' and hoped that the Cabinet would fall into line with the other nations, and withdraw any reservations.[141] As for the other major criterion in solving the disarmament dilemma – recognition of French fears – Snowden seems to have been a positive liability. MacDonald observed that Snowden's method of negotiation was 'to throw daggers', that he upset the French delegation to the Dawes Conference in 1924 to such an extent that the Conference almost collapsed, and that Herriot, the French Prime Minister, saw Snowden as an enemy.[142]

Lord Parmoor[143] was an ecclesiastical lawyer, whose pacifism brought him into the ranks of Labour, and in MacDonald's first administration he was made responsible for League of Nations affairs.[144] Parmoor felt himself in complete agreement with MacDonald on foreign and international questions, but that he was a 'cuckoo in the nest' at the Foreign Office where his enthusiasm was not shared.[145] He sought reassurance from MacDonald before agreeing to join his government, that the Labour Party would adopt a new foreign policy on new lines 'substituting friendliness and goodwill for the war spirit', and that a generous, but firm, policy would be adopted towards France.[146] As far as the League itself was concerned, Parmoor inclined more to the view that it could not be regarded as a superstate, and also believed that it would not be effective 'until there has been reduction in armaments and a more inclusive policy of equality among all countries on questions of right'.[147] As Head of the British delegation to the Fifth League Assembly he was instrumental, along with Henderson, in drawing up and pressing for the acceptance of the Geneva Protocol. He deeply regretted that MacDonald would not allow him to sign it.

J.H. Thomas,[148] former trade union activist and member of Labour's right wing, would seem to have been a somewhat pugnacious individual to represent Britain at the opening of the Disarmament Conference in February 1932. Cecil, for instance, records that Thomas's suggested method of persuading the Australian Prime Minister to take a more reasonable view at the Paris Peace Conference, was to hit him between the eyes,[149] and on meeting the principal delegates to the Disarmament Conference in Geneva commented that he had enjoyed it 'better than bull fighting'.[150] Thomas did not appear to see the intrinisic link between security and disarmament; when, following the inaugural sessions of the Conference in February 1932, the French Prime Minister, André Tardieu explained to him France's need for greater security, his only comment was 'Oh 'ell'.[151] This remark Cadogan translated to Tardieu as 'Mr Thomas had listened with great attention and interest and would report faithfully to his colleagues'.[152] Thomas was apparently going to need an extremely diplomatic interpreter if he was to appear to understand the key issues at the Conference![153]

The Service Ministers in MacDonald's Labour administrations took little part in the disarmament question, whether because MacDonald gave them little scope to exert their own personalities, or because they had nothing to contribute in that area. Lord Thomson, Secretary of State for Air in both Labour administrations until his death in the R101 disaster in October 1930, was one of MacDonald's few close friends, and perhaps shared his goals and ideals more than anyone, but his other colleagues had far less to recommend them. According to MacDonald, Viscount Chelmsford, First Lord of the Admiralty in the 1924 Labour government, was weak and the commendations of him, put forward by Haldane, the Lord Chancellor, had been 'falsified'.[154] Chelmsford's successor in MacDonald's second administration, A.V. Alexander, fared little better, being, in Lord Thomson's opinion, a 'mere agent of the admirals' and playing no decisive part in naval disarmament.[155] MacDonald also queried Alexander's ability to keep the Admiralty in check;[156] for example, in criticising a naval reduction scheme Alexander and the Admiralty had produced, he asked 'Are you sure we have cut as far as is possible? In 1924 the Admiralty said they were going to the bone; in 1925/6 a Tory 1st Lord cut deeper. That was bad for our reputation'.[157] Tom Shaw,[158] Minister of War from 1929–31 was, according to Major-General A. C. Temperley, 'by conviction a pacifist' who did not wish 'to have anything to do with war or military operations',[159] and according to Liddell Hart became a joke at the War Office – no more than a 'rubber stamp'.[160]

Non-elected policy-makers

It was not only the elected representatives who exercised power over policy-making and hence, disarmament. Sir Maurice Hankey, Secretary to the War Cabinet, the postwar Cabinet and the Committee of Imperial Defence for the whole of the period under review, was a man of great influence. Clemenceau called him the real master of ceremonies at the Peace Conference,[161] and Sir Henry Wilson, Chief of the Imperial General Staff, remarked in relation to the disorganisation of meetings from which Hankey was absent, 'If you once lose hold of Hanky-Panky you are done, absolutely done'.[162] Hankey's influence, however, was more than organisational; in discussions on the naval enquiry in December 1920, Lloyd George remarked that 'we must watch Hankey very carefully, for this sort of enquiry has a knack of coming out the way he wants'.[163] Hankey did not approve of the League of Nations; he rejected the offer to become its first Secretary-General, stating that the 'British Empire is worth 1,000 Leagues of Nations'.[164] Similarly his views on disarmament were clearly set out in his 'Introduction to the Study of Disarmament',[165] in which he stated that disarmament was responsible for 'decline of the military spirit' which had led to the crumbling of all the early empires. He believed that the 'perspective of the Peace Conference was somewhat warped by the recent struggle', and that the speed at which Britain had reduced her armaments after the Conference was largely responsible for the 'present weakness of trade and unemployment'. Hankey maintained that 'our first task is to re-establish the sinews of war which provided such an important element in the victory of the Allies in the late war'.

Another of the non-elected policy makers was Sir Eyre Crowe, Permanent Under-Secretary at the Foreign Office until his death in 1925. Crowe was another who thought that the reduction in armaments carried out by Britain was a weakening process, believing that the rather precarious peace which existed in postwar Europe was maintained by the armies of France and of the Little Entente, whilst Britain was unable to reap the fruits of her victory over Turkey because of her military impotence.[166] In particular, he argued that the signatories of the League Covenant were not, in fact, committed to arms reductions under Article 8; what Article 8 really meant was that the maintenance of peace required national armaments not to exceed the needs of national safety.[167] Even Hankey, Crowe maintained, had fallen into the trap of believing that the nations of the British Empire, as signatories of the Covenant 'are definitely committed to the principle of limitation of armaments'.[168] Crowe firmly believed that the practical difficulties inherent in any scheme of limitation of armaments had never been surmounted and that no one had ever been able to work out a practical plan of disarmament. One reason for this was that general confidence in the good faith of all parties did not exist. 'There is good reason', he maintained, 'why it should not exist. History and the nature of things and men afford the explanation. Nor [was] there any prospect that it [would] exist in the future.'[169] Thus, if a clause in a treaty was 'incapable of execution' it was not good policy to insist on it being carried out. No one, he argued, would seriously claim that His Majesty's government should insist on the surrender and trial of the Kaiser simply because they had committed themselves to it under the Treaty of Versailles; therefore discretion should be exercised in implementing clauses which were impractical.[170] Crowe's solution to the disarmament dilemma was that, rather than drop the matter altogether – too heroic a step – British policy ought to be to criticise any plans for disarmament or guarantees which might be offered![171]

Another influential, non-elected official with strong views on disarmament was Sir Robert Vansittart, Permanent Under-Secretary at the Foreign Office from 1930–8. Vansittart did not believe in disarmament through international conference; indeed he disapproved of the Washington Conference of 1922, describing it as 'an endless process of bargaining about guns and tons and categories, which ended by nearly costing us our very existence'.[172] There was only one possible basis for the multilateral limitation of armaments, and it was 'confidence not categories'.[173] Unfortunately, as far as Vansittart was concerned, there could be no confidence without 'permanent unilateral disarmament of the aggressors', by which Vansittart meant Germany. The Disarmament Conference, which in his opinion should never have been called, would fail for lack of this confidence; but having been summoned, Vansittart saw the conference as perhaps offering the breakthrough in persuading the government to stiffen its commitments to France, the only way he could see to deter the Germans.[174]

Towards the end of the period under review, a champion of the disarmament cause emerged in the ranks of the non-elected representatives. Sir Alexander Cadogan was head of the League of Nations section at the Foreign Office, and chief adviser to the British delegation at the Disarmament Conference of 1932–4. In 1927 he wrote a Memorandum on the current disarmament situation, in which he stated that 'States maintain their present armaments because they consider them indispensable to secure them against the dangers with which they are or might be threatened', and drew the rather pessimistic conclusion that not even a Protocol 'which must depend for its efficacy on absolute good faith . . . would effect such a radical improvement as to change the whole mood of Europe'.[175] Chamberlain criticised the memorandum as 'consistently negative' and concluding 'on a note of despair'.[176] By 1933, however, Cadogan had recognised the increasingly imperative need for Britain to take the lead in saving the Disarmament Conference, and with Eden and Temperley drew up the British Draft Convention known as the MacDonald Plan. The hardest part was to persuade Simon that it should be presented to the Conference. Cadogan's diary for the period is full of cries of frustration at Simon's reluctance to commit the Cabinet to this course of action. 'Here we are', he lamented at one point, 'left alone to do Simon's work for him . . . '[177] A few days later he complained that Simon had rung him from London, 'only to wrangle about texts – not to give any guidance'.[178] 'Simon says P.M. has gone to country', he wrote, 'so what can he do?' and, as an afterthought, wrote '(Shoot himself)'.[179] But Cadogan was adamant that, in spite of the lack of support from senior colleagues, the Draft Convention would be presented to the Conference, and he and Eden exerted tremendous pressure until MacDonald and Simon accepted their point of view. 'You have both been so right on this', Simon told the two most junior members of the British delegation.[180]

Conclusion

The foregoing representative sample of individual members of the policy-making élite during the period under consideration demonstrates the breadth of views held. They range from the militarism of Churchill to the pacifism of Parmoor, and all shades in between. As far as Conservative Ministers are concerned, in general they did not understand disarmament, and held the 'insane view . . . that the people who must be obeyed on any question of disarmament are the fighting services'.[181] Never, during the 1920s, was disarmament an item of priority among Conservative ministers. Baldwin, in concentrating on his own particular fields of interest – holding the Party together, and striving for industrial peace – left matters of foreign policy to successive Foreign Secretaries, notably Austen Chamberlain (1924–9). But whilst Chamberlain did recognise that disarmament meant reduction by international agreement, his approach to gaining such international agreement differed greatly from that of Cecil, the man to whom he left most of the work until the latter's resignation in 1927. Despite his gradually dawning respect and support for the League, and his desire to offer some tangible form of security to the French, Chamberlain's approach to disarmament was *re*active, whereas Cecil's was *pro*active. He would *not* provide a positive lead. Neither, as might be expected, was there a lead from the Conservative Service Ministers, whether in the Baldwin administration of 1924–9, or the National government of 1931–5.

Labour Ministers predictably held much stronger views on the necessity to achieve a measure of disarmament, but their individual potential during two periods of minority administration was very much subordinated to the policy of Ramsay MacDonald and to the need for Liberal support. Only Henderson achieved any individual success, working tenaciously both as Secretary of State for Foreign Affairs to achieve acceptance of the Optional Clause and General Act, as well as in his role as President-elect in preparing for the Disarmament Conference. MacDonald himself, as shown above, worked for peace rather than disarmament, believing wholeheartedly that one would follow the other. In this respect there are great similarities between MacDonald and Chamberlain; both wanted to improve what MacDonald referred to as the international 'weather'.

The Liberals had their own problems of unity and direction. Lloyd George, whilst ostensibly supporting the idea of a general reduction in armaments, was given more to grand gestures and speeches than to the patient negotiations which were needed to achieve such reduction. He avoided the League, preferring his own personal, flamboyant style of diplomacy. Even his notable overruling of the Admiralty at the Washington Naval Conference was more a gesture than a real conviction. Simon, preoccupied as he was with his own position within the predominantly Conservative National government of 1931–5, did not have the necessary strength of character to make any impression on the Disarmament Conference, which was arguably the last hope of success for disarmament in the inter-war period, whilst Samuel, no matter how strong his ideological support for disarmament, was not in a position to make any impression on the proceedings of the Conference or the policy of the National government.

If any of the above elected politicians were in doubt as to the direction which British policy should take, they would, of course, take the advice of the permanent Whitehall officials – and would, in no uncertain terms, be warned not only of the dangers of Britain reducing her level of armaments but of the further dangers of multilateral negotiations under the League. But for most of the period under review this was unnecessary. The Conservatives dominated the governments, and individually as well as collectively, they were inclined to hinder rather than pursue disarmament. It was a problem which, with any luck, would simply fade away; and if it would not, it would be better to adopt a policy of avoiding responsibility for the anticipated breakdown of negotiations rather than continue making concessions.[182]

It was significant that the only men who truly recognised the seriousness of the disarmament question were those ministers and representatives who worked for any length of time at Geneva. At the highest level, Cecil and Henderson came into this category. The work of more junior representatives, however, should also be noted, particularly Eden and Cadogan, who were close to the heart of the problem during the Disarmament Conference of 1932–4. During this period, they exerted whatever pressure they could on their superiors in London to go at least to Geneva and try to retrieve the rapidly disintegrating conference. At the same time, they were unable to instil the real nature and urgency of the problem into the minds of those who actually made the policy decisions.

The views of the foregoing cross-section of the policy-making élite demonstrate that whilst there was no one consistent view on the desirability and/or feasibility of reaching an international disarmament agreement, the supporters of, and believers in, such a cause were considerably outnumbered by those to whom disarmament was either a utopian dream or a severe threat to British power. In the following chapters it will be demonstrated just how important the views of these individuals were in influencing successive British governments' reactions to the dilemma in which they found themselves in the aftermath of the Great War.

4

THE LLOYD GEORGE COALITION GOVERNMENT, 1918–22

Victory in war was bought at a considerable price; Britain was almost bankrupt as a result of the colossal expenditure demanded by the war effort, yet Lloyd George's electioneering pledges in November 1918 promised a more socially just order and the creation of a 'fit country for heroes to live in'.[1] The fulfilment of these pledges would appear to demand that Britain, for a time, should become more inward-looking, and should concentrate on channelling her resources into rebuilding her social and economic fabric. But as a result of the Paris Peace Conference, Britain had acquired greater overseas commitments; her Empire had increased considerably and now included Tanganyika and South West Africa, the extensive new mandated territories in the Middle and Near East resulting from the dissolution of the Ottoman Empire, Transjordan, Mesopotamia and Palestine, whilst the Dominions themselves had acquired further responsibilities in New Guinea and Samoa.[2] By June 1920 the Secretary of State for War, Winston Churchill, was questioning Britain's ability to continue to meet her responsibilities. 'I am sure we are trying to do too much with our present forces and certainly it is impossible, within the present financial limits, for me to continue to meet the varied and numerous obligations of our policy . . . .'[3] He asked 'Are we to defend Persia, to go on reducing the garrison in Mesopotamia, reduce military responsibilities there and in Palestine, who is to be responsible for civil administration of Mesopotamia etc.?'[4] The list of current responsibilities cited by Churchill included India, Egypt, Ireland and Aden, as well as the commitments mentioned above, but another new dimension had been added to British interests, including the Army of the Rhine, the Army of the Black Sea and the proposed Anglo-American guarantee of French security, as well as the internal defence of Great Britain.

In addition to her increased Empire commitments, Britain also had a new commitment to the continent of Europe, something which she had always striven to avoid. Europe was in chaos, needing a strong hand to guide it towards stability, and this was a challenge on which Lloyd George could not to be expected to turn his back. Besides, he could not afford to concentrate purely on domestic matters. Not only was his undoubted expertise needed abroad, his position at the head of the Conservative-dominated Coalition depended increasingly on successes in foreign policy. This posed a considerable dilemma; how to juggle the demands for social and domestic reform, decreased military expenditure, increased military commitment and the political and economic reconstruction of Europe? It is very important to bear all aspects of this dilemma in mind when looking at the steps which the Lloyd George Coalition was willing, or able, to take towards meeting the commitment to international disarmament. In the latter respect, during the course of his administration, two particular problems were of major importance: naval rivalry with the United States and Japan; and the establishment by the League of Nations of the Temporary Mixed Commission on Armaments.

Naval rivalry

In mid-1919 Sir Maurice Hankey, as Secretary to the Cabinet and Committee of Imperial Defence, reported that it was vital to cut down expenditure 'otherwise bankruptcy stares us in the face'.[5] At the same meeting at which this conclusion was reached, another important and far-reaching decision was made; that the Service Departments should frame their estimates on the assumption that the British Empire would not be engaged in war with a major Power for ten years. The famous, or infamous, Ten-Year Rule was later to be rolled forward year by year until it was finally abandoned in March 1932. Economic necessity thus dictated that, in spite of Britain's increased military commitments, drastic reductions should be made in the level of her fighting forces. She was, of course, not alone in this type of reduction in the wake of the Great War; demobilisation and arms reductions for reasons of economy were carried out by all the victorious Allies. In Britain's case it was certainly done with a careful eye on the security both of the British Isles themselves, and of the needs of the Empire. But one aspect of arms reductions caused much concern, both amongst politicians and the Service concerned: the ongoing supremacy of the British navy.

In March 1919, the First Lord of the Admiralty, Walter Long, wrote to Lloyd George in Paris to inform him of the progress of the navy vote through Parliament. Long summed up the Admiralty's, and the government's, predicament thus:

> the feeling in the House of Commons is in favour of an adequate Navy, sufficient to protect our island country, and to do its duty throughout the Empire . . . but that at the same time every effort must be made to secure strict economy, great reduction in expenditure, and that nothing must be done, consistent with our safety, which would prejudice our position in carrying out our domestic reform programme. . . .[6]

When Long was informed of the decision that there should be no increase in naval shipbuilding, and that only £60 million would be available for the navy in the coming year, he, according to Hankey, 'took it well'.[7] By February 1920, however, although the estimates had risen to £84 million, also with no allowance for any new programme of construction, the Admiralty Board was protesting that naval supremacy was under severe threat.[8] The main threat came from the United States which, in 1916, had adopted a naval programme designed to give her a navy second to none. This aim was not only a reflection of the United States' growing share in world trade, with a consequent need for a larger mercantile navy with appropriate defensive support, but also a result of British and German 'disregard for American interests on the high seas' during the early part of the Great War.[9] There was no place for Britain's traditional standing as the world's dominant naval power in Wilson's new world order.

In July 1920 a British Admiralty Memorandum pointed out that, unless the Americans could be persuaded to abandon their 1916 naval building programme, the following spring was the latest date at which Great Britain could 'take steps to prevent the Empire from occupying a position of absolute and marked inferiority at sea by the year 1924'.[10] Whilst the Admiralty was prepared to accept some inferiority in post-Jutland battleships, they were not prepared to go below a margin of nine of this class as compared with the twelve to be possessed by the United States.[11] Since economy was the over-riding aim of the postwar government, a naval building race was an unacceptable prospect. As Sir Arthur Balfour, Lord President of the Council, said, the government 'had to choose between the Scylla of financial embarrassment on the one side, and the Charybdis of an unsatisfactory naval position . . . on the other'.[12] A Cabinet Memorandum also questioned the 'place and usefulness of the capital ship in future naval operations'.[13] Lloyd George, according to Hankey, wanted 'to be able to prove that the Capital Ship is doomed – which would be very convenient politically',[14] although the Admiralty had produced a very powerful memo to show that this was not the case. But perhaps the final straw was the statement by Lloyd George to the Committee of Imperial Defence that as soon as Britain embarked on a naval race, the United States would demand payment of the £1,000,000,000 owed to her in war debts, which would be on top of the money to build the ships.[15]

The potential naval race was not confined to the two largest naval Powers; the Japanese were also rapidly increasing their naval strength. The United States naturally saw a threat from Japanese economic expansionism in the Pacific and East Asia, and this increased their commitment to the idea of a Big Navy. By 1921 the Americans had seven battleships and six battle-cruisers under construction. Britain was also very concerned over the prospect of an increase in the Japanese navy, and as Lloyd George pointed out, whilst Japan was not as affluent as the United States, she had no debt and 'her people were of a lower standard than the European, and they might be prepared to make greater sacrifices'.[16] A large Japanese navy was not only a threat to Britain's overall naval supremacy, but her larger and more numerous cruisers would enable her to challenge Britain's position as far as her Asian possessions were concerned.

In 1902 Britain had concluded an alliance with Japan, essentially as a safeguard against Czarist Russia; this alliance had been renewed in 1905 and 1911, and was due to expire in 1921. The situation in the Far East had changed a great deal since 1902. Soviet Russia, torn by war and internal revolution, was not the threat it had been in 1902; the Japanese were now seen as economic competitors, and there was concern that Japanese envy of Britain's world-wide Empire might well develop along the lines of Germany's pre-war jealousy. Curzon thought that if this were the case, there could be no doubt that the Anglo-Japanese alliance 'has enabled us to exercise a very powerful controlling influence on the sometimes dangerous ambitions of Japan'.[17] A Foreign Office Memorandum, however, maintained that the *raison d'être* of the alliance had ceased to exist, and furthermore that, in its present shape, it was probably incompatible with the League of Nations. It was suggested that it either be modified to meet the requirements of the League or dropped entirely.[18] The Foreign Office Memorandum concluded that Britain's aims were 'above all things peace and the rehabilitation of China; to work in full harmony and co-operation with the United States, and: to preserve, if possible, friendly relations with Japan and to secure her genuine co-operation in the peaceful development of the Far East'.[19]

If the *raison d'être* of the alliance had, in fact, ceased to exist, there were those who believed it ought to be renewed from a strictly strategic point of view to maintain the friendship of one who could turn into a formidable enemy.[20] But in the final analysis, if the alliance was not directed against the Soviet Union, the only other possible opponent must be the United States, and in the light of deteriorating relations between America and Japan, and the apparently inevitable onset of a naval race with both Britain and Japan, the US did not wish to see a renewal of the alliance.[21] There were thus two powerful reasons for reaching a closer understanding with the United States; the impending naval race and the question of the Anglo-Japanese alliance.

An opportunity to address outstanding differences with the United States appeared to present itself with the swearing in of a new American administration in March 1921. At first sight the prospects of reaching an understanding on levels of armaments with the new President Harding seemed remote. In December 1920, before taking office, Harding had proclaimed the need for a Big Navy and a big merchant marine, and was believed to hold the view that the United States should wait until its naval strength had exceeded that of Britain, in approximately three years' time, in order to be able to negotiate from a position of strength.[22] Britain, of course, could not afford to sit back and wait for this 'position of strength' to become a reality. However a sign of hope came on 14 December 1920, when the powerful Republican Senator Borah introduced a resolution in the Senate which called for a 50 per cent reduction in the naval building programmes of Britain, Japan, and the United States. The CID immediately instructed Curzon to write to the British Ambassador in Washington instructing him to 'do his best to ascertain, unostentatiously' how the new administration would view a discussion on this question.[23]

On 11 July 1921, the day after the Naval Appropriations Bill, including the Borah resolution, was approved by Congress, President Harding announced his intention to summon a conference in Washington. Harding's haste in taking the initiative was to prevent the British government from summoning a conference in London; in Washington the Americans could set the agenda. In the event, this suited Britain in that she was merely called upon to respond to whatever the Americans proposed. In all, nine states were invited; in addition to the five great naval Powers, China, Belgium, The Netherlands and Portugal would attend in order to discuss the Far Eastern and Pacific situation. The British tried to persuade the US to hold a preliminary conference with themselves and the Japanese in order to 'arrive at a common understanding on the wider principles which should underlie the future Pacific policy of the three powers'.[24] They had not, in fact, intended that the two subjects – disarmament and Pacific security – be discussed at the same time, preferring that the latter point be discussed earlier, in London. But misunderstandings and poor communication between Curzon and Secretary of State Hughes led the latter to conclude that the British government were trying to 'hoodwink' the United States by taking the initiative from them, and this, in turn, led to the 'extremely hurried nature' of the American government's actions in pressing ahead with arrangements for the conference.[25]

The Washington Conference

The Washington Conference opened on 12 November 1921; Lloyd George himself did not attend, being totally preoccupied with the problems of Ireland. It is possible to suggest, as Erik Goldstein does,[26] that the Irish question merely provided a very useful excuse for Lloyd George not to attend, but the understanding of the British Empire Delegation was that Lloyd George would travel to Washington should his presence be required. In early December Hankey wrote to the Prime Minister that 'Nothing has exercised my mind more than the question of whether it is essential for you to come out or not' and the conclusion he reached was that 'it is not at present indispensable'.[27] Hankey did observe, however, that 'from a more public and general point of view I think your arrival here would be an inestimable advantage', one reason being that Hughes had slowed down the

Conference, and Lloyd George's presence might speed things up, as Hughes 'will be very frightened of your being too clever for him, and on his guard against the hustle'.[28]

In the absence of Lloyd George, the British delegation was more than ably led by Balfour, assisted by Hankey and representatives of the Admiralty. Balfour dealt with the difficult business of reconciling instructions from the Cabinet and Foreign Office and dealing with the Admiralty representatives and technical experts attached to the British delegation, as well as with the conflicting demands and personalities of US, French and Japanese delegates, all in his own inimitable style. At one point he summed up his somewhat difficult position in a telegram to the Foreign Office:

> I am to try, if possible to induce the French to agree to a very small battle fleet so as to leave us free to accept American proposals without modification. Having persuaded them to deprive themselves of their form of naval defence I am then to persuade them that they really require no submarines because a war between France and England is unthinkable. This task being successfully accomplished, I am then to ask them to reduce the number of their aircraft seeing that we cannot sleep securely in our beds lest in a war with France, London should be burnt to the ground! For a task as complex as this I fear a trained diplomatist is required. But I will do my best.[29]

Balfour did more than his best: he scored a triumph. He negotiated, drafted, smoothed ruffled feathers and was, as Auckland Geddes observed, 'in great form' and 'a hit with the Americans'.[30] Harding's secretary remarked to Hankey, 'I am just gone on Balfour'.[31] Even so, instructions from Lloyd George and the Cabinet crossed the Atlantic on a daily basis.[32]

It has been suggested that Britain was less than enthusiastic about the conference, in that little preparation appears to have been made in advance.[33] However, as early as August 1921 the Cabinet decided that the British case 'must be prepared in a most serious and hopeful spirit',[34] and the Standing Defence Sub-Committee of the CID was immediately charged with gathering together a large amount of material for the use of the British Empire Delegation on all subjects likely to be raised. In addition, the Foreign Office had been engaged for some months on the preparation of memoranda on the many political questions which were liable to arise at the Conference.[35] Admittedly the date on which the Standing Sub-Committee produced its terms of reference (24 October), was very close to the opening date of the Conference (12 November), but it spelt out the government's position very clearly. First and foremost, the aim of the British Empire Delegation at the Washington Conference is to achieve the largest possible reduction in expenditure on armaments, subject to two fundamental considerations:– First, that the vital interests of the British Empire are safeguarded. . . . Second, that the conclusions of the Conference are of a stable character and are not liable to be dislocated by any miscalculation of national or political elements concerned, such as occurred after the Paris Peace Conference, owing to the refusal of the Government of the United States to ratify the instruments drawn up.[36]

The British government were not prepared to be caught out again by United States isolationism!

The document clearly highlighted 'the vital importance of disarmament from the standpoint of the British Exchequer', and went on to deal with political problems such as the preservation of the status of Hong Kong and Kowloon, the freedom to develop the naval base at Singapore, and the importance of Wei-Hai-Wei as a 'sanatorium to the fleet in the China Seas'. As early as June 1921 the Standing Defence Sub-Committee had reached the conclusion that, whilst accepting current financial constraints, it was vital that Singapore be developed as 'a base of concentration, repair, and supply for the British fleet'.[37] The Sub-Committee also reached the conclusion in relation to the Washington Conference 'that the strategical interests of the British Empire would be best served by a maintenance of the territorial *status quo* in the Far East' and that any attempt to raise the question of the regulation or limitation of methods of warfare should be resisted. Submarines, however, were open for discussion since a ban on their unrestricted use 'could not fail to be of importance to British commerce'. Particular emphasis was placed on the extent to which Britain had already unilaterally disarmed. While the United States and Japan had been steadily building up their navies, Britain had not laid down a single new ship since the Armistice. Similarly, in the case of the army and air force, Britain's levels were far lower than those of France.

These instances, which are mentioned to illustrate broadly how far we have gone in disarmament, can be supplemented by the technical missions should the British Empire Delegation find it desirable to develop this aspect of disarmament.[38]

A further guideline came from the Committee of Imperial Defence, where Winston Churchill proposed that the 'Naval delegates should go to Washington with a clear statement of our proposed annual building programme, based on the one-power standard'.[39] Britain could then offer to cut out the ships included in the 1924 building programme and abandon the programmes of 1922–3. This would avoid the appearance of Britain conceding nothing whilst the United States would be asked to reduce her published building programme. Whilst the abandoning of the two-power standard was 'regretted',[40] it was a financial necessity. As far as practical measures of disarmament were concerned, however, the final instructions to the British Empire Delegation contained no positive proposals. The aim was to 'allow the other delegations to put forward their proposals, and submit them to criticism'.[41] At the same time, the Delegation's terms of reference were clearly set out; safeguard the Empire, maintain the *status quo* in the Far East, refuse to talk about reduction of land and air armaments, but press for the total abolition of submarines.

The British Empire Delegation arrived in Washington on 10 November 1921, after a moderately rough voyage, during which Balfour avoided sea-sickness by remaining in bed almost the whole time. He did, however, work very hard and 'absorbed the mass of detail . . . involved in the Conference and [was] extraordinarily well up in the whole question'.[42] Sir Maurice Hankey's correspondence with Lloyd George during the conference provides a very useful picture of the proceedings, both from a political and diplomatic point of view, and also from a more personal angle. He observed, for instance, that the cavalry escort which conducted them to their lodgings on their arrival was noted for its apparent inability to remain mounted, someone having told him that 'the troops always fall off their horses . . . and sure enough one of them did on this occasion'.[43] Whilst many of Hankey's observations are businesslike and politically impartial, his somewhat acerbic temperament led him to describe President Harding 'as being a very sincere, likeable sort of man, but not very "quick in the uptake"'.[44] Similarly, Secretary of State Charles Evans Hughes was 'very suspicious by temperament',[45] and Colonel Roosevelt, Chairman of the Technical Sub-Committee 'a tremendous babbler',[46] a point which had some interesting repercussions later in the proceedings.

The Conference opened on Saturday, 12 November 1921, with what Balfour described as a 'dramatic announcement' by Hughes. None of the visiting delegations had had any idea of the content of Hughes' speech in advance; even when pressed by Balfour on the previous evening 'he had smilingly asked me not to press him as to the contents of his opening statement'.[47] In his address, Hughes referred back to the first Disarmament Conference convened by the Emperor of Russia, and told the Powers that they were 'admonished by the futility of the earlier efforts'.[48] He stressed the waste involved in constantly designing and producing ever more advanced weapons.

> Moreover in proportion as the armaments of each Power increase so they less and less fulfil the object which the Governments have set before themselves. . . . To put an end to these incessant armaments

and to seek a means of warding off the calamities which are threatening the whole world, such is the supreme duty which is to-day imposed on all States.[49]

The disarmament plan put forward by Hughes laid down four general principles: that all capital ships on the building programme, either actual or projected, should be abandoned; that a further reduction should be made through scrapping certain older ships; that, in general, regard should be had to the existing naval strength of the Powers concerned; that the capital ship tonnage should be used as a measurement of strength for navies and a proportionate allowance of auxiliary combatant craft prescribed.[50] Under Hughes' proposal, Britain would cease construction of four new ships of the 'Hood' type and scrap all her second and first line battleships up to the 'King George V' class. Japan would abandon the plans for two battleships and four battlecruisers not yet laid down, and scrap three capital ships, four battlecruisers in process of construction, and all ten Dreadnought battleships of the second line. It was further proposed that no capital ships should be laid down during the next ten years and that the maximum replacement tonnage should be fixed at 500,000 tons for the United States and for Great Britain, and 300,000 tons for Japan. Under this programme, America would have to scrap fifteen battleships under construction and fifteen older battleships.[51]

The reaction of the First Sea Lord, Lord Beatty, to the American proposals was generally favourable on the question of the limitation of capital ships, but he refused to consider acceptance of the ten-year shipbuilding 'holiday', pointing out that it would 'result in decay of naval ship construction and armament industries unless firms were heavily subsidised' and would mean that these industries would have to be re-created at the end of the period, at great expense. The 'holiday' would only result in 'bursts of feverish shipbuilding competition' when it ended. He suggested an alternative scheme 'substituting slow and steady replacement for spasmodic building'.[52] The British Empire Delegation fully discussed both Hughes' proposals and Beatty's views, gave 'a warm welcome in principle to the American proposals',[53] and decided to accept the American plan as regards number of capital ships. Balfour did, however, propose to emphasise the 'widespread and special responsibilities of the British navy' and indicate 'that certain aspects of [the] scheme [would] require further examination'.[54] In other words, the British Empire must retain a number of cruisers and auxiliary merchant cruisers over and above the ratio agreed for capital ships.

The question of the naval holiday led to a great deal of heated correspondence between the Admiralty delegation in Washington and the Prime Minister and government in London. Beatty had asked the American Naval Delegation what they intended to do with their shipyards during a naval holiday, and Colonel Roosevelt had, in Hankey's words, 'let the cat out of the bag' by stating that they would be building cruisers and seaplane carriers, and the armour-plate plant would be kept busy 'reconstructing our old battleships'.[55] As Hankey pointed out, this would be 'out of harmony with the whole spirit of the scheme',[56] with the result that the Americans changed tack, privately suggesting that the naval holiday scheme 'was not well thought out' and that the British should help them recover from the consequences of their own indiscretion.[57]

Within the British government the whole question of a naval holiday was blown up out of all proportion by a telegram which Lloyd George sent to Balfour in which he accused the British naval experts of undermining the 'holiday' proposal and 'helping the Americans out' by pointing out to them the 'disadvantages of their own proposal from their point of view'.[58] Lloyd George stressed that

> the ten year absolute naval holiday in capital construction originally proposed by the United States ought to be accepted definitely as the policy to which Great Britain will subscribe. . . . The failure of the naval holiday through the attitude of our experts and the financial consequences which it will entail [will] be severely criticised in the House of Commons.[59]

He intimated that whilst governments and peoples on both sides of the Atlantic wished to see the naval holiday accepted, the admirals on both sides 'no doubt wish for a continuous, progressive, competitive construction on an agreed scale in capital ships'.[60] Thus, in a telegram to Balfour, Lloyd George pointed out that the Cabinet were adamant that the 'advantages of a ten year absolute naval holiday in capital ships are so great for the cause of peace and disarmament throughout the world, that we are prepared to face the technical objections and inconveniences inseparable from it'.[61] Hankey and Balfour immediately responded, saying that Beatty and his naval colleagues had, in fact, been 'scrupulously correct and loyal' and that nothing had been done to 'commit the British Empire Delegation against the scheme, or to hamper Mr Balfour in adopting the Cabinet's present policy of accepting the full plan for a naval holiday'.[62] Having received the Cabinet's decision Hankey intimated that 'our naval people will be very much upset', but, in his heart of hearts, he thought the Cabinet was right.[63]

Whilst Britain appeared quite ready to accept the proposed proportion of capital ships allotted to her, the Japanese were rather less than happy. Baron Kato Tomasaburo, the Japanese representative, had instructions from Tokyo to accept not less than 70 per cent of the British and American levels. He did, however, indicate to Balfour that an agreement to maintain the *status quo* in the Pacific in regard to the matter of fortification might help him in accepting the proposed 60 per cent ratio.[64] Kato explained that, as in the United States and the British Empire, there had been a 'certain reaction in Japan against the burden of armaments',[65] and that this had been accompanied by an improvement in the somewhat strained relations between Japan and the United States, which had been especially marked since the present American administration had come into office. He added that, while he was optimistic of reaching an agreement on arms reduction, he did not see how he could persuade his government, nor the Japanese people, to accept a reduction to 60 per cent, which would involve the scrapping of their latest battleship, the *Mutsu*, which had been completed only two days previously.

In conversation with Balfour and Hughes, Kato pointed out that every time news of the erection of fortifications in the Americans' islands in the Pacific was received in Japan, 'it had caused a feeling of alarm and apprehension'.[66] He therefore thought that an agreement to maintain the *status quo* in the Pacific in regard to the fortification and creation of naval bases – the United States 'could agree not to increase the fortifications or the naval bases at Guam, the Philippine Islands and Hawaii'[67] – might influence government and public opinion in Japan. In response to Kato's statement, Hughes explained the thinking behind the proposed 60 per cent for Japan. Japan, he said, had no great naval power as a near neighbour, had nothing to fear from any country in her vicinity, and was not nearly as dependent on sea communications as was Great Britain.[68] He believed it was fair to take existing naval strengths as a base, and pointed out that Japan was not actually in a position to change her relative strength, 'for if Japan built more ships the United States was also able to build and to maintain the ratio as it was'.[69] The sacrifice of the *Mutsu* was of little significance when compared with the three American ships which were almost completed. Balfour, when asked for his opinion, said that if precise figures were to be rigidly adhered to, the British Empire definitely would come off worst, but in the interests of reaching an agreement Great Britain was prepared to accept the American proposals. He pointed out that Japan, 'owing to geographical and economic considerations, was perfectly secure under this ratio',[70] and if the proposed quadruple arrangement for a new security agreement to replace the Anglo-Japanese alliance were accepted, would be even more so.

Given the Japanese position on the *Mutsu* and the 70 per cent ratio, it became clear than an agreement would only be reached if the British and Americans were prepared to make concessions. In the event, the Japanese demand for an agreement on Pacific bases in return for acceptance of the 60 per cent ratio in capital ships was accepted; but the demand to retain the *Mutsu* was met by British and American counter-demands to retain their own most technologically advanced vessels. Within the overall agreed ratio, the Americans demanded two additional Marylands and Britain two of the new Hoods, which were already in hand but not yet constructed. This was a classic case of an increase in arms being necessary to stabilise the international situation, but, as Lloyd George pointed out, it would result in a relatively stronger British fleet and favourably affect the unemployment position on the Clyde and Tyne.

There were rumours that the French also were unhappy with their proposed ratio, and wanted the same level as Japan. Britain was horrified at this demand, seeing an overturning of the *status quo* in the Mediterranean, and Balfour suggested that in order to prevent an 'irreparable breach of [the] Entente' the Prime Minister should 'renew offer at any rate for 10 years which Lord Grey made to France in July 1914 that England would guarantee . . . security of French coasts against naval aggression'.[71] In practice, the demand for parity with Japan turned out to be no more than a rumour, but the French Admiralty did strongly object to parity with Italy. However, this objection was over-ruled by Briand, leading Balfour to observe that 'the French Delegation were probably in the embarrassing position of receiving conflicting instructions from M. Briand in London [where he was discussing with Lloyd George the question of an Anglo-French guarantee] and from the French Admiralty in Paris'.[72]

On 12 December Hankey informed Lloyd George that Balfour had successfully drafted a Quadruple Treaty which would replace the Anglo-Japanese Alliance and make it easier for Kato to 'explain yielding on the 70 per cent demand'.[73] Under this treaty, Britain and the United States undertook to confine the development of naval bases in the Pacific to Singapore and Pearl Harbour respectively. This agreement increased Japanese security by preventing Hong Kong, Guam and Manila from being developed as naval bases. By 22 December Hankey was able to report that the Quadruple Treaty had been signed, and the ratio in regard to capital ships had been settled. The French, thanks to Balfour's diplomacy and Briand's over-ruling of his naval staff, accepted parity with Italy. The ratios agreed for both capital ships and aircraft carriers were 5:5:3:1.67:1.67 for the United States, Great Britain, Japan, France and Italy respectively.

Agreements on other naval questions proved more elusive. The American plan had originally proposed that auxiliary combatant craft be restricted in the same proportion as capital ships, but whilst Britain had been quite happy to accept this ratio for cruisers, she added the proviso that 'a number of cruisers and auxiliary merchant cruisers are essential, over and above the proportion agreed upon for use with the fleet'.[74] This was because of the vast lines of communication which Britain had to maintain with her Empire, and because the United Kingdom 'is so dependent on the free use of the seas that starvation would follow six weeks' deprivation of the sea routes to its ports'.[75] As a counter-proposal the British Delegation suggested that cruisers be limited to a maximum tonnage of 10,000 tons per ship, whilst Beatty tentatively put the required number, for fleet and other purposes, at 50 (which was less than the existing complement), although it was not intended to make this number public.[76]

Britain was not alone in refusing to accept the proposed ratios for cruisers and other auxiliary ships. Having over-ruled his Admiralty on the question of capital ships, Briand maintained his government would never accept the extension of ratios to lighter vessels. He also vehemently opposed the abolition of submarines, suggested by Britain. Had the cruiser question been examined in isolation it might perhaps have been possible for a compromise to be reached, but it was not. The more the French dug in their heels over submarine tonnage, the more obstinately did the British stick to their demands for more cruisers than anyone else.[77] The French position on cruisers was, however, effectively the same as that of Britain since they maintained the right to superiority over Italy in this category, because of their colonial commitments. Thus they effectively supported the British in their refusal to accept absolute ratios in cruisers and auxiliary vessels. In the circumstances, no agreement was reached on quantitative limits, though qualitative limits were established for individual cruisers.

There was also failure to reach an agreement on the limitation – or better still from the British point of view – the abolition of submarines. The British Delegation claimed they did not put forward the proposal for abolition from 'unworthy or selfish motives', since they understood that the weaker powers viewed submarines as a legitimate weapon and an effective and economical means of defence.[78] Rather, they stressed the vulnerability and unsuitability of the submarine for these tasks in view of on-going developments in counter-offensive measures against submarines.[79] Britain also maintained that the only measure of success submarines could achieve was, as demonstrated in the recent war, against merchant shipping, and that could by no means be viewed as defensive. This view was challenged by the Italians, who viewed the submarine as 'an indispensable weapon for the defence of the Italian coasts'; by the Japanese and French, who saw submarines as 'efficient, useful for fighting war fleets and merchant marines'; and by the Americans who put forward a lengthy report which supported the 'legitimate use' of submarines.[80] Thereupon the Committee on Limitation of Armament and the Sub-Committee on Limitation of Naval Armament, set up by the conference, discussed the pros and cons of submarines over many meetings and eventually drafted rules designed to regulate their use. Apart from this provision, submarines were not limited at Washington.

The Washington Conference was not initially intended to be confined to naval matters. In addition to questions of security in the Pacific and the Anglo-Japanese alliance, it was envisaged that reductions in land and aerial armaments would be considered. But it almost immediately became clear that neither of these would, in fact, be discussed. Before the conference began, the Standing Defence Sub-Committee of the Committee of Imperial Defence accepted the Army Council's view that the British army has been reduced to a level which leaves no margin beyond what is barely essential for the discharge of our Imperial commitments, and that our military forces provide no basis on which to found proposals for any measure of military disarmament which includes Great Britain.[81]

This was the position which the British Delegation was instructed to adopt at the conference. The Air Ministry also stressed the 'extreme difficulty of achieving much in the direction of aerial disarmament. . . .'[82] The argument put forward by the Air Staff was that, having been debated by the League of Nations for many months without obvious result, there was little chance of the conference reaching any agreement. They also questioned the validity of a conference of only the major powers reaching a binding compact:

> when the question is that of abnegation of the right to use new and potent weapons of war, it is plain that the first essential is that *all Powers* must be in agreement; it is not for a few first-class powers to deny themselves the use of weapons with which a lesser Power may well entirely defeat them. It is hoped, therefore, that the British delegation will have express instructions that this matter is not to be discussed in any form.[83]

The Standing Defence Sub-Committee endorsed this view, and instructed the British Delegation that they were 'unable to suggest any effective means of aerial limitation of armaments' but that they should attempt to gain some concessions from the French to reduce their extensive aerial armaments. However, it was agreed that the matter 'should be left to the discretion of the British Empire Delegation' having regard to the development of the work of the conference and further information to be furnished by the Air Ministry.[84]

The British were not alone in preferring to concentrate on the question of naval armaments and, in particular, the French delegation to the conference strongly objected to any discussions on land armaments. Given the collapse of the proposed Anglo-American guarantee in 1920, this is hardly surprising. Briand took the position that 'unless other Powers were willing to share the risks of the French government and give a guarantee to come to the aid of France in the event of unprovoked aggression by Germany, France could not admit their right to discuss the provision which she deemed necessary for the defence of French territory'.[85] Briand insisted that any discussion on effectives and war material could only be directed against France, and that the 'French Chamber and Senate had given him explicit instructions to the effect that without a guarantee he must not allow France's land armaments to be discussed'.[86] Lloyd George criticised Briand's disingenuous reference to the threat of German revival, when all knew that Germany was disarmed and no threat at all, and stressed to Balfour that France's overwhelming superiority made a real settlement impossible.[87] France's attitude, however, coupled with the absence of many of the principal military Powers of Europe, did not, in Balfour's words, 'encourage the hope that this Conference can achieve much in this direction'.[88] In the circumstances, having read despatches from Balfour at the Conference, the CID decided that if France were unwilling to discuss land and air forces, and were determined to develop submarines, it would be 'undesirable for the British Empire to disarm by sea, land and air, while France was given *carte blanche* to keep up large armaments of all sorts'.[89]

> The Committee were unanimous in thinking that in the future a very dangerous situation might arise if France were strong on sea, land and air, while Great Britain were weak in all directions, and that in such circumstances the Empire would be merely existing on the goodwill of its neighbour – a situation which had not been tolerated in the past and could not be tolerated in the future.[90]

On the non-naval side, three technical sub-committees were appointed at the Conference to cover aircraft, poison gas and rules for the conduct of land war, but Balfour was forced to admit to Curzon that, whilst wishing to obey Cabinet instructions on the matter of aerial disarmament as far as France was concerned, his technical advisers were unable to 'suggest any means by which this object can be satisfactorily attained'.[91] The experts had a number of reasons for reaching this conclusion. France, they said, was always 'likely to be superior to Great Britain in civil aviation',[92] because her better meteorological conditions and greater area of country were more conducive to the development of civil aviation. The French also were always going to have more and superior air mechanics simply because compulsory military service would allow them to train air mechanics whilst organising, perhaps secretly, a civil aviation system. If asked to limit aviation, France would 'urge that many of these arguments apply also to the case of Germany',[93] and would therefore be unwilling to agree to any limitation. The only answer, the technical experts believed, was the creation of a strong air force in order to meet any potential threat from France. However, the British Delegation did not have to make these views public in Washington, because the Americans were equally keen to develop coastal aircraft, and consequently did not favour any restrictions.[94] Hankey informed Lloyd George that 'foreign technical opinion is as strong as British that you cannot limit air armament in the present state of civil aviation, which can so easily be converted for military purposes' and for that reason 'we are not going to get any result in regard to the air'.[95] This conclusion was echoed by the experts on the Sub-Committee on Aircraft,[96] and no agreement was ever reached on this subject. Hankey wryly observed, 'It is profoundly disappointing to think that at the moment when we are getting rid of naval competition, we are about to be plunged into a competition in aerial armament . . . '.[97]

The final agreement between the five major naval powers was signed on 6 February 1922; as well as the ratios for capital ships and aircraft carriers agreed earlier, the agreement stated that no country could possess a capital ship exceeding 35,000 tons, whilst gun calibre on capital ships must not exceed 16 inches. Aircraft carriers were restricted to a maximum of 27,000 tons, with a maximum gun calibre of 8 inches, and no other 'vessel of war' – in reality, cruisers – was to exceed 10,000 tons or to carry guns of more than 8-inch calibre. Also on that day a Nine-Power treaty in regard to China, a treaty embodying resolutions in regard to poison gas and submarines, a treaty on Chinese tariffs, and a treaty between China and Japan in relation to Shantung were added to the Naval Treaty itself.

The Quadruple Treaty had been completed earlier. On 6 February 1922, Balfour informed Lloyd George that his 'mission to the Washington Conference has reached its conclusion'.[98] His assessment was that the agreements reached had solved all the outstanding problems as far as security in the Pacific and the question of the status of China were concerned. He also pointed out that

> It may be worth observing that if the Secret memorandum submitted to the Cabinet by the Standing Committee of the Committee of Imperial Defence No. 280-B be compared with the Naval Treaty it will be found that in all essentials the safe-guards of our Naval position therein enumerated have been fully secured. Nor has this result been achieved at the cost of any other nation. The financial burdens of the great Naval Powers have been alleviated with no injury to national honour or diminution of security.[99]

Herein lies the reason for the apparent success of the Washington Conference. All the Powers involved desperately needed an agreement, both on grounds of economy and security. The naval race, at least as far as capital ships were concerned, was halted, although the repercussions of the failure to limit cruisers were to be very serious. The tension between the United States and Japan, who had been 'almost at daggers drawn'[100] when the conference began, had been replaced by a feeling of goodwill, and the removal of the Anglo-Japanese alliance, to which the Americans had shown 'violent antipathy', had been replaced by a system which, on paper at least, offered security to all concerned in the Pacific. Agreement was politically vital to all governments concerned; the naval representatives were over-ruled by the politicians in a number of instances; for example Briand insisted that the French Admirals accepted parity with Italy, Kato accepted the 60 per cent ratio against the wishes of the Japanese Admiralty, and Lloyd George insisted that the British Admiralty accept the ten-year naval 'holiday'. But Washington was only a partial success: there were areas in which there was no political consensus, and hence no agreement. In essence, the conditions for a successful, if limited, naval agreement had been present but not the conditions for agreement over land and aerial armaments.

Land armaments: the security–disarmament equation

The key to the negotiation of the Washington treaties was the ability of the three leading naval powers to adjust not only their armament relations but their security relations in line with contemporary changes in the distribution of international power. At Washington the Japanese had demonstrated the connection between security and disarmament by making their acceptance of the 60 per cent ratio in capital ships contingent on American and British acceptance of the Pacific bases agreement. Similarly, the French had demonstrated the connection by categorically refusing to discuss land and air disarmament unless some sort of security guarantee were offered in return. The question now was whether a similar adjustment of security relations could be agreed for Europe which might facilitate the general disarmament envisaged in the Preamble to Part V of the Treaty of Versailles and Article 8 of the Covenant of the League of Nations.

There were some indications that this might be possible. Immediately prior to the Washington Conference, the British Cabinet had agreed that in the event of a renewal of the Anglo-American guarantee being brought up at Washington, the British Empire Delegation 'should be authorised, and was in honour bound, to support and promote in every way the ratification by the United States of America of the Paris Agreement of June 27th 1919' and that the French, in gratitude for this support, should be persuaded to agree to a limitation of aerial armaments.[101] Similarly, in December 1921, when Briand approached Lloyd George on the question of a separate Anglo-French Alliance – as distinct from Anglo-American guarantee – Sir Eyre Crowe, Permanent Under-Secretary at the Foreign Office, pointed out that in the event of concluding such an alliance the French would 'enter at once and with determination into the path of military disarmament'.[102]

Perhaps surprisingly, given Crowe's position, when considering the question of an Anglo-French alliance the British government put little emphasis on the question of general disarmament. When Lloyd George met Briand at the Cannes Conference in January 1922, they discussed the possibility of a British guarantee to France, the initial draft of which did attempt to tie the question of French disarmament to the British offer of security. Viscount d'Abernon, British Ambassador at Berlin, stated that the original document 'laid down a number of conditions from the standpoint of Great Britain's interest' including, amongst other things, that France would renounce the submarine. 'The submarine consideration, in particular', d'Abernon commented, 'would have removed a serious danger to our overseas communications'.[103] The Cabinet wholeheartedly supported Lloyd George's inclusion of the submarine question, demanding, if anything, that greater emphasis be put on that question and on the prevention of naval competition between France and Britain.[104] These conditions, however, were not pressed upon the French, Briand having, in d'Abernon's words, 'prevailed upon Lloyd George to omit the . . . conditions'.[105]

In the event, other factors predominated. In particular, the hard-line Poincaré replaced Briand as *Président du Conseil*, and the British Cabinet expressed the view that although Britain was 'under moral obligations to defend the soil of France against unprovoked aggression by Germany',[106] this would not best be met by the Military Convention demanded by the new French Premier since such a convention would involve Britain in maintaining an army up to the level desired by France. In other words, such an agreement might result in French *dis*armament but British *re*armament. In the event Lloyd George informed Poincaré that the Military Convention he required would not be offered, and that 'the French should trust to the honour of England'.[107]

The implications of Britain's stand over the alliance with France would appear to be inevitable. France would never agree to reduce the level of her armaments as long as she continued to be insecure. The consequence of this, as shown by Britain's position during the Washington Conference, was that Britain would not agree to any further reductions as long as France remained superior in armaments. There was little point in Lloyd George's criticising Briand's disingenuous attitude over the potential German threat, and waiting for France to adopt a more reasonable frame of mind if the British were equally entrenched in their own position. It was not that Britain did not recognise the connection between security and disarmament; it had been clearly demonstrated by the Japanese and the French at Washington, and accepted by Crowe in his assessment of a potential alliance. There appeared, however, to be a two-fold problem which was to determine the course of disarmament negotiations throughout the period under review. The first problem was that Britain would not accept the depth of French insecurity, and always tended to be more sympathetic towards Germany. From a French point of view Britain's fear of making any military commitment to Europe was as illogical and unreasonable as French fear of Germany to the British. The second problem was that Britain, at least British Conservatives, did not understand the meaning of international disarmament. They conflated the *uni*lateral reduction of armaments for financial reasons – a matter of *in*ternal policy – with *multi*lateral reductions for reasons of international security – a matter of *ex*ternal policy. From an internal point of view, they were willing to accept arms reductions to the 'lowest level consistent with national [and Imperial] safety'; but from an external point of view they failed to accept that international disarmament implied compromise and recognition of the position of other states, and that other states framed their armaments policy on the same basis as the British: that of minimum perceived requirements.

The disarmament problem was not something which was to be left to Britain and France to solve. The League of Nations had been charged with the responsibility of formulating plans for the reduction of national armaments. In order to carry out this task the League Council established two bodies. The Permanent Advisory Commission (PAC), established in May 1920, was set up under Article 9 of the Covenant in order to advise the Council on military, naval and air questions. It consisted of military, naval and air experts, who, in Cecil's opinion, 'had to do what their professional superiors at home desired, and that was almost invariably that they should do nothing themselves and if possible prevent anyone else from doing anything'.[108] The first report of the PAC offered little prospect for achieving disarmament, but, as Cecil later pointed out, 'it is as useless to expect most military and naval experts to be in favour of disarmament as it is to expect cobblers to be opposed to the use of leather'.[109]

The second body to be set up, in September 1920, was the Temporary Mixed Commission for Disarmament (TMC), the aim of which was to formulate plans for the reduction of armaments under Article 8 of the Covenant. The TMC was not composed of official representatives, although its members were chosen by their respective governments from individuals 'possessing the requisite competence in political, economic and social matters'.[110] As far as Britain was concerned, the chief personalities were Viscount Esher and Lord Robert Cecil. The TMC achieved little in its first year, but in 1921 the Disarmament Committee of the League Assembly issued a report which urged the TMC to formulate a definite scheme for disarmament; a disarmament section of the League Secretariat was created and the TMC was enlarged. Cecil considered that the TMC, unlike the PAC, 'did excellent work'.[111] Esher, however, was less certain on this point. He criticised the Commission's decision to appoint a purely technical subcommittee, which indicated that the views of the non-technicians were of no importance.[112]

General disarmament and the Esher Plan

The Temporary Mixed Commission was initially charged with the task of preparing a draft treaty 'or other equally definite plan' for the reduction of armaments.[113] Esher had, at first, been sceptical about the League, predicting that it would be a 'Holy Alliance under another name'.[114] He did, however, accept that the level of popular support for disarmament would mean that Lloyd George must choose between the risks of a disarmed nation and internal revolution. The League, therefore, must be carried 'to its logical conclusion and rely upon the moral law that [was] its base'.[115] Esher's assessment of the TMC is interesting: 'It is curious', he wrote to his son, 'but only the representatives of the Great Powers talk. The others are dumb'.[116] The Great Powers, therefore, were still in charge of negotiating a disarmament agreement, in spite of the façade of involvement by all states under the League system.

Esher soon found that the TMC had made no progress in drafting a treaty on disarmament, and his own fears of another 'aimless war' led him to take matters into his own hands. He collaborated with the dissident soldier, Major-General Frederick Maurice, and on 23 February 1922 they put forward proposals which Esher considered to be drastic. When he discussed them with the French soldiers they, in his words, 'nearly had a fit'.[117] The Esher Plan, as it was known, was, according to Esher himself, 'put forward to show that a scheme of disarmament could be practically handled, if the good will was there'.[118] It proposed that standing armies should, in peace time, be restricted on a numerical basis 'by a ratio following the Naval precedent at Washington'.[119] This ratio would be confined to metropolitan military and air forces, leaving each country to fix the forces required by it for colonial and overseas defence. The ratios were based on a unit of 30,000 men of all ranks serving either voluntarily or compulsorily, including all permanently armed police forces and permanent staffs of reserve or territorial forces.[120] The Esher proposals would have restricted the land and air forces of European states to the following units:

Belgium	2
Czecho-slovakia	3
Denmark	2
France	6
Great Britain	3
Greece	3
Italy	4
Jugo-Slavia	3
Netherlands	3
Norway	2
Poland	4
Portugal	1
Roumania	3
Sweden	2
Spain	3
Switzerland	2

The forces of Germany, Austria, Bulgaria and Hungary were to remain as defined in the Treaty of Peace.[121] There was no attempt to limit reserves, colonial forces, or, indeed, armaments themselves, although Esher believed that a workable system of budgetary limitation *could* be drawn up, not perhaps in regard to men, because a conscripted man would always cost less than a volunteer, but certainly in regard to material. Esher's reasoning was that, although he had never contended that to limit armaments was to end the possibility of war, he did contend 'that it brings within narrow limits the possibility of sudden attack by one nation upon another. For this reason the experiment is worth trying, always assuming that the people of the world are serious in desiring to reduce the chances of war'.[122]

But were the people of the world serious? There is no evidence of any British Cabinet involvement in the drawing up, or even in discussion of, the Esher Plan, which speaks volumes for government commitment – or rather lack of commitment. The proposed figures would have meant substantial reductions by some countries, notably France, and as Esher said, 'I cannot imagine what *our* War Office will say'.[123] The only official reference to the Plan is in a Committee of Imperial Defence Memorandum (No. 339-B dated 3 April 1922) which set out Esher's own version of the Plan, and a reply from the War Office to Hankey which stated that the 'ratio allotted to Great Britain under Lord Esher's proposals will certainly not suffice'. The Paper also concluded that it did not appear that 'Lord Esher's proposals are likely to be received with much sympathy by the Council of the League of Nations' because they 'lay outside the duty of the Temporary Mixed Commission, a view with which the Council are in full agreement'.[124] Neither of these papers was ever discussed by the CID itself; the nearest they came to recognition was when they were tabled, but not referred to, during a subsequent debate on the proposed Treaty of Mutual Guarantee.[125] It would appear that Esher was appointed to the Temporary Mixed Commission and left to get on with it!

There is, of course, a question over whether the Esher Plan could have worked, even if it had had the backing of the government. Whilst making no overt concessions to French security it did give an advantage to Britain and France in that it excluded colonial forces, and it did not attempt to limit reserves, a point on which France remained adamant.[126] The Plan also provided for the reconstitution and strengthening of the Permanent Advisory Commission of the League, 'under a president to be appointed by the Government of the French Republic'.[127] These concessions were perhaps insufficient to persuade the French to accept the Plan as it stood, though Esher himself maintained that he found the French to be very sympathetic and helpful.[128] Poincaré discussed his difficulties with Esher most amiably, and Esher offered advice, including the suggestion that the French should become protagonists of the land plan of disarmament.[129] Nevertheless, it is difficult to see how the French could have accepted the Plan without some modification; it required a reduction of almost 50 per cent in her European forces, though still leaving her the chief military power. Nor is it conceivable that Germany would have accepted 'a Franco-German ratio of 6 to 3.3 armed men in Europe indefinitely',[130] though an agreement based on the Esher Plan could perhaps have temporarily answered the disarmament problem.

The fate of the Esher Plan is somewhat obscure. Salvador de Madariaga, the head of the League disarmament section, stated that, officially, it was rejected by the Permanent Advisory Commission, the body made up of military experts, 'on the ground that no practical criterion existed to determine a unit of armament having a reasonable degree of comparative value'.[131] He maintained, however, that though there were numerous and substantial technical reasons against the plan, the 'impulse that brushed it aside – somewhat curtly – was political' in that it was directed too exclusively towards land forces and neglected sea armaments, and the French and the Italians would never separate the two.[132] Esher himself, perhaps naturally, denied that this was the case,[133] and it does seem unlikely to be the real reason for its precipitate abandonment, as the Washington Naval Treaty had successfully dealt with sea armaments only a few months earlier. Esher himself later explained, in a letter to the then Prime Minister, Ramsay MacDonald, that the reason his plan had not been pressed was that Cecil, who had great influence with the Commission, was 'so keen on adopting a different procedure' that Esher had 'regretfully' given way.[134] He believed there was no chance of progress being made with Cecil's proposed Treaty of Mutual Guarantee and even suggested that his colleague's proposal actually stood in the way of disarmament. Cecil himself makes no reference to Esher's proposals either in his autobiography, *A Great Experiment*, or in his collected papers.

Fundamentally, however, it was lack of government support which caused Esher to withdraw from the Commission, though he still insisted that the principles embodied in his plan were more likely to succeed than the system of guarantees which formed the basis of Cecil's. Philip Towle maintains that '[t]he Esher proposal was the most realistic British paper on land disarmament in the inter-war years. Nor is that very surprising; Esher was the only British strategist of such distinction who applied his mind to the problem at the League. He knew what was possible and what was advantageous. But the moment, if it ever existed, was lost.'[135] If the Esher Plan did, in fact, represent the most realistic proposal for land disarmament in the inter-war years it must surely have deserved some government support, especially in view of Lloyd George's professed commitment to disarmament. It received none.

Conclusion

The record of the Lloyd George Coalition government between 1919 and 1922 demonstrates the aspects which ensure success or failure in disarmament negotiations. The Washington Conference was undoubtedly a success in the areas of importance to the participants; the elimination of competition in capital ships, the replacement of the Anglo-Japanese alliance and the question of security in the Pacific. It also addressed the problem of security in Europe in that it stabilised the naval positions of France and Italy, and still left the British navy supreme in that area. Where there was no consensus of ambitions or necessity to co-operate — submarines, auxiliary craft, land and aerial armaments — no agreement was reached. The Washington Treaties have been blamed for upsetting the naval balance in the Pacific and enabling the Japanese to gain in superiority and confidence, thus allowing them to attack Pearl Harbour in 1941. But it is difficult to accept this criticism in the light of the technological developments which occurred in the twenty years between the signing of the Treaties and the entry of the United States into the Second World War. Even in 1921 it was becoming evident that the capital ship was losing its strategic importance in view of developments in aircraft and aircraft carriers, factors which perhaps contributed to British and US willingness to forgo the development of naval bases close to the Japanese mainland. Other factors, too, undermined the balance achieved at Washington; the world-wide economic depression of the early 1930s, the rise of Chinese nationalism, German and Italian Fascism, and the growing importance of the Soviet Union, all served to destabilise the international situation in a way which the negotiators at Washington could not have foreseen. At the time of its negotiation it was a vital element in stabilising deteriorating relations between the three major naval powers, and curbing their soaring expenditure.

If Washington demonstrates the effect of political commitment to disarmament, the Esher plan effectively demonstrates the effect of its absence. There was no British commitment to an internationally negotiated arms agreement; as far as the Cabinet was concerned, they had done all the reducing they intended to do on a unilateral basis, and were determined to go no further. Esher received no support from either the government or the Fighting Services. His plan was dismissed in favour of another, which, as will be demonstrated in the following chapter, may have received more publicity, but in the end suffered the same fate.

5

THE CONSERVATIVE
GOVERNMENTS, 1922–3, AND
THE FIRST LABOUR
GOVERNMENT, 1924

The two separate administrations, Conservative and Labour, are dealt with together in one chapter first because they were both of short duration, and second because there is a great similarity in their approaches to the question of disarmament. Both were responsible, at least in theory, for overseeing attempts to achieve *indirect* systems of disarmament through the League of Nations, and each was responsible for undermining the attempts of the other, although in the case of the Labour government the attempt was destroyed by the incoming 1924 Conservative administration. For the sake of continuity, the Conservative administrations of Bonar Law and Baldwin are treated as one, as there was nothing to distinguish the foreign policy, at least as far as disarmament is concerned, of one from the other.

The Conservative governments of Bonar Law and Baldwin

The Conservative government of Andrew Bonar Law which took office in October 1922 firmly repudiated the interference in international affairs which, it was believed, had helped in the downfall of Lloyd George. Its election manifesto declared that 'The nation's first need . . . is, in every walk of life, to get on with its own work, with the minimum of interference at home and of disturbance abroad'.[1] Bonar Law carried this lack of interference to the running of the country; his ministers, including Curzon who remained at the Foreign Office, were very much allowed to get on with their own business. On the resignation of Bonar Law in May 1923, Stanley Baldwin largely retained the Cabinet, and the policies, of his predecessor.[2] The Conservative Party at this time was split between those who supported the decision to remove Lloyd George from office, and those who still supported the Coalition ideal. The Conservative administrations of 1922–3, therefore, were restricted in their make-up by the unwillingness of the two factions to work together. Austen Chamberlain, Balfour and Birkenhead, as Coalition

Conservatives, were excluded from office during the Bonar Law and Baldwin governments of 1922–3.

The Conservative administrations made little progress in either the field of multilateral disarmament or arms reductions on a unilateral basis. Their aims were divided between the ever-present need for economy, and the fear of being unable to meet the needs of the Empire and of falling behind the French in aircraft numbers. The Cabinet Minutes of 20 January 1923, for example, record the First Lord's desire for urgent attention to be given to the navy's need to design and undertake preliminary work (amounting to about £10,000 in all) preparatory to the laying down of a new type of submarine, whilst asking the Cabinet to 'note with satisfaction' that the Admiralty had reduced their Estimates within the figure proposed by the Chancellor of the Exchequer.[3] The conflict between the Treasury and the War Office was even more marked. The regular army had been reduced to the 'furthest limit compatible with national safety',[4] and the Secretary of State for War, the Earl of Derby, asked whether there was anyone who could say that the time had come when 'a further weakening of our land forces' would make for peace.[5] The General Staff produced what amounted to 'a simple balance sheet of liabilities and assets' and asked that a decision on the 'degree of finality with regard to the size, composition and distribution and establishments of the Army' be made.[6] Baldwin, then Chancellor of the Exchequer, agreed that 'it would be false economy to reduce our military strength below the margin of safety' but pointed to a 'disproportionate development of the non-combatant services' and questioned its effect – greater efficiency or 'merely increased elaboration of administration with a diminishing return of military efficiency'.[7] More economies must be made.

Whilst the soldiers and sailors were repeatedly asked to make economies, the junior service, the air force, was a different matter. The Cabinet was conscious that 'a considerable increase in the air force will in all probability be required',[8] and by June 1923 they bowed to the 'melancholy necessity' of creating a Home Defence Force 'of sufficient strength adequately to protect us against Air attack by the strongest air force within striking distance of this country'.[9] The decision to provide for a strength of 600 first-line machines was accompanied by an 'affirmation of the desire of the government to secure a reduction of aerial as well as other armaments by means of an international agreement'.[10] The problem emanated from the strength of the French air force. France was the only Power which could seriously menace Britain, and whilst a war with France would be a 'world calamity' which was almost unthinkable, where national policy was concerned, 'even the unthinkable must be faced'.[11] The French air force outnumbered the British by 1,178 aircraft to 371 in May 1923, and the gap was forecast to increase to 2,180 to 575 respectively by 1925. The air menace was a problem which increasingly preoccupied the Conservative government. As Balfour said, in relation to a surprise attack from France:

Have we any adequate methods of parrying a blow so sudden and so deadly? I cannot think so. The proper reply to aerial attack is aerial defence, and aerial counter-attack; and our relatively insignificant air force is incapable of either.[12]

The General Staff, of course, were unhappy with the proposed expansion of the air force to 52 squadrons and 594 machines: they argued that more could be done from existing resources, and that the problem of Home Defence was a single problem to be solved 'by the whole of our available forces and resources, and not by the sudden expansion of a single arm'.[13] If the army and navy were to be cut, they could not accept with equanimity the expansion of the new air force; but the 'melancholy necessity' of creating an Air Home Defence Force won the day.

The Treaty of Mutual Guarantee

If the efforts of the Conservative government towards reductions in levels of land armaments stemmed from motives of economy rather than the pursuit of multilateral agreement, the attempt to achieve a substantial measure of indirect disarmament via the League of Nations which was made, at least in their name, was a more significant one. The Esher Plan, proposed under the previous administration, was abandoned in favour of a proposal drawn up by Lord Robert Cecil, and his opposite number in France, Colonel Réquin, for a general security treaty. The TMC, in rejecting the Esher Plan, had agreed that the exclusive object of any arms reduction treaty should be the limitation of forces maintained in time of peace, and that the question of reserves could be safely neglected, a point which the French had always insisted upon. But the important point, according to the TMC, was not the limitation of the total force which any country could ultimately put into the field, rather the 'force which it could mobilise during the first few months of war'.[14] In these circumstances the most practicable plan to secure a reduction of armaments was by means of a world-wide Treaty of Mutual Guarantee.

In September 1922 the Third Assembly accepted the principle of a general security treaty in its Resolution XIV. In the same resolution, the Assembly accepted the intrinsic link between disarmament and security:

[n]o scheme for the reduction of armaments within the meaning of Article 8 of the Covenant, can be fully successful unless it be general.

And

[i]n the present state of the world, many Governments would be unable to accept the responsibility for a serious reduction of

armaments unless they received in exchange a satisfactory guarantee of the safety of their country.[15]

A guarantee of security, it was felt, could be found in a 'defensive agreement which should be open to all countries, binding them to provide immediate and effective assistance in accordance with a prearranged plan'.[16] This assistance should be provided by countries situated 'in the same part of the globe' unless a country was in special danger, for historical, geographical or other reasons, in which case 'detailed arrangements should be made for its defence in accordance with the above-mentioned plan'.[17] The prime objective of the proposed security treaty, however, remained a reduction in armaments, either by means of a general disarmament treaty, which was the generally preferred method, or by means of partial treaties, which was the method preferred by the French. With this in mind, the Assembly asked the TMC to draw up a Draft Treaty of Mutual Guarantee.

It was Cecil who eventually drew up the proposed Draft Treaty, with the co-operation of Réquin. It began by stating that

> The High Contracting Parties hereby agree that if any one of them is attacked all the others will forthwith take such action as they may respectively have agreed to take in accordance with this treaty.[18]

Any state which felt itself to be 'menaced by the preparations or action of whatever kind of any other State' should submit a case to the Council, and if the Council decided, by not less than a three-fourths majority, that there was 'reasonable ground for thinking that the said preparations or action constitute a menace as alleged' they would make provision for military support for the menaced State in case of attack. The guarantee, however, would only become operational if the victim of aggression had reduced its peace-time military forces in accordance with plans prepared by the League Council. Any State which did not reduce the level of its armaments to the permitted level would have its rights under the treaty suspended, and risked the imposition of financial and economic sanctions until such time as it conformed with the terms of the treaty. If it failed to do so, and the Council, again by a three-fourths majority, decided that it constituted a menace to another of the High Contracting Parties, a supplementary treaty would be drawn up for the defence of the menaced party.

On the question of aggression, the Draft Treaty envisaged that the League Council would decide, within four days of notification being addressed to the Secretary-General, which of the Parties were the 'objects of aggression and whether they [were] entitled to claim the assistance provided under the Treaty'. The other signatories would accept the decision of the Council and immediately take the 'measures necessary to fulfil their obligations under this treaty'. They undertook not only to defend the state under attack, but also to take 'offensive measures required to reduce the aggressor State to submission'.

The measures required to be implemented in the event of aggression included an immediate and complete economic and financial blockade, and, much more contentiously, a commitment to accept the military command of any State chosen by the Council to organise military measures, and to place an agreed proportion, 'not being less than one-quarter', of its naval and air forces at the disposal of such military command. In respect of such military obligations, the Draft Treaty stated that:

> Nothing in this treaty shall oblige any of the High Contracting Parties not being a European State to furnish any military forces in Europe, or not being an American State in America, or not being an Asiatic State in Asia, or not being an African State in Africa, provided that this article shall not apply to the naval forces mentioned . . . above.[19]

The treaty was to last for ten years, and would come into force when ratified by certain Powers: in Europe by Britain, France, Germany, Italy and Russia, or by the first four of these countries to do so; in Asia by Japan and one other Power, and in America by the United States and one other Power, provided that these states had reduced the level of their armaments in accordance with the figures laid down by the Council. An annexe to the draft explained that air forces and tanks should only be furnished by those states situated in the same continent as the state under attack, and that in the case of Powers with colonial possessions 'only those forces actually situated in the same continent should be called upon'.

This was the essence of the proposal which was put before the member governments for comment and, hopefully, approval. As Cecil pointed out, the Draft Treaty did not go into actual detail of levels of disarmament, but by confining the guarantee to those who had disarmed, he believed 'that thereby sufficient inducement to disarm would be given'.[20] He summed up the implications of the Treaty thus:

> without an effective guarantee of security, there could be no hope of disarmament and . . . without a reduction and limitation of armaments, a guarantee of security was impracticable.[21]

Thus only those states which first reduced the level of their arms would be eligible to be protected by the Treaty, which meant that those who remained heavily armed, and would consequently be seen as a threat, remained outside, neither offering nor receiving the promised assistance. It would seem that the weaker states, as far as arms levels were concerned, must band together to protect themselves against those who remained outside the Treaty.

The Draft Treaty was not well received by the British government, who, as Cecil commented, followed their usual attitude towards the League; for example, he received no technical help from the War Department 'such as we got from the French', although they had been kept informed of the progress of negotiations.[22] Eyre Crowe commented that the Draft Treaty put the 'cart before the horse' in that the 'nebulous' object of disarmament would be achieved by the implementation of a 'satisfactory guarantee of national safety'.[23] The Admiralty attacked it on the grounds that, by a three-fourths majority, the League would determine whether action had to be taken against an aggressor, and that as early as October 1921 they had objected to any proposal whereby a state should take military action at the instance of the League of Nations.[24] They also maintained that the demand to 'maintain certain elements of armed forces for use at the call of the Council of the League' meant that naval forces would probably be the first to be called upon and that 'a very large proportion of the burden arising from this Treaty of Mutual Guarantee will fall upon the British navy' which had already been reduced to the minimum to enable it to meet the demands of the Empire.[25] The regional limitations suggested by the Treaty hardly applied to Britain because the extent of the British Empire would commit her 'to possible operations in all parts of the world', and far from leading to a reduction of forces, any further commitments imposed by the Treaty would make it necessary to increase her naval forces.[26] The Admiralty also raised the question of the United States: should the US menace Mexico – 'a not improbable contingency' – Britain should then be liable to supply naval or other forces 'to coerce the United States of America'.[27] They concluded that they did not, in fact, 'advocate any guarantee additional to that already provided in Article 10 of the Covenant'.[28]

The General Staff also objected on a number of grounds. They did not like the proposed definition of an aggressor,[29] pointing out that 'violation of territory might be purely a matter of defensive strategy, and therefore a measure of self-preservation'.[30] The demand for a force for an offensive campaign implied an almost unlimited commitment, and there were serious objections to the provision of military assistance for a state which had been attacked, first because the War Office could not commit themselves blindly to placing British troops under the command 'of some foreign General Staff' and second because the delay in taking action would give valuable time to an aggressor which 'may be almost fatal'.[31] The four days specified for the Council to determine the victim of aggression was unacceptable; time was of vital importance, and they quoted Napoleon – 'Ask me for anything in war but time'.[32] They also pointed out that if a state were itself attacked 'it would have no certainty as to the assistance it would receive'.[33] The War Office concluded that:

It is considered therefore that the General Treaty does not afford satisfactory and definite guarantees for immediate and effective assistance, and, consequently, does not provide a sound basis for a scheme for the Reduction of Armaments.[34]

The Committee of Imperial Defence drew together the criticisms of the armed services in order to give instructions to British Delegates to the Permanent Advisory Commission who were to discuss the question in Geneva on 16 April 1923. Lord Salisbury emphasised that there were two sides to the proposed Treaty, the political and the technical, and the CID was not qualified to give its comments on the former; that must be left to the Cabinet. He did, however, express the opinion that accepting the obligation to provide a proportion of British naval and air forces to deal with an attack on another Treaty signatory, 'would be a definite renunciation of our right as a nation to take such action as we considered proper'.[35] By a three-quarters majority of the League Council, Britain would be deprived of her freedom of action. The First Lord, Amery, expressed the opinion that the technical questions were actually tied up with the question of principle, but that whilst the general Treaty of Mutual Guarantee was unworkable, special regional arrangements might be possible. The Secretary of State for Air, Sir Samuel Hoare, agreed with Amery, pointing out that the naval agreements reached at Washington showed that special regional agreements were in the realms of possibility.[36] The CID eventually recommended that the armed services should instruct the British Delegates to leave the political initiatives to representatives of other nations, to decline to deal with political issues and to attempt to confine discussion to the practical difficulties raised by the proposed Treaty.

If, understandably, the technical aspects of the Treaty of Mutual Guarantee were rejected by the armed services, the Draft Treaty fared no better on political grounds. Within the Cabinet, Amery recommended against acceptance of the Treaty as drafted by Cecil on the grounds that

> such a treaty can only add unnecessarily to our military commitments and increase the danger of dragging us into wars in which we have no real interest, without in the slightest degree promoting either our own peace and security or those of other nations or leading to any reduction of armaments.[37]

Amery maintained that it was not armaments as such which brought about wars, 'but the conflict of interests and ambitions'.[38] Any guarantee must, in fact, be a guarantee of the *status quo* established by the peace treaties; that would be the only course which the late Allies would accept, and would automatically be unacceptable to 'any of our late enemies'. He also highlighted fundamental differences in interpretation between Britain and her former allies; with France over the Ruhr question for example. If Britain could not even agree with her European neighbours, where there was no danger whatever, why should Britain 'get committed to intervening in conflicts which we should otherwise keep clear of' in the Pacific, Afghanistan, the Middle East or Africa for example, where Britain was likely to obtain no help.[39] Cecil's idea of confining the guarantee to separate continents would mean, in Amery's view, 'the dissolution of the British Empire, and its replacement by a political organisation of the world in continents'.[40] By accepting a 'rigid compact' for the maintenance of the *status quo*, and the intervention in every case of aggression, the people of this country and of the Dominions would decide that the United States had been right to reject the League of Nations, and would come to regard it as they regarded the Holy Alliance 'as a league for repression and interference of which we should do well to wash our hands as speedily and as completely as possible'.[41]

Amery was not the only member of the Cabinet to express strong objections to the proposed Treaty. Viscount Peel, the Secretary of State for India, expressed the opinion of the Indian government that 'none of India's potential enemies in Asia is a member of the League of Nations and . . . consequently the immediate result of India's reducing her armaments would be to weaken her military position *vis-à-vis* a definite and proximate danger'.[42] Lord Salisbury, Chairman of the CID (and the brother of Lord Cecil), set out his own views of the proposed Treaty of Mutual Guarantee in an official Note of 7 May 1923. He supported the objections raised by the Admiralty and War Office, and asserted that Empire commitments meant that Britain would be involved in all corners of the globe. Moreover, an 'inelastic military establishment' was incompatible with the British system of working with a bare minimum, the four days' delay gave an unacceptable advantage to an aggressor, and 'the *casus foederis* might arise at the very moment when we have upon our hands domestic troubles' which would make involvement in external affairs undesirable.[43] Salisbury did, however, point to the CID suggestion that the League Council might like to consider the possibilities of a system which contained less specific obligations, and which, whilst still 'constituting a sufficient condition for the disarmament which is so desirable', would not incur 'the grave practical objections which are presented by the draft Treaty'.[44]

Cecil tried, on many occasions, to explain his Draft Treaty, and to answer its critics. He pointed out that French objections to the draft were diminishing as a result of constructive discussions, and the Italians were not averse to a settlement. His answer to the CID was that Britain's acceptance of the Covenant of the League of Nations meant that she was already bound by many of the terms of the Treaty; blockade action against an aggressor, for example, was already a binding commitment. Cecil believed that the arms reductions, which were the starting point of the Treaty, would greatly reduce the chance of aggression, and furthermore that if any serious breach of the peace occurred Britain would certainly be drawn into it, with or without the existence of a treaty, and if the aggression was by a small power, it would be 'snuffed out' under the treaty with very little trouble. Of what he called the 'other smaller objections' Cecil did not underrate the difficulty of defining aggression, but overall he maintained that:

> In this as in the whole problem the question is how vital do we think disarmament to be. I believe its importance cannot be exaggerated, and I am therefore ready to advocate the acceptance of considerable obligations to secure it.[45]

This, of course, was the crux of the problem: how vital did the British governments, of whatever political hue, think disarmament to be?

In May 1923 ill-health forced Bonar Law to resign, without any decision on the proposed Treaty having been taken. In September 1923 the Fourth Assembly of the League of Nations recommended its member governments to give 'further consideration' to the proposals contained in what had now become known as the proposed Treaty of Mutual Assistance (TMA). The new British Prime Minister, Stanley Baldwin, uninterested in disarmament and, according to a member of the Foreign Office, 'only concerned to keep the peace between his colleagues',[46] prevaricated. Memoranda continued to emerge from the Service Departments on the TMA, but the Cabinet took no decisions on the subject. Baldwin's government was defeated on 6 December 1923 over the issue of Free Trade, and the fate of the TMA was left to Ramsay MacDonald's minority Labour government which took office in January 1924.

MacDonald's government, as will be shown later, changed very little as far as defence policy was concerned; it still, of course, listened to the experts who had advised its predecessors. Sir Eyre Crowe, the Permanent Under-Secretary to the Foreign Office, continued to advise against acceptance of the Treaty: it involved much more commitment to Articles 10 and 16 of the League Covenant than was currently the case, and, since British naval and military authorities wished to see these commitments 'whittled down . . . to the narrowest limits', His Majesty's government should not 'countenance or support any scheme involving the more far reaching obligations' which would be imposed by a treaty of guarantee.[47] The Foreign Office, in a memorandum prepared at almost the exact moment of the change in administration, commented that the government was placed in a difficult position in that 'the draft treaty is not merely championed by Lord Robert Cecil, the principal British representative in the League, but is largely his work. It is arguable whether Lord Robert or His Majesty's government are placed in the more invidious position – assuming the latter to endorse the criticisms now offered.'[48] The criticisms centred on those of the General Staff and War Office, with the additional observation that Cecil's position on the 'so-called Temporary Mixed Commission' was unsatisfactory in that he, and other members of the Commission, were not official representatives of their governments. 'The difficulty is accentuated in Lord Robert Cecil's case', the memorandum continued, 'by the fact that the scheme originally proposed by him when in the position of an irresponsible member of a committee, not representing his government, has now assumed final form at a moment when he has become the official representative of His Majesty's Government'.[49] The Foreign Office saw no evidence that a guarantee which was so 'obviously precarious' would offer any inducement to reduce armaments, and indeed concluded that 'if the treaty be scrupulously carried out it will mean an increase in armaments all round, whereas the express object of the treaty is to pave the way to disarmament all round'.[50] It also maintained that the proposed treaty amounted to an expansion of Article 10 of the Covenant 'in its most stringent and now discarded interpretation' and as such would 'form an insuperable barrier to the entry of the United States into the League'.[51]

Hankey privately prepared a document for the Lord Chancellor of the incoming Labour government, Viscount Haldane, covering some preliminary suggestions as to the lines of the British reply to the League. In this document he asked two main questions: 'Are the guarantees contained therein sufficient to justify a State in reducing its armaments?' and 'Are the obligations towards other States of such a nature that the nations can conscientiously undertake to carry them out?'[52] He pointed out that the time taken to define the aggressor, and then to mobilise the appropriate forces to deal with the aggression, raised the question of the effectiveness of the Treaty, and if states did not believe the system would work, they would be unwilling to reduce the level of their armaments. The obvious reluctance of many nations to accept the proposed Treaty was evidence that they did not feel this particular system would work, and from the criticisms and suggestions offered by these nations, a more suitable system could be devised. Hankey concluded that the British government felt that

the real force of the League is moral rather than material; that the League should aim at the elimination of causes of friction between nations, the settlement on equitable lines of longstanding differences, and the prompt consideration and public ventilation of disputes which have reached an acute stage. The development of material force, for which international organisations are but ill adapted, should be contemplated only in the last resort, and up to the present time has not been shown to provide a convenient basis for a scheme of limitation of armaments.[53]

In other words, the removal of the sources of tension would provide a greater sense of security, and hence a reduction of armaments, than the threat of force on which many would hesitate to depend.

As with the previous Conservative government, Cecil tried every argument he could to persuade the new Labour administration that the Draft Treaty involved Britain in no further commitments, even going to the extent of stating, in the face of anticipated Dominions objections, that the Treaty at first would not be likely to extend beyond Europe 'where alone it is urgently wanted'.[54] The security offered by the Treaty would, he believed, persuade France seriously to reduce her army and aircraft, and to limit her submarines. He railed against his critics: the 'militarists like Amery who wish to rely on our own right arm', 'the bureaucrats like Crowe who are against all new-fangled plans of organisation and particularly against disarmament and arbitration', the 'pro-Germans like Mrs Swanwick[55] who cannot bear the thought that those who have been . . . so unjustly treated by the Versailles Treaty should be precluded by enforcing by arms a more righteous settlement', and those who expounded all the traditional objections to 'entangling alliances'.[56] But despite Cecil's conviction that Britain had entered into international obligations to 'make some effort for reduction and . . . limitation of armaments' his proposed Treaty of Mutual Assistance was not accepted as the answer to these obligations.

Before assuming office, MacDonald had written to Cecil giving his comments on the proposed Treaty. He pointed out that he thought 'any attempt to remove the fear of France by military guarantees [would] fail', and that the contemplated series of military conventions could 'quite easily become military alliances capable at any moment of being cut away from League of Nations obligations and being made independent powers'.[57] He felt that the fact that the Council of the League was to be the arbitrating authority meant 'the big powers only'. MacDonald preferred to attack the problem 'from the other end', as he described it. 'I do not believe', he stated, 'that we can get a political condition which will make a policy of disarmament successful until we get a more complete political settlement', a point which he repeated when in office: 'My own feeling about Disarmament is that we ought to advance the political side a bit further before we can expect any good result from a direct approach to the problem'.[58] His fear was that Cecil's scheme would degenerate into 'a renewed edition of the balance of power'.[59] His Cabinet finally made the decision to reject the Treaty of Mutual Assistance on 30 May 1924, in line with Foreign Office recommendations. At the same time, Ministers felt that in submitting their decision to the League 'greater prominence to the constructive side of the government's attitude towards the Treaties of Mutual Assistance' should be given, and that their support for an International Conference on the Limitation of Armaments should be stressed.[60]

The first Labour government

The Labour government came into office on 22 January 1924, with little prospect of remaining in power for any length of time. The General Election had given 258 seats to the Conservatives, 191 to the Labour Party, and 158 to the Liberals; Liberal support was therefore necessary for MacDonald's government to survive. A.J.P. Taylor maintains that there was little to distinguish the policies of Baldwin and MacDonald. 'The things on which they agreed were becoming more important than those which divided them, and many great issues were settled far from the bitterness of party strife.'[61] Defence, Taylor maintains, was an 'outstanding example' in that the Labour government of 1924 ignored its pacifist wing and carried on the policies of its predecessor. To some extent this is true. On 17 January 1924, for example, the Baldwin Cabinet approved the allocation of £5,000,000 for the construction of light cruisers.[62] Not only did the incoming Labour administration not overturn this decision, it concluded that 'having inherited from [its] predecessors certain responsibilities in regard to air defence', it would '[carry] on the administration for the present without any break in continuity of policy'.[63]

MacDonald, however, had a number of reasons for avoiding radical changes in policy. One reason why it appeared that the pacifist wing of the Labour Party had so little effect on the policy of the 1924 government is that MacDonald had so little faith in any of his colleagues. Because he saw the Labour Party in 1924 as badly lacking in first-class talent, he took almost all the responsibility on his own shoulders. When faced with the formation of his first Cabinet he lamented that 'some weak appointments seem to be necessary; whole not as good as I would wish; must have some specialist outsiders'.[64] The pool of Labour MPs from whom he could select his second-ranking appointments was equally poor; for example, the position of Under-Secretary for Air was occupied by a close friend, the pacifist, William Leach, who struggled hard to justify to himself the bombings in Iraq. Leach could only salve his conscience by seeking reassurance from the Air Ministry that during his term in office 'not a single man had been killed by our punitive action', and that sending in the army instead could have been 'a very costly business, particularly in British lives'.[65]

Having made the appointments MacDonald was subsequently dissatisfied with them. 'The Admiralty is specially weak', he wrote in his diary on 28 April 1924. 'This service will never be controlled until a strong genius is found, but where is he?' The Admiralty, indeed, was singled out for special criticism: 'It has been so long accustomed to have its own way and is so incompetent . . . when placed in a general scheme of defence policy, that it stands in the way of everything that is politically wise'.[66] He confessed to being 'amazed at military mind. It has got itself and the country as well in a rut where neither fresh air nor new ideas blow'.[67] The civil service was also not immune from MacDonald's criticism; within a month of taking office he commented, 'I begin to see how officials dominate Ministers', though he did think that he perhaps 'had good men' at the Foreign Office if he treated them better than they had been treated under Curzon.[68] Having made the necessary Cabinet appointments, MacDonald asked Hankey how far, as Prime Minister, he 'could expect to control their policy', and was relieved to learn that 'through the medium of the CID he could do a good deal'.[69] All in all, then, MacDonald *was* the First Labour government, at least apparently in his own mind. Unable to trust anyone else with the responsibility, he took on the role of Foreign Secretary as well as that of Prime Minister.

MacDonald quite deliberately chose a more conservative approach than might have been expected. He was well aware of the trepidation with which many – from the King to the financial establishment – viewed the prospect of a radical Socialist government. On meeting MacDonald, the King hoped that he 'would do nothing to compel him to shake hands with the murderers of his relatives', and MacDonald recognised that it 'would be a miracle' if the King had not been apprehensive.[70] Hankey also relates an anecdote concerning the 'establishment's' attitude towards MacDonald. On MacDonald's first night in office he 'was at a loose end for dinner' and Hankey took him to the United Services Club, where they had to walk past tables of retired Colonels and Admirals of a highly Tory hue.

Many of them looked at us open mouthed, pausing twixt cup and lip, as I filed down the room followed by the tall, frock-coated figure of the new and sinister Labour Prime Minister. That he should dine in their club on his first night of office![71]

It was not only the Establishment with whom MacDonald had to contend; his own Party was less than supportive. He continually had to endure what one of his closer friends and supporters called the 'sniping' of the ILP.[72] His bitter frustration with many of his own Party colleagues caused him, in William Leach's words, 'to begin to despise far too many of his own Parliamentary friends'.[73]

MacDonald's desire not to rock the boat extended to his decision to maintain the existing Cabinet Secretariat, with Hankey as its Chief, and to take an active interest in the CID. At their initial meeting he informed Hankey that he had made many personal enquiries about him, and having heard nothing but good, begged him to remain, hoping that they would become friends as well as associates.[74] The influence exercised by Hankey was undoubtedly a factor in the continuity of policy.

Another reason why there was little change in direction was that, whilst disarmament was high on his agenda, MacDonald recognised that, in his own words, 'the 'weather' must be improved' before results could be expected.[75] He came to power when relations with France were at a low ebb as a result of British disapproval of the French occupation of the Ruhr; but though mistrusting the French, he had decided that 'France must have another chance'. He would offer co-operation but France must be reasonable and 'cease her policy of selfish vanity. This is my first job'.[76] Significantly, he declared that 'Armaments and such problems that are really consequences must wait'.[77] For this reason MacDonald channelled most of his energies during his first period in office towards improving the 'weather'. The improvement would take years of steady work, and MacDonald was very much aware that his 'official life' might only be one of months.[78]

The bitter animosity between France and Germany, fuelled by the reparations question, must be tackled before any measures of disarmament could be considered. One of MacDonald's first acts on taking office was to write to the French Premier, Poincaré, that he grieved to find 'so many unsettled points causing us trouble and concern' and hoped it would be possible to 'be frank without being hostile and defend our countries' interests without being at enmity'.[79] Poincaré replied that he would do his utmost to solve the problems 'by friendly agreement and to our mutual advantage'.[80] When Poincaré's government fell, to be replaced by that of the Radical Socialist, Herriot, relations between Britain and France became even more cordial. MacDonald also extended his personal approach to Mussolini in order to improve relations with Italy.[81]

MacDonald always believed in the personal approach to diplomacy, an approach which was certainly successful in his handling of the parties and issues involved in the London Conference on reparations which took place between 11 and 16 August 1924, and led to the acceptance of the Dawes Plan. A solution to the problem of reparations had been MacDonald's top priority; his first attempt to improve the 'weather'. The success of the London Conference was, according to Hankey, due largely to MacDonald's good handling and resource,[82] and even his political opponents gave him credit for that particular achievement. On the fall of the Labour government, Baldwin told MacDonald 'You have done at least one big thing . . . – the London Conference'.[83]

The Singapore naval base

If MacDonald maintained that the 'weather' must be improved before the question of armaments could be tackled, he did make one dramatic gesture in the area of unilateral reduction. In May 1921 the CID had agreed that Singapore should be 'regarded as the main British naval base for operations in the Far East' as it was impossible to guarantee the defence of Hong Kong.[84] It was felt that, now that the German threat had been removed, 'the most likely war for some time to come would be one between the white and yellow races whose interests lay in the Pacific'.[85] The Dominions would be approached for a contribution to the cost of the development, and it was felt that Australia and New Zealand would 'expect something more tangible in the way of insurance for defence than reliance on the Anglo-Japanese alliance'.[86] The Washington Naval Conference, of course, saw the replacement of the Anglo-Japanese Alliance, and the development of Singapore was implicit in the security arrangements reached at Washington. In a later discussion on the limitation of naval armaments, the CID 'endorsed the view of the Admiralty that the development of Singapore as a naval base could be defended as a defensive measure'.[87] Accordingly in December 1922, under Bonar Law's Conservative administration, it was decided that

> the decision of the late Government in June 1921 that a base should be established at Singapore on the understanding that no considerable expenditure need to be incurred for the next two years should be reaffirmed by the Cabinet.[88]

On 5 March 1924, six weeks after taking office, MacDonald read out a statement to the Cabinet on the government's policy in regard to Singapore, with the warning 'not to mention the matter outside until the announcement was made in Parliament',[89] and on 17 March the Cabinet approved a revised Statement on Policy on Singapore. It had been decided that to ask Parliament to continue with the scheme 'would exercise a most detrimental effect on our general foreign policy'.[90] It was felt that such development would conflict with the policy which MacDonald had outlined to Poincaré, that 'our task . . . must be to establish confidence, and this task can only be achieved by allaying the international suspicions and anxieties which exist today'.[91] To continue with the development at Singapore 'would hamper the establishment of this confidence and lay our good faith open to suspicion', and further development would suggest that the government had doubts about the success of its own policy.[92] Should a return to a condition of world politics which required the maintenance of security by armaments occur, the position would be reconsidered, but it was the duty of the government to prevent such a condition from arising.

The Dominions had been consulted on the question, and whilst the Canadian and Irish Free State governments had wished to 'refrain from any advice on the problem', the governments of Australia and New Zealand, quite naturally, were unhappy with the decision. The Australian government, whilst expressing sympathy with the government's foreign policy generally, and the quest for arms reduction in particular, felt that the abandonment of Singapore would jeopardise rather than promote that policy. It would result in the reduction of the mobility of the fleet, which in turn would reduce the government's influence in the 'Councils of Nations'. The decision not to proceed ought to be part of an international agreement rather than a unilateral declaration of principle. The New Zealand government echoed Australia's view; whilst recognising that the base would have a defensive rather than offensive role, it was felt that 'the interests of the British Empire in the Pacific [would] be endangered' if capital ships were not allowed to operate in those waters, and that 'the time has not yet come to rely solely on the influence for peace of the League of Nations'.[93] The

New Zealand government even offered a contribution of £100,000 towards the cost of the base, but MacDonald's decision had been made for reasons of principle, not of economy.

The Dominions, of course, were not the only ones to object. Admiral of the Fleet, Earl Beatty, declared that if the government intended to abandon the development of Singapore 'they must in consequence release the Admiralty of the responsibility of protecting the empire and the trade',[94] and threatened to resign if the decision was carried. Beatty said that since the Washington Conference the situation from the naval point of view had altered; the United States was no longer able to operate in the Western Pacific, and the responsibility therefore fell to the British Empire. 'Without Singapore we should be swept out of the Western Pacific and have no means of countering a naval offensive by Japan' and such an offensive was not inconceivable in the future.[95]

A Cabinet Committee had earlier been set up under the Chairmanship of J.R. Clynes, the Lord Privy Seal, to deal with the replacement of fleet units other than capital ships and Singapore, and at its first meeting on 27 February 1924, Beatty outlined the history of the commitment to Singapore. He enumerated the many decisions taken to proceed with the base, stressing that agreement had been reached at Washington only because the decision had been taken to develop Singapore. The balance of power in the Pacific had altered, he said, and British existence in the Western Pacific now rested 'on the sufferance and goodwill of another power'.[96] This was an unacceptable situation. Lord Olivier, the Secretary of State for India, and J.H. Thomas, the Dominions Secretary, both queried the need for the base as there was no evidence of any hostile intent on the part of Japan, but Beatty was adamant that the base would enable Britain 'to revert to [her] traditional naval policy' and increase her naval forces in the Far East. At a later meeting Beatty maintained that the British delegates to the Washington Conference had 'light-heartedly' agreed to restrictions on the improvements at Hong Kong only because they knew that the base at Singapore was to be strengthened. MacDonald rigidly stuck to his line that 'It would be wise policy and strategy to take the opportunity now presented of attempting to reach agreement on the problem of limitation of armaments'.[97] The announcement that the government intended to proceed with the development of the base would be 'disastrous', and would undermine the creation of international confidence. Should the new policy not succeed, then the question could be re-examined. By the third meeting of the Committee on 5 March 1924 it was concluded that there was no point in going further into the financial considerations of abandoning the project, since the introduction of financial considerations 'would detract from the moral standpoint of the government'.[98] The Report drawn up at this meeting of the Committee was that which MacDonald read to the Cabinet that same day, and which eventually was announced as his government's policy. For Beatty the whole question might well have been one of 'loyalty to party taking precedence over loyalty to country',[99] but for MacDonald it was undoubtedly a question of principle.

The Geneva Protocol

Having made his stand on the principle of unilateral disarmament as part of internal policy, at least as far as the Singapore base was concerned, MacDonald was faced with the problem of an international agreement in the shape of a replacement for the Treaty of Mutual Assistance. As noted earlier, in rejecting this Treaty, his government had referred to the 'constructive side' of their attitude towards treaties of mutual guarantee,[100] and the Labour government thus set to work to help the League draw up a plan which would remedy the faults of the TMA. A team of seven was sent to Geneva to carry out this work, led by Lord Parmoor. At the Fifth Assembly of the League, the work of drafting a protocol was given to a sub-committee of the Third Committee (Reduction of Armaments), and in view of his other commitments, Parmoor delegated the leadership of the smaller team on this sub-committee to Arthur Henderson, the Home Secretary. The draft Protocol for the Pacific Settlement of International Disputes which emerged was a result of discussion and compromise, most notably with the French and with the Dominions of the British Empire.

The Geneva Protocol was an attempt to close the 'gap' in the Covenant which had always left the Powers the final option to use force should economic sanctions fail, and to remove one of the major criticisms levelled against the TMA, its failure to define an aggressor. The question of this definition was one of the most complicated areas of the Protocol, but a solution to the problem was found through the concept of compulsory arbitration. Basically, states which refused to mediate or arbitrate in international disputes, or refused to accept an award, would be presumed aggressors, and made liable to sanctions under Article 16 of the Covenant if they resorted to war. With this in mind, a complex system for the submission of disputes to various bodies, including the League Council, Permanent Court of International Justice and *ad hoc* tribunals was drawn up.

The system of compulsory arbitration formed the essential link between security and disarmament, although the Protocol went further than the TMA in the matter of disarmament, Article 17 specifically requiring the signatory states to participate in an international conference for the reduction of armaments, to which all other states should be invited. The date for this conference was set for Monday, 15 June 1925, and the Protocol would not come into force until a disarmament agreement had been reached. On the security side of the equation, in the event of an application of sanctions, states would be required 'to co-operate loyally and effectively in support of the Covenant of the League of Nations, and in resistance to any act of aggression, in the degree which its geographical position and its particular situation as regards armaments allow'.

France, and nine other countries, signed the Protocol before the close of the Assembly, Briand, the head of the French delegation, declaring that 'France is honoured in adhering to the Protocol, and for myself . . . the most memorable event in the whole of my political career is that I have come to this platform to bring you my country's adherence to the Protocol . . . '.[101] Parmoor bitterly regretted that he was unable to follow Briand's example, but MacDonald had requested that he did not sign on behalf of the British Delegation. Whilst accepting that 'it was consistent with the British Constitution that before the Protocol was signed the House of Commons should have an opportunity to give its verdict', Parmoor believed that the withholding of his signature as head of the British Delegation was a prominent cause in the final rejection of the Protocol by the incoming Conservative government,[102] the Labour government having fallen over a relatively trivial matter, in November 1924.

Whilst discussion of the disarmament policy of the incoming Conservative government belongs in the following chapter, it is important to examine here the reasons for its rejection of the Protocol. It has been said that the Protocol was 'rarely read and constantly misunderstood',[103] and it certainly appears to have been the victim of wilful misinterpretation, both on the part of the Conservative government and the British press. For example, at the 190th Meeting of the CID, Lord Curzon insisted that the proposals contained in the Protocol involved the future security and almost the existence of Britain and the Empire. He queried the impartiality of the International Court, whose judgement on arbitration must be accepted, and maintained that the Protocol would involve heavy commitments which would 'place the British navy in an ambiguous, a false, and . . . a humiliating position. . . . All sorts of obnoxious duties would be placed upon its shoulders; it would begin by being the watch-dog, and would end in all probability by being the scape-goat, of the world'.[104] Curzon further asserted that the major criticism contained in all the papers presented to the CID on the subject, was that the Protocol 'cuts a slashing gash into the root of national sovereignty' and converts the League into 'the very thing we have always been trying to avoid, namely, into a sort of super-state'.[105]

The Board of Trade and Treasury both objected strongly to the Protocol on the grounds that economic sanctions would involve great injury to British trade. The Service Chiefs said remarkably little, pointing out that the majority of the previous objections to the TMA applied to the Geneva Protocol. The Chiefs of Staff did, however, feel compelled to point out that it was

> their solemn duty unanimously to state that, in their opinion,
> acceptance of the Protocol will be fraught with grave danger, not

only to the security, unity and sovereignty of the Empire, but also to its honour and good name.[106]

A sub-committee of the CID was formed to consider the question of acceptance or rejection of the Protocol in the light of the objections received from Curzon, the Foreign Office and the Service Departments. However, it based its remit on the premise that 'it was impossible for the Government of this country to turn it down without making a serious effort either to amend the present form of the Protocol or to substitute something else for submission to the League of Nations in its stead'.[107] The committee further raised the question of adherence by the Dominions, without which, it was argued, the home government could not accept the Protocol, even though – as Parmoor pointed out – the Dominions had been closely involved with every step of its formulation. Another notable criticism was that the Protocol did not meet with the approval of the United States, since the Americans feared that they might be 'declared aggressor to the League and that attempts might be made to enforce sanctions against them'.[108] In view of the American attitude, Austen Chamberlain suggested that a public announcement of the American attitude should be made as this 'would obviously have a great effect upon the nations which were now considering their attitude towards the Protocol'.[109]

The view that the Protocol involved greater commitments, both economic and military, and surrendered national sovereignty to the League Council, was the one which dominated all discussion on the subject. Supporters of the Protocol insisted that this was not its intention, nor would it have this effect. Parmoor pointed out that, in reality, the Protocol contained no more commitments than the powers had already signed under the League Covenant. He stressed that the Protocol involved no extra commitment to sanctions than those contained in Article 16 of the Covenant, and that, in any event, 'the creation of a common confidence and goodwill [was] of greater importance than penalties of any kind in the form of sanctions'.[110] He also regarded the substitution of the words 'call upon' in place of the word 'recommend' in the application of military, naval or air force sanctions, as merely a change of procedure; it certainly did not mean that the Council was thus empowered to 'prescribe the particular method which particular nations should follow'.[111] Parmoor quoted the opinion of Sir Frederick Pollock, a great international legal authority, in relation to the recommendations of Article 16, that the League Council could give no orders, and still less dictate to the Powers. Pollock concluded that:

The risk of a British Fleet or a French Army, not to speak of contingents from the Dominions, being ordered about under some foreign command is fabulous, and not less so because the fable has been accepted by some persons who ought to have known better.[112]

The fable was, in fact, widely spread by the British press, one notable example being that of a newspaper correspondent who, having discussed the implications of the Protocol with Parmoor, wrote to him in great disappointment because his paper would not publish his communication 'since it was not in accord with their political views'.[113] The former editor of *The Times*, Wickham Steed, supported this view, being able to recall no instance within the last ten years 'of the country having been so seriously misled by its Press as it was . . . about the Geneva Protocol'.[114] Parmoor attributes the attitude of the press to a distrust of the foreign policy of the Labour government, but points out that the Protocol was supported by many who could 'in no sense be regarded as favourable to the general policy of the Labour Party', including Lord Hardinge and Sir Edward Grey, now Viscount Grey of Fallodon. Grey was surprised to see a headline in a London newspaper stating that he opposed the Protocol, when, in fact, he had expressed no such sentiment, believing rather that it gave no power to any foreign tribunal to give orders to the British navy, and that the Protocol was simply a reinforcement of the understandings to which nations had committed themselves when they signed the League Covenant.[115]

Misrepresentation of the opinions of politicians and others was not, however, confined to the press. Austen Chamberlain, for example, maintained that Ramsay MacDonald had privately declared to him that he himself 'would never have signed [the Protocol] in its present form'.[116] However, Chamberlain admitted that MacDonald had explained to him that under the terms of the Protocol 'We do not incur new obligations, but all our old obligations are very much tightened up and rendered more precise and specific',[117] and whilst it may well be true that MacDonald would not have signed the Protocol in the form in which it emerged from Geneva, he insisted that whilst it 'may be faulty in this provision or that, in this or that mode of expression . . . [it] can be altered as the result of reflection and arrangement'.[118] MacDonald believed that when the Protocol had worked once or twice, 'it will be impossible for a nation to defy it – impossible not owing to the menace of force, but to habit and other psychological and moral reasons . . . '.[119] Even Cecil, whose own Treaty had been rejected by those who put forward the Protocol, accepted that there was no truth in the suggestion that the Protocol would put the British Fleet at the disposal of the League, and that the Conservative Opposition's attack on the Protocol 'was largely unfair'.[120] Recent historical analysis tends to confirm this view.[121]

In practice, however, the Cabinet eventually decided to accept the view of the Committee of Imperial Defence and the reactions of the Dominions and India 'that the Geneva Protocol is open to grave objection and cannot be accepted'.[122] At the same time, they recognised that to reject the Protocol without offering any alternative would 'prolong the present state of insecurity and tension in Europe', and began to draw up a 'draft formula on security' – which will be considered in a later chapter. The decision to reject the Protocol led Sir Gilbert Murray, the President of the League of Nations Union, to comment:

> Looking back, I am convinced that the rejection of the Protocol was a tragedy, and illustrates the almost incredible frivolity with which people allow considerations of party advantage to outweigh realities.[123]

There certainly seems to be no other convincing explanation for the Baldwin government's decision to reject the Protocol. It conducted what can only be described as a propaganda campaign against its acceptance; there was little substance in its professed fears of hugely increased commitments. As MacDonald remarked, its strength was psychological and moral, and involved *no* new commitments. The professed unwillingness of the Dominions to accede to the Protocol was no more than an excuse, as none of them had expressed an adverse opinion on the subject. In essence, the Conservative government was afraid of those obligations to which it was already committed, and did not wish to have them, as MacDonald put it, 'tightened up'. It preferred to bow to the pressure of the Service Departments rather than to international opinion. The spectre of the Geneva Protocol was to haunt the search for disarmament throughout the inter-war period; the French had pinned their hopes on the Protocol, and were to remain resentful of what they saw as Britain's arbitrary decision to deny them the security they so desperately needed.

Conclusion

Little real progress was made towards disarmament during the short-lived governments of 1922–4. The two attempts at indirect disarmament through international agreement failed, at first sight, for almost identical reasons: fear of loss of sovereignty and an apparent increase in commitments. There were significant differences, however, between the two proposals. The Treaty of Mutual Assistance, as Crowe commented, did put the cart before the horse. States were expected to disarm before a guarantee of assistance could be implemented. No one was prepared to put any faith in such a guarantee, and whilst Cecil claimed that national sovereignty would not be handed over to the League, the overwhelming opinion from both sides of the political spectrum, was that the TMA would involve further commitments and an increase in the level of armaments. It is difficult to see how the Treaty could have been accepted by a Conservative government any more than by the Labour government which eventually rejected it.

The Protocol, on the other hand, although very much tied to a reduction in armaments, aimed to create a feeling of security by implementing a system of compulsory, all-encompassing arbitration: the horse was definitely before the cart! In the event of an aggressor failing to accept the results of such arbitration and resorting to force, sanctions would be instantly and automatically applied by all other signatories. In answer to criticisms over loss of sovereignty, the supporters of the Protocol maintained that it contained no more commitments than those to which Britain was already bound by her signature of the League Covenant. Certainly the fighting services objected to the Protocol on exactly the same grounds as the TMA, but whereas MacDonald might well have been willing to over-ride their opinion, the Conservatives, as Cecil remarked, held the 'insane view' that 'the people who must be obeyed on any question of disarmament [were] the fighting services'.[124] As MacDonald said, with amendments the Protocol could have worked. And, most importantly, it was supported by the French. It is difficult not to support Gilbert Murray's view that the Conservative government rejected the Protocol for reasons which had much more to do with Party advantage than because of any real disadvantages as regards British security.

As far as attempts at direct disarmament are concerned, nothing was achieved by the Conservative and Labour administrations of 1922–4. MacDonald's stance over Singapore was little more than a symbolic gesture, believing as he did that he would not be long in office. Inevitably the development of the naval base suffered only a brief setback: it was re-commenced immediately Baldwin's government took office again. MacDonald undoubtedly obtained the 'improvement in the weather' which he saw as a pre-condition for any negotiated agreement on disarmament, through his determined, yet patient, handling of Franco-German differences over reparations at the London Conference. But the weather, especially British weather, as the next chapter will show, is changeable!

6

THE CONSERVATIVE
GOVERNMENT, 1924–9

The new Conservative administration took office in November 1924, with Baldwin once again at its head, though in other respects it was a very different administration from that which lost to Labour in late 1923. By playing the protectionist card in 1923 Baldwin had 'detached its supporters' such as Austen Chamberlain from the Lloyd George Coalition, but by renouncing protectionism in 1924 he 'detached its opponents also' and had won Winston Churchill to the Conservative side.[1] Chamberlain was appointed Secretary of State for Foreign Affairs, while Churchill became Chancellor of the Exchequer. The rifts in the Conservative Party were beginning to heal, though Baldwin had to spend a considerable amount of time and effort in ensuring that his team pulled together.

The security problem and the Locarno Treaties

As far as foreign affairs was concerned, security took precedence over disarmament. Thus one of the first acts of the new government was to reverse MacDonald's decision over Singapore. The proposed base was supported as a defensive measure by both the First Lord of the Admiralty, W.C. Bridgeman, and the new Chancellor of the Exchequer; and although its cost had been underestimated,[2] the decision to proceed was taken by the Cabinet on 6 April 1925.[3] However, the First Lord and Chancellor were less in harmony over the question of the Naval Estimates which the Admiralty put forward in January 1925. Bridgeman admitted that the estimates represented a 'large increase over last year's figures', but pointed out that the programme envisaged had already been agreed at a meeting of the CID in November 1921, which was presided over by Churchill, and endorsed at a Cabinet Committee meeting in February 1922, also chaired by Churchill.[4] The decision reached by these committees was that

> the number of British cruisers must be based not upon the number
> of Cruisers maintained by other Powers, but upon the length and

variety of sea communications over which food and other vital supplies for the UK must be transported.[5]

This decision that Britain's cruiser requirements were absolute, rather than relative to the fleet of any other Power, was to have important repercussions. Bridgeman put forward an estimate of £65,500,000, an increase over the figure which the then First Lord, Amery, had put forward for 1924–5 (£62,250,000, subsequently reduced by the Labour government for that period to £55,800,000). The increase of £9,700,000 could be accounted for partly by 'accounting technicalities', partly because of extra expense incurred by the development of the Singapore naval base, and partly because the charge for the Fleet Air Arm (£1,323,000) was to be included in the navy estimates for the first time. But the bulk of the difference (£6,405,000) was chiefly due, in Bridgeman's words, to 'expenditure which must be regarded as automatic and uncontrollable'.[6] Although the policy of vessel replacement adopted by the last Conservative government was to be followed, the 8 cruisers which Baldwin had agreed should be laid down at the close of 1923–4, had he remained in office, had been reduced to 5 by the Labour government, and Bridgeman proposed that the figure should also be 5 for the current year rather than the 6 proposed by the Admiralty. The overriding consideration, however, was that the One Power Standard should be genuinely maintained.

The new government thus quickly resumed the course set by Baldwin's previous administration, although there is no indication that it would have adopted Cecil's Treaty of Mutual Assurance as a solution of the security problem. Even so, the majority of the Cabinet were well aware that some measures must be taken to increase the level of European security. As the new Secretary of State for Foreign Affairs commented in relation to the European obsession with the question, 'it is not the negative absence of security, it is the positive presence of insecurity that creates this troublesome and difficult situation'.[7] A Foreign Office memorandum which he circulated immediately the Conservatives returned to office, stated that 'though temporarily dormant' the question of French security 'is likely to be one of the most important, if not the most important, issue in foreign politics with which the new government will have to deal'.[8] This assertion was queried by some Cabinet members. Lord Curzon, for example, maintained that as the most powerful military country in Europe, France had no reason to feel insecure; Germany was disarmed, and all that was necessary was 'to induce a pacific feeling in Germany herself so that she may abandon ideas of revenge'.[9] Balfour was also 'cross with the French', as their obsession with security was so 'intolerably foolish'; Chamberlain, however, summed up the situation by asserting that whilst France's *reasons* for feeling insecure were questionable, her actual feelings were genuine.[10] Thus the prevailing view was that 'something must be done' to remedy the situation.

It was not only the politicians who saw a need to address French fears. The General Staff felt that a mutual defensive pact or alliance against Germany was an essential condition of French, Belgian and indeed British security. They recognised that French fear of Germany was 'profound and universal' even if the question at issue was not understood by the majority of the British people.[11] In the circumstances, the General Staff was not averse to taking on new commitments; in a very revealing statement they declared:

> For us it is only *incidentally* a question of French security; essentially it is a matter of British security. . . . France's fear of Germany is the dominating psychological military factor in Europe at the moment. It can only be allayed by the influence and active support of Great Britain.[12]

A pact with France, they felt, would help the moderate elements in Germany to develop the conditions essential to lasting peace. The development of these conditions was not, however, a military problem. 'The allied forces can only hold the ring so that statesmanship may have a free hand.'[13] What was more, the General Staff recognised that France would be unwilling to reduce the level of her military and air forces whilst having to rely on her own resources for security. The suggested pact, they maintained 'might thus pave the way to a first stage in disarmament'.[14] The military men *did*, in fact, recognise, as Crowe had done in 1921, that a willingness to make commitments to France could be the first step in an international reduction in armaments.

However, if there was a consensus among the politicians that something had to be done to improve European security, there was no consensus over the means by which that improvement should be made. Chamberlain would have preferred to negotiate a pact with France alone; without a pact with Britain, he asserted, France would feel deserted, would continue the occupation of Germany, pursue her own way and drag Britain 'impotent and reluctant in her wake'.[15] Churchill, on the other hand, preferred that Britain should keep out of the equation altogether: Britain could exert more influence over France 'if she had still at every stage to convince us of her own rectitude and moderation. . . . When France has made a real peace with Germany,' he declared, 'Britain will seal the bond with all her strength'.[16] Hoare was also inclined to leave the matter to France: 'France must say what it is that she wants' and if Britain was to make any offer to her, she must receive in return 'some counter advantage for the British Empire'.[17] The majority of the Cabinet occupied various intermediate positions between the Chamberlain and Churchill views, and in general the whole question of security was complicated by the need to take a firm public stance on the Geneva Protocol. The question of Belgium also began to creep into the equation, the Channel ports being seen as vital to British security. At the same time, a Sub-Committee of the CID, chaired by Curzon, originally set up to look at the question of the Protocol and security in December 1924, concluded that 'a guarantee involving France and Belgium would be more acceptable to public opinion if Germany were to be involved'.[18]

On 20 January, the German government, worried that Britain might accept the Protocol or enter a bilateral pact with France, put forward its own scheme for a settlement of the security problem – a quadrilateral pact involving Britain, France, Belgium and Germany. The Cabinet initially greeted the proposal with suspicion, believing (rightly) that it was aimed at dividing Britain from France. The Foreign Office offered their assessment of the situation. 'One half of Europe is dangerously angry; the other half is dangerously afraid', declared a memorandum prepared in February 1925.[19] The only sound line of British policy, this document maintained, was the path of British interests, but the policy of 'splendid isolation' was not a real option. It was necessary to Imperial defence to offer a guarantee to France and Belgium. If Germany knew that by invading France she would inevitably 'incur the hostility of the British Empire' it was most unlikely that she would 'make any such endeavour'. Similarly, if France knew that her ultimate security was of direct interest to the British Empire 'the provocative policy inspired by her present uncertainty will tend to diminish'.[20] The memorandum concluded that

> until we can quieten France, no concert of Europe is possible, and we can only quieten France if we are in the position to speak to her with the authority of an Ally.

On 2 March the Cabinet officially accepted the view of the CID that the Protocol was open to grave objections but that a straight rejection was likely to prolong the state of insecurity in Europe.[21] Chamberlain's appeal for an Anglo-French alliance, however, was also rejected, after vigorous opposition by Churchill, who was supported by Curzon, Hoare, Amery and Birkenhead, among others.[22] All that could be agreed, as a basis for further consideration, was a formula based on the German proposals of 20 January. This became official British policy at a Cabinet meeting on 20 March, though it needed a threat of resignation by Chamberlain before the Churchill group finally fell into line.[23]

On 6–7 March, Chamberlain broached the idea of a quadrilateral pact with Edouard Herriot, the French Prime Minister, as a possible alternative to an Anglo-French alliance. Herriot's initial reaction was unfavourable, 'ominous of future trouble' in Chamberlain's words;[24] but gradually, in the realisation that nothing better was on offer from Britain, the French Prime Minister began to view the German proposals as a basis of possible agreement. Discussions opened which were to pave the way to the Locarno agreements in October. There were, of course, a number of what

Chamberlain referred to as 'difficult questions' to be overcome first, including French proposals to incorporate the principle of universal arbitration into the proposed pact, and also an extension to Poland and Czechoslovakia of the guarantees which, in the German proposals, would be confined only to the frontiers between Germany, France and Belgium.[25]

Cecil raised the question of disarmament during discussions on the proposed pact,[26] but Chamberlain refused to consider any question of reduction until security was achieved; 'the road to disarmament', he maintained, 'lies through security'.[27] Even then, he suggested, 'the new pact does not touch Russia, and Russia is the key to the problem'.[28] Although he recognised that sooner or later Britain would have to face the question of disarmament, it was preferable to wait, 'and it would be well that we should prepare ourselves for such a discussion by an examination of what is practical'.[29] Hankey's response to this was to ask the Chiefs of Staff 'to formulate principles and constructive suggestions as to the methods and stages by which reduction and limitation of armaments [could] be pursued'.[30] 'It should be impressed upon them', he stated, 'that we and our late Allies are pledged by the Covenant and the Treaty of Versailles to further measures of general disarmament'.[31]

On 26 June 1925 Chamberlain put before the Cabinet the draft of a Treaty of Mutual Guarantee, which would guarantee the borders between France, Belgium and Germany.[32] Once France had agreed that Germany's eastern borders would not be subject to the same guarantees as the western borders, the Cabinet agreed to France's right to guarantee arbitration treaties between Germany and her eastern neighbours.[33] The basis of an agreement having thus been accepted by the British Cabinet, arrangements could be made for a conference between the interested parties. Even before the conference took place, further problems became evident. Bruce, the Australian Prime Minister, registered his disapproval in a letter to Amery, the Colonial Secretary, claiming that 'It is impossible for Great Britain, without striking a fatal blow at Empire unity, to enter into a Security pact without the support and concurrence of the other self-governing parts of the Empire; and that it is impossible to obtain the concurrence of those other self-governing parts to any Security Pact that might be contemplated'.[34] In fact the final draft imposed no obligations on the Dominions, but the interchange highlights the extent of opinion which had to be considered in drawing up any kind of agreement. Another problem of a somewhat different nature was caused by the Germans' 'amazing gaffe', as Baldwin described it,[35] in repudiating the War Guilt Clause of the Treaty of Versailles almost on the eve of the Locarno Conference; scarcely a good omen for the standard of German diplomacy. However, despite the problems, negotiations went on through the summer of 1925, culminating in agreement in the Swiss town of Locarno, on 16 October 1925 – Chamberlain's 62nd birthday.

The most important of the Treaties signed at Locarno was the Rhineland

Pact, under which France, Belgium and Germany recognised the inviolability of their common frontiers. Germany also accepted the demilitarisation of the Rhineland. Britain and Italy specifically guaranteed these agreements. Any violation was to be reported to the League, and if the League judged that aggression had taken place, the other Powers were to come to the aid of the victim. In cases of flagrant aggression the response would be immediate, without recourse to the League Council. Germany further signed arbitration treaties with France and Belgium, under which any disputes would be settled by negotiation or arbitration. She signed similar treaties with Poland and Czechoslovakia, whilst refusing to recognise her borders with these two states as definitive. France, however, obtained agreement that in honouring her alliances with Poland and Czechoslovakia she would not be breaking the Locarno guarantees; thus if she crossed the Rhineland to assist Poland or Czechoslovakia she would not incur the displeasure of the guarantors of the Rhineland – Italy and Britain. In an additional agreement, Germany was given a permanent seat on the League of Nations Council, although she pointed out that in her disarmed state she could not be expected to implement sanctions under Article 16 of the Covenant.

Disarmament itself did not arise during the discussions leading up to the conclusion of the Locarno Treaties. However, a clause was added to the final Protocol of the Conference expressing the 'firm conviction' of the governments involved that the agreements would provide a climate in which the negotiation of an international convention under Article 8 of the Covenant could take place.[36] The clause was inserted at the instigation of Cecil, and was seen by the advocates of disarmament within Britain as 'a further governmental commitment to the concept of disarmament.'[37] In themselves, the Locarno Treaties created neither security nor disarmament. Indeed, the guarantees contained within the treaties were perhaps too vague to be meaningful; how could Britain, for example, draw up concrete military plans if she did not know against whom they would be directed, or with whom joint planning arrangements should be made? The general atmosphere, however, improved markedly. America approved of the treaties, as they seemed to herald a period of stability in Europe; the Italians approved, because their international status was enhanced; Britain and the Dominions approved because stability had been achieved without any precise military commitments having been made. For their part, the Germans were once again legitimate members of the European community and had protected themselves against renewed incursions by the French. The French gained an illusion of security.

A further significant consequence of the Locarno Treaties was that Germany renewed the Treaty of Rapallo, the joint treaty of friendship and mutual co-operation signed with the Soviet Union in 1922. The Soviet Union feared that Germany was moving too far towards the West, and the West, as Chamberlain had pointed out, feared the influence of the Soviet

Union. If the Locarno Treaties were not examined too closely, it would seem that a large step had been taken towards addressing the problems of German revisionism and French security. In reality the commitments contained in the Treaties, were hollow: France had been given no firm military commitment – in the sense of British or Italian forces allocated specifically to the defence of France, or even staff talks – whilst Germany had retained her freedom to revise her Eastern frontiers. In spite of the apparent euphoria which followed the signing of the treaties, and the stress placed on the 'Locarno spirit' during the next five years, France was not fooled by the illusion. In June 1927, the Foreign Office was to observe 'a certain change of temper' on the part of France and Belgium in regard to their relations with Germany in that they were 'informed less completely than formerly by the Locarno spirit'.[38] In response to this observation, the Marquess of Crewe, British Ambassador at Paris, stated that 'the Locarno treaties have never been considered here to provide a complete solution of the problem of French security' but that 'the better informed sections of French public opinion are fully aware that the Locarno guarantees are as much as any British government is ever likely to be in a position to concede to France'.[39] France was thus making the best of the little she had been given, but was in no way sufficiently secure to consider any weakening of her position.

The Preparatory Commission

At the Sixth Assembly of the League in September 1925, at the instigation of the French, a Committee of the Council was set up to pave the way for the establishment of a Preparatory Disarmament Commission. Chamberlain thought the move premature, believing that it was prompted merely by a desire to forestall an American initiative and to look good in the eyes of international opinion.[40] Nevertheless, he acquiesced in the move, since resistance would have brought accusations of hypocrisy and bad faith both from other Powers and from sections of British public opinion.

The feeling within the CID which met to consider the proposed committee on 17 November 1925 was hardly positive. Balfour, for example, maintained that, having 'disarmed' already, it was not Britain's business to take a leading part, 'only a helpful part' in the forthcoming deliberations. Chamberlain's main thought was that Britain should prevail on 'the Power which was highly armed', that is, France, 'to cut down her armaments and so bring influence to bear on others'.[41] Again, Chamberlain stressed the importance of Russia in the equation, a point supported by Beatty, who believed that whilst not a great naval Power at the time, Russia was in a position 'to increase her naval forces if she so desired'. Essentially, therefore, it was agreed that Britain should stand on her record of unilateral arms reductions, and not take a leading position in public sittings. Rather, as Chamberlain put it, she should 'take a leading part behind the scenes'.[42] It is difficult to see how Britain could maintain her distance from public involvement, and still expect to exert any influence over proceedings, but this appeared to be her suggested policy towards the Preparatory Commission.

In December 1925 the Cabinet decided that the Sub-Committee on the Reduction and Limitation of Armaments (RLA), established in the previous month, should advise as to the course to be followed.[43] However, before commencing its examination of the resolutions adopted by the League Council in setting up the Preparatory Commission, the Sub-Committee pointedly restated the extent to which Britain had already reduced her armaments, concluding that the size of the navy and the army were not dependent on the strength of the forces of other countries, and therefore should not be reduced further 'in consequence of a general agreement'. It further asserted that Britain's air forces were so 'markedly inferior to those of France' that 'any measure of reduction which would bring about a condition of greater equality' should be welcomed. In other words, all reductions must be made by other Powers; Britain could go no further.

The Sub-Committee, which became known as Cecil's Sub-Committee, sat throughout the years of the Preparatory Commission, chiefly responding to problems arising in Geneva rather than offering any concrete policy. At its first meeting it attempted to prepare answers for the questionnaire submitted by the League Council, and came to a number of conclusions. 'Armaments', it decided, should be defined as 'Forces immediately available on the outbreak of war and the material maintained for their use', while the expression 'reduction and limitation of Armaments' should be broken down into two separate definitions; 'reduction' to mean reduction of 'Armaments' to a certain standard, and 'limitation' to mean restriction of 'Armaments' within a certain strength. On the question of by what standards it was possible to measure the armaments of one country against another, it concluded that the naval side was 'comparatively simple', and should mean the number and size of ships and the calibre of the guns carried. As far as land forces were concerned, Britain would like to see the abolition of conscription, which would of itself 'impose a certain measure of Disarmament'. The Sub-Committee accepted, however, that this was unlikely to be acceptable to those continental powers for whom conscription was the basis on which their armed forces rested.[44]

The Sub-Committee came to negative conclusions on many other questions: for example, the difficulty of limiting military aircraft, because of the ease with which civil aircraft could be converted to military use; the impossibility of distinguishing between offensive and defensive armaments, and the impracticability of devising an index figure to represent all factors involved in drawing up a scale of armaments permissible to various countries. The collective security system implicit in Article 16 of the Covenant was again examined, but the conclusion was reached that dealing with acts of aggression after they had taken place, as laid down by Article 16, did little towards the removal of the menace of competition in armaments. The Sub-Committee recommended that the government should only 'contemplate contributing to additional or more precise guarantees of security in exchange for definite and substantial guarantees that a genuine scheme of Disarmament will be enforced, and that the degree to which this country would assist an attacked State should be made dependent on the extent of the policy of Disarmament agreed upon by the Conference and on the measure in which that policy is put into effect'.[45] In other words, a disarmament agreement must come before any guarantees which would increase the level of security. The final item on the questionnaire under consideration was in direct contrast to the foregoing conclusion; 'Admitting that disarmament depends on security', it asked 'to what extent is regional disarmament possible in return for regional security?' The Sub-Committee's response was that, in view of the fact that Locarno had increased Britain's commitments, but had made wars less likely and thus diminished her commitments, 'Regional security does make a measure of regional disarmament possible'. In relation to the questionnaire, a Foreign Office memorandum produced in October 1927, and criticised by Chamberlain as being too negative, declared: 'Assuming that it was necessary to appoint prematurely a body to "prepare" a conference for which the world was not yet ready, there could probably have been devised no better means of keeping it occupied for an almost indefinite period'.[46]

The Preparatory Commission for the Disarmament Conference was actually set up by the League Council in December 1925. It initially consisted of representatives of the members of the Council and, by special invitation, The United States, Germany, the Soviet Union, Bulgaria, Finland, The Netherlands, Poland, Romania and Switzerland. It was eventually to include, in addition, Argentina, Chile, Colombia, Salvador, China, Canada, Cuba and Greece. The Commission met for the first time on 18 May 1926, its first task being to consider the questionnaire set by the Council. In order to answer this questionnaire, the Commission set up various sub-committees, the most important being Sub-Committee 'A' which was composed of military, naval and air advisers who were to tackle the technical questions, and Sub-Committee 'B' which would deal with questions of an economic nature. Cecil was appointed to represent the British government, and went prepared with the instructions drawn up by his Sub-Committee.

Throughout the life of the Preparatory Commission, Cecil was to complain bitterly and often about the attitude of the Service Departments, and the reluctance of the government to send senior officials to raise Britain's profile at Geneva. His argument, supported by Chamberlain, was that if more senior officers were present at meetings, decisions could be taken without reference to the home authorities.[47] In refusing Cecil's request, the Service Ministers 'stressed the difficulty in parting with senior people for long periods of time';[48] in reality, of course, leaving matters in the hands of lower-ranking officers coincided with Britain's policy of not taking a leading part in public. Whatever happened, there was to be no positive British input to the proceedings.

In reporting to the CID on the first session of the Preparatory Commission, Cecil declared that the opening debates had been 'rather unsatisfactory . . . every Delegation seemed to be waiting to see what the other Delegations proposed'.[49] At the same time, he added, 'Disarmament was no longer within the range of academic talk only and something definite would have to be done'.[50] In agreeing with Cecil, Chamberlain maintained that Britain was, in fact, doing something; 'the object of the Locarno treaties', he said, 'was to give security which would make disarmament possible'.[51] For his part, Cecil stressed that the French would agree to limit their armaments 'if they knew for certain that the armaments of Great Britain would come to their assistance'.[52] The old argument again reared its head; if Britain wanted France to reduce her armaments then Britain must make concrete commitments to France.

It is not within the scope of this study to examine the Conservative government's policy towards the Preparatory Commission in detail; this has been done elsewhere.[53] The important point to note is the government's general attitude towards the Commission. Having agreed that disarmament could no longer be merely academic talk, the government wavered between paying lip-service to the Commission and panicking when it appeared that this attitude would bring about its collapse. The position was complicated, however, by the presence of Cecil, whose pro-disarmament views were at odds with the majority of his colleagues.

In March 1927 Cecil, tiring of the interminable technical discussions of Sub-Committee 'A', produced a draft convention, revised and approved by the CID and Cabinet, and presented it to the Commission. In it, he attempted to lay down the principles of reduction and limitation of armaments, rather than precise figures, which would be discussed and filled in when the disarmament conference actually met. The French then put forward their own draft convention, which highlighted the main points of difference between the two countries. On the naval side, Britain insisted on limitation by numbers and classes as well as tonnage, whereas France would only consider a limitation of total naval tonnage, irrespective of classes of vessel. On the question of land disarmament the French refused to accept that the limitation of effectives must apply to reserves as well as to the effectives actually serving with the colours.[54] This was to prove a major sticking point; not even Cecil could move the French. 'I have done my best and I have been a complete failure', he declared. 'As we cannot get a unanimous view in favour of the opinion I put forward, it is no good persisting'.[55]

There were a number of other significant points of difference between the British and French drafts; air armaments, land *matériel*, budgetary limitation, and supervision were all questions on which the British and French points of view were in direct opposition. Arguably, these differences were inevitable and merely reflected the underlying strategic differences between the two states. The French wanted to limit air and naval effectives; the British did not. The French wanted to limit land *matériel* indirectly, through budgetary limitation; the British were inconsistent, but basically opposed any quantitative limitation of land *matériel* and openly objected to budgetary limitation. The French wanted strict verification procedures; the British resisted any form of investigation or control by an international body. While both Powers wanted to ensure their security, for France security meant retaining the military superiority she had over Germany while for Britain, an island state barely concerned with military invasion, the retention of naval supremacy in home waters was all-important.[56] These strategic differences would not disappear, but they did not preclude agreement at political level if the British and French governments were willing to make mutual concessions, with Britain conceding to France on land armaments in return for France conceding to Britain on naval armaments.

On 26 April 1927, the Preparatory Commission adjourned for six months, partly to allow the so-called Coolidge Naval Disarmament Conference to take place, partly so that private negotiations could be held to break the Anglo-French deadlock. The omens, however, were not auspicious. Certainly, as far as the British government was concerned, there was a great amount of concern at events at Geneva, but not because of the lack of progress in negotiations, rather because of its potential impact on Britain's defence policy. Lord Eustace Percy, for example, went so far as to accuse the Commission's proceedings of being 'a positive menace to the peace of the world' as all the powers were doing was directing attention towards the British Navy, in order to conceal their own 'mutual jealousies'.[57] Far from looking towards concessions to France, Percy advocated a stiffening of the British position and even withdrawal from the negotiations. The Admiralty too refused to discuss any movement towards the French position. At one point, Cecil complained to Chamberlain that the First Lord, W.C. Bridgeman, had adopted an attitude of 'malevolent neutrality' towards all proceedings in Geneva.[58] At the time of the adjournment it appeared that only a real change of heart on both sides could end the Anglo-French deadlock, and without the wholehearted support of the British government, such a change of heart appeared unlikely.

The Coolidge Naval Conference

In February 1927 the new American President, Calvin Coolidge, decided to try to emulate his predecessors in organising a successful naval disarmament agreement, and invited the five major naval powers to a conference with the aim of extending the ratios for capital ships achieved at Washington to the remaining classes of vessel. The Washington agreement had not been a total success, having merely channelled the naval race into the classes not covered by the agreement, and causing the larger powers to re-assess their naval strategy to take advantage of these unrestricted classes. The United States, with large expanses of ocean to cover, and few naval bases, built up to the Washington limit of 10,000 tons for cruisers. Britain, with long lines of communication with her Empire to protect, but numerous naval bases, preferred a larger number of smaller cruisers. Japan, seeing the United States as her chief potential enemy, chose to concentrate on large high-speed submarines with which to disrupt the American fleet, and wished to increase the ratio which was allowed to her. When they agreed to meet in Geneva, therefore, the three major naval powers had very different naval strategies in mind.

Italy and France, the other two major naval powers, declined to attend a conference which was aimed specifically at limiting naval power; they maintained that land, sea and air disarmament were inseparable and should be discussed together or not at all, and in any event, such discussion should be carried on under the umbrella of the Preparatory Commission rather than independently. Also, they were engaged in their own smaller-scale naval race in the Mediterranean at the time, and were thus reluctant to discuss naval limitation at whatever level. Nevertheless, there was a certain feeling that if the Coolidge Conference achieved its objectives, it would help the work of the Preparatory Commission.

The chief British representatives at the Conference, which opened on 20 June 1927, were Bridgeman and Cecil, and Bridgeman was keen to be 'first in the field' with the British programme.[59] Whilst well aware that the Americans were looking merely to extend the Washington ratios to all other classes of vessel, the British had their own plan. Bearing in mind the success of Charles Evans Hughes in Washington, in presenting a plan apparently out of the blue, Bridgeman felt that similar success could be achieved by not disclosing anything in advance. He did not, in fact, achieve the same success. When the conference opened, the representatives of the three participants each stated their own case, and these cases differed widely. The Americans, as already stated, thought it would be a simple matter to extend the Washington ratios to cover other classes; this would include cruisers in the range 3,000 to 10,000 tons, and destroyers in the range 600 to 3,000 tons. Primarily for financial reasons, however, Britain wished to see cruisers divided into two categories: the Washington standard of 10,000 tons maximum, armed with 8-inch guns, and a smaller type up to 7,500 tons armed with 6-inch guns. Whilst willing to see the former type limited in the Washington ratio, Britain did not want any limit to be placed on the smaller type. When the larger cruisers reached the end of their lives, they would be replaced by the smaller type. Britain also proposed that submarines be divided into two classes, 600 and 1,600 tons, and destroyers and destroyer leaders limited to 1,400 tons and 1,750 tons respectively. The

Japanese approach was to use the end of existing construction programmes to limit the total tonnage of submarines and other auxiliary craft. This would effectively give them the 70 per cent ratio which they wanted with the United States.[60]

The implications of Britain's insistence on two separate classes of cruiser, in line with her own needs, were to be of crucial importance. In April, the Naval Staff had categorically stated that 'it is very undesirable that the British Empire, which is peculiarly dependent upon the security of the trade routes for its very existence in a way that bears no comparison whatever with the circumstances of other Powers, should agree to a limitation in the number, as opposed to the size and armament, of cruisers to be allowed'.[61] By a complicated system of 'multiplying the tonnage normally at sea on defined ocean routes by the length of the route to be traversed', the naval staff arrived at a figure of 70 cruisers for Britain, 47 for the United States and 21 for Japan. The needs of the Empire, they maintained, were absolute, and not relative to the size of fleet of any other power. These figures would, in fact, involve an increase in both tonnage and vessels, and would deny the Americans' claim to parity. In May, the Cabinet accepted the Admiralty's proposals as the basis for negotiations at Geneva, and though they agreed that the British Delegates 'should be given a reasonable latitude in regard to details',[62] the inclusion of Bridgeman in the delegation effectively ensured that the Admiralty's needs would be stoutly defended.

The question of the Americans' demand for parity was a further complication. The American delegation claimed that Balfour had conceded parity in cruisers at Washington, even though no formal agreement had been reached. Hankey checked this claim, and found that, in fact, no such concession had been made; the British Delegation had always claimed that their unique position as an island 'so dependent on the free use of the seas that starvation would follow six weeks' deprivation of the sea routes to its ports', made it essential that they had sufficient cruisers to protect these routes.[63] Significantly, included in Hankey's memorandum were extracts from the 55th Conference of the British Delegation to the Washington Conference, which stated that 'the grand total of cruisers for fleet purposes and for other purposes was put by Earl Beatty tentatively at fifty', although this number was never actually submitted to the Washington Conference. It could be asked, therefore, what had changed so dramatically in less than six years to cause Britain's *absolute requirement* in cruisers to rise from 50 to 70, more especially since the relations of the three great naval powers had improved dramatically since 1922.

Parity of itself was not the main problem. Even the Admiralty did not take a 'grave view' of the United States building up to their limit, but they must, according to Bridgeman, 'resist a limitation by total tonnage'.[64] This was pure pragmatism. The Admiralty were aware that, as with capital ships pre-Washington Conference, should the United States choose to out-build the British navy, they were in a position to do so. The Cabinet was, however, asked 'not to adopt the *principle* of parity of naval strength in so many words, as this was contrary to previous policy and was believed to be strongly opposed by the Admiralty'.[65] The instruction which the Cabinet sent to Bridgeman read:

> For diplomatic reasons we think it most desirable to say publicly and at once what we believe to be your view, namely, that, while we mean to build cruisers up to our needs, we lay down no conditions limiting [the United States'] cruisers to a smaller number. Do you see any objection?[66]

Before this telegram arrived, however, Bridgeman had, in fact, made a statement to the American press which specifically conceded parity:

> Great Britain has no intention of contesting the principle of parity between the naval strength of the United States and Great Britain. . . . It is true that we think our special needs demand higher number in certain types of vessels but we do not deny the right of the United States to build up to an equal figure in any type of warship if she thought it necessary.[67]

The Cabinet accordingly agreed with Bridgeman's statement, instructing Howard to inform the United States government that they did not 'dispute or contest in any way' America's claim to absolute parity. But Beatty and Churchill both strongly disputed such parity; Beatty complained that Bridgeman could not possibly have meant to concede parity in all classes, he must only have referred to the Battle Fleet and not to cruisers required for the protection of trade. The Admiralty were, Beatty conceded, prepared to consider parity in regard to cruisers of the 10,000 tons category but not to cruisers necessary for the protection of sea communications and trade.[68] Churchill's argument was that 'there can be no parity between a Power whose Navy is its life and a Power whose Navy is only for prestige'.[69] It was simply that the Big Navyites in the United States pressed for equality with Britain, not that American requirements matched Britain's in any way.

The question of whether Britain had, or had not, in fact conceded parity in *all* classes of cruiser was to be a constant source of argument. The view that the United States demanded parity merely because she *wanted* it, rather than *needed* it, exerted a negative effect on the whole of the negotiations. Britain did not 'admit a moral right to parity in small cruisers' but recognised that she could not prevent the Americans building to parity if they insisted on so doing.[70] But parity was a complicated issue; for the Americans it meant equality in total tonnage, for Britain it meant numbers and classes of vessel, and there appeared to be no point of contact between the two viewpoints. A year after the failure of the conference, Allen Dulles, legal adviser to the American Delegation, was forced to admit in a speech at the Royal Institute of International Affairs, that neither country wanted to be put in a position of inferiority 'whether from a sense of prestige or – call it what you will'.[71] Dulles maintained that the main problem at the Conference had been the 'lack of knowledge of each other's intentions'; whilst it was not for the United States to question Britain's perceived need for 70 cruisers, the fact that at the time she had only possessed 50 meant that any agreement would be 'fixing a limit for the future and not the present' which would, in fact, encourage, rather than discourage, building.[72]

The essence of the problem was thus two-fold: the Americans believed that a simple extension of the Washington ratios was all that was required, whilst the British were quite prepared to accept that ratio in the larger, 10,000 ton cruisers, but reserved for themselves the right to build as many smaller cruisers as were necessary to protect the Empire. On top of the technical difference was the perception of each side that the other was not playing wholly fair; the Americans did not *need* a navy as large as Britain's, but the British were apparently reneging on their concession of parity. The proposals put on the table by each side immediately highlighted the problem.

The American proposal to extend the 5:5:3 ratio agreed at Washington would give to the two main parties a cruiser tonnage of between 250,000 and 300,000 tons, a destroyer tonnage of between 200,000 and 250,000 tons and a submarine tonnage of between 60,000 and 90,000 tons; the Japanese would be allowed 60 per cent of each of these figures. Britain's scheme, in contrast, would have entailed a total tonnage of cruisers alone in the region of 650,000 to 700,000 tons, even though, for Britain, it would have achieved a reduction of £50,000,000 over her estimated normal naval expenditure.[73] Chamberlain complained that having made a frank statement of her needs in the experts' committee, Britain was met with the United States' persistent refusal to reciprocate. The United States stubbornly maintained that 'such a statement involved political considerations unsuitable to [the] expert committee'. They at last produced a document 'almost in form of an ultimatum' indicating that of the total tonnage they proposed, 250,000 tons would be devoted to the largest class of cruiser. At present Britain had built, or was building 14 of these cruisers, with another in the approved programme, whilst the United States had 2 and were contemplating construction of a further 6, but if the US' proposals were adhered to, they would have to increase her programme of 8 to a total of 25. 'This American proposal' maintained Chamberlain, 'would force us into a great new building programme of most costly and most menacing class of vessel . . . and would result in an increase of expenditure and armament instead of a reduction of either.'[74] If the Americans demanded equality in all classes, they would have to justify an increase in their demands from the 300,000 of their proposals to 500,000 tons.[75]

The technical and political complexities were further compounded by clashes of personality. The Coolidge Conference is a classic example of the importance of the interaction of individuals in putting forward, or holding back, a government's policy. Bridgeman was distinctly unimpressed by the calibre of the American delegation, complaining that it was 'not of sufficient authority or position, as was that of Japan and Britain, to move without advice from home'.[76] Whilst it may be true that the American delegation was 'intentionally less distinguished' because they did not want to appear to be too anxious,[77] the effect on the British and Japanese delegations was to convince them that the Americans were not as committed to achieving a result as they were themselves. In Bridgeman's opinion Hugh Gibson, the leader of the American delegation, was 'a plausible but not very experienced diplomat' who was 'totally ignorant of naval affairs' and could not control the naval delegates. Bridgeman's initial reactions to the Naval representatives, Admirals Long and Jones, were, respectively, a 'nonentity' and 'a very charming man, but absolutely determined to get everything the Big Navy party wanted, or nothing'.[78] By early July, his patience was wearing thin and he wrote to Baldwin that the people at home had not the 'faintest notion of the difficulty we have with these cursed American Admirals [who] understand nothing of our position and very little of their own'.[79] 'All they do', he complained, 'after puzzling over obvious facts for hours is to wake up occasionally and murmur 'total tonnage', but how we are to say what our total tonnage can be if they won't say what ships they want to build, I am at a loss to know'. Having declared that Job was his pattern in patience and Washington 'whose virtues seem not to have descended on his countrymen' for truthfulness,[80] Bridgeman finally burst out, 'If Job had encountered Admiral Jones instead of Elihu, I doubt if he could have held out'.[81] Whilst these observations are obviously of a personal nature, they do demonstrate the tensions which were present between the members of the British and American delegations.

Further pressure was put on the British delegation by the machinations of the American press who, from the outset, appeared determined to wreck the conference. Bridgeman reported that as soon as the British plan was presented, the American press 'set to work to read into [it] all sorts of Machiavellian devices for retaining superiority', claims which the American delegates did nothing to contradict.[82] There was, of course, a great deal of truth in this accusation, although Britain would argue that she did not want superiority for its own sake, but only because it was necessary to protect the Empire. Cecil believed the attitude of the press reflected a propaganda campaign by the big steel and armament manufacturers to prevent a reduction in armaments, and had been informed that the Bethlehem Steel Company 'were prepared to spend up to $1,000,000 in propaganda'.[83]

While Cecil concluded that this was no doubt an exaggeration, there was certainly a great deal of evidence to implicate at least one individual, the 'high-pressure and high-salaried lobbyist William B. Shearer who did his suave best to promote discord at Geneva'.[84] The suspicion that Shearer was working for the Big Navy lobby and steel interests was confirmed two years later when he brought a lawsuit against the three shipbuilding and armament firms which had hired him to work against the conclusion of any agreement in Geneva.[85]

This, then, was the atmosphere in which the Coolidge Conference took place. The mutual, almost harmonious, interests of Washington were completely absent at Geneva. After the initial clashes of programme and personality, the British delegation raised the question of capital ships; they were looking for a substantial reduction in future expenditure, but as capital ships were still subject to the Washington agreements the Americans refused to discuss the subject in the absence of France and Italy, at least until substantial agreement had been reached on cruisers.

At one point Bridgeman telegraphed to the Cabinet that the 'Americans made it plain that they and the Japanese could reach agreement on total tonnage tomorrow' and that Gibson felt sure that, if the British and Japanese delegations could find some 'mutually acceptable' basis of agreement, it would be possible for the American delegation to complete an agreement.[86] In response, the Cabinet reinforced their instructions to Bridgeman:

> Although . . . ready to agree to a ratio for the 10,000 ton 8" cruisers we could not agree to fixing *by treaty* a permanent total tonnage limit for all classes of ships whether specified in classes or lumped together. But we are ready to approve an agreement fixing the actual units of the annual programmes of new cruisers for the three Powers during say the next five years or if absolutely necessary up to 1936, and of course tonnage of these units when added up could be embodied in the agreement. Such programmes would naturally enable America to reduce her leeway in cruisers up to the point beyond which she would stimulate further building on the part of Japan. Should the three Powers be able to agree to such actual programmes a further scaling down all round might then be discussed and finally agreement be signed.
>
> As to period of agreement we should much prefer the shorter as it better safeguards our position and affords better chance of agreement. The longer the period the nearer the Americans might come to equality of numbers in practice as distinguished from theoretical right to parity, and . . . equality of numbers in the case of nations with such different needs and perils would result in actual inferiority for us.[87]

At this point Britain can hardly be criticised for sticking so rigidly to her position, for it was far from clear what the American position actually was. Lord Jellicoe pointed out that the Americans continued to talk about tonnage 'without it having been decided of what the tonnage was to consist'. At the back of their minds was the question of armed merchant ships; 'the Americans', he said, 'had in mind that the Cruisers we required for trade protection could hold up neutral shipping: in other words, they were harking back to the old story of freedom of the seas'.[88] If the Americans' meaning was unclear as far as tonnage was concerned, there was equal confusion over numbers. Chamberlain pointed out that the American State Department seemed to be completely unaware that Admiral Jones had 'mentioned the intention of the United States of America to build 25 10,000-ton Cruisers'; the American delegation, he concluded 'was not reporting fully to the State Department what was happening at the Conference'.[89] Until the Americans actually made their requirements and intentions clear, it was perhaps illogical to expect Britain to move from her own programme.

In an effort to close the gap between Britain and the United States, Bridgeman and Cecil agreed to take up Gibson's suggestion of coming to a prior agreement with Japan. This was done, and on 16 July it seemed that a tripartite agreement could be reached on the basis of the Anglo-Japanese proposals.[90] Beatty and the Admiralty, however, backed strongly by Churchill, resisted agreement on the basis proposed on the grounds that it would mean inferiority *vis-à-vis* the Americans. Accordingly, the British delegation were called home, under protest, while a new set of instructions was hammered out by the Cabinet.

On the delegates' return, a number of acrimonious discussions took place and many new factors were brought into the equation, including duration of the agreement, life of over-age vessels and replacement conditions. The chief protagonists were Bridgeman and Cecil on the one hand (advocating flexibility), and Churchill and the Admiralty on the other (advocating resistance). In effect the latter won by pitching the proposed terms of acceptance at a level they believed the Americans would reject. Thus, although the Admiralty dropped their insistence on a new class of 6-inch gun cruisers, they agreed to do so only if 1931 was adopted as the termination date of the agreement and provided they had the right to arm the smaller types of cruisers with 8-inch guns, in order to avoid pre-1931 6-inch cruisers becoming obsolete.[91] Overall, they emphasised that the Anglo-Japanese scheme, even as revised, meant Britain was 'accepting a principle of inferiority on the sea' with the United States, and a combined cruiser and destroyer tonnage with Japan which was 'below the safety ratio'. 'As a result', the Sea Lords complained, they 'felt it incumbent upon them to point out that if the United States of America and Japan exercise their full rights under the Agreement, they will not be able, with the means left at their disposal, to fulfil the responsibilities hitherto resting upon them'.[92] The Sea Lords were thus serving warning on their political masters; have it your way, but we can take no responsibility.

Even while the politicians were attempting to reach a compromise through the Anglo-Japanese discussions, the Admiralty were working to their own agenda. On 19 July Beatty revealed that the Admiralty considered that all proposals so far raised for discussion in Geneva were unacceptable, and in consequence the Admiralty 'had completed a new scheme as an alternative to be put forward in the event of a breakdown on all the other proposals'. This had been sent to Geneva in a sealed envelope, 'with instructions that it was not to be opened unless the need arose'.[93] The alternative scheme had not been discussed with anyone outside the Admiralty. This was exactly the type of conduct which had caused Cecil to complain of the Admiralty's 'high-handed' attitude during meetings of the Preparatory Commission, in persisting 'in giving direct instructions to their representatives in Geneva'.[94]

On 12 July the British government issued a Draft Statement, again setting out the justification for their case, and attempting to deflect blame for failure to make progress. The British Delegation then returned to Geneva to discuss the Anglo-Japanese proposals. Bridgeman believed most difficulty was likely to arise over the limitation of the guns in the smaller cruisers to a 6-inch calibre.[95] The Japanese and Americans were both opposed to this limitation, but as the Japanese did not intend building until after 1931 any 8-inch gun cruisers beyond the 10,000 tonners provided for, they were thus unlikely to object seriously. There was a further complication in that Britain possessed four cruisers of the 'Hawkins' type which carried 7.5-inch guns, and had laid down the 'York', a cruiser of 8,000 tons with 8-inch guns. The Japanese had four cruisers of the 'Furutaka' type which also carried 8-inch guns. The Americans were therefore justified in contending that if their 8-inch gun cruisers were confined to the proposed 12 10,000 tonners they would be reduced to a definite inferiority to Britain and little better than equality with the Japanese. As regards the length of the agreement, Britain preferred the treaty to terminate in 1931 rather than 1936 'because the shorter the period the more of the nature of a *modus vivendi* will the arrangement appear to be'.[96] The main fear, on this question, related to the Japanese rather than the Americans; the figures conceded to Japan were actually much larger than the Admiralty's proposed strategy for war against Japan would allow!

The final proposals presented by Bridgeman at Geneva envisaged a combined total tonnage of cruisers, destroyers and submarines of 590,000 for Britain and the United States, and 385,000 for Japan, but in addition each power was to be allowed to retain a quarter of the foregoing tonnage in over-age vessels. Britain would retain the four 'Hawkins' class ships, the 'York' and two 'Emerald' class, the Americans could retain her ten 'Omahas' and Japan her four 'Furutakas'. All other cruisers were to be divided into two classes; 10,000 tons and a maximum gun calibre of 8-inch, and 6,000 tons, not exceeding 6-inch gun calibre. Britain and the United States were to have 12 10,000-ton cruisers and Japan 8.[97] These proposals contained the factor to which the Americans had objected all along; limitation on size and armament rather than total tonnage. It is hardly surprising, therefore, that the Americans rejected the final, and only slightly amended, British proposals. Gibson was later to complain that the British had 'put forward one plan after another . . . but in each instance, after the false whiskers were removed, we found the old . . . building programme grinning at us'.[98]

The Americans insisted throughout the conference on the 8-inch gun, even in a smaller class of cruiser – the calibre agreed at Washington on British initiative. On this point, Britain had no effective response, though Bridgeman put the government's case that 'unless [the] treaty provided for limitation of 8-inch gun it would be a treaty not for limitation but for an increase of armaments'.[99] Gibson's reply was that there was no hope that the Americans would give way on the question, and the Japanese would agree to whatever America accepted. In the circumstances, the only alternative Bridgeman saw was to compromise somewhere between a 6-inch and 7.5-inch gun 'which would eliminate argument with which Americans are obsessed about armed merchantmen'.[100] Cecil confirmed Bridgeman's view that without some compromise on the 8-inch gun there was, in the opinion of the American delegation, no hope of an agreement.[101] The Cabinet replied that nothing had occurred 'to cause them to alter their previous decision about 6 and 8-inch guns', and they could not authorise any offer of compromise.[102]

The failure of the conference had been almost inevitable from the moment it began. Bridgeman was adamant in blaming the Americans; they had said that if the British and Japanese could reconcile their differences, they would have no difficulty in agreeing, and then, when Britain and Japan had worked on a compromise, had refused to join in.[103] He went further, maintaining that the Americans were clearly determined to refuse everything, being too afraid of the American press and the Big Navy supporters, who were against any kind of agreement.[104] Cecil was equally adamant as to where the blame lay; Britain had reneged on her concession of parity and had, in effect, said to the Americans that we proposed to 'limit the larger cruisers which may be inconvenient to us but we decline altogether to limit the small cruisers because they are the things that matter to us'.[105] He had warned the Cabinet before returning to Geneva that if they 'insisted on their irreconcilable attitude about the 8 inch guns' the conference would fail and he would resign.[106] He was careful to state afterwards that 'on the actual issue on which . . . the Conference broke down . . . the Americans were wrong and we were on our merits right', but by refusing to negotiate over the 6-inch gun 'we got nothing whatever, whereas if we had given way we should have got a good deal'.[107] To the dismay of his colleagues, Cecil did, in fact, resign, his resignation merely serving to convince the Americans that they were right, and undermining Anglo-American relations even further. The official British line was to blame the Americans:

> [the] American argument (as far as they have consented to argue) appears to be as follows: We claim equal tonnage with you. As we do not need small cruisers with six inch guns for commerce protection such as British Empire does, we shall use our tonnage to build only big cruisers with biggest permissible gun such as are the proper adjuncts of fighting fleets and incomparably superior to your commerce protectors. We do not need those in such numbers for security and their construction will not promote economy but prestige demands that we build to parity tonnage irrespective of need for security or fighting strength.[108]

It certainly would appear that the Americans did not wholeheartedly support an agreement. Esmé Howard confided to Baldwin, on 3 August, that Kellogg had adopted an air of 'wearied disinterest' and had always 'refused to admit that our needs were at all different to those of the United States'.[109] Bridgeman maintained that the Americans had 'made a great political blunder by calling the Conference merely to help them in electioneering'.[110] This view is supported by Brian McKercher who states that Coolidge was desperate to repair Republican fortunes, and so adopted the mantle of peacemaker. His efforts to secure naval disarmament, however, 'were geared solely to making a favourable impression on American voters and had little to do with allaying the fears that disarmament meant to other Powers.'[111]

Recent analyses of the Coolidge Conference highlight a number of reasons for its failure. Stephen Roskill believes the 'fundamental cause of the failure of the conference undoubtedly lay in the differing strategic requirements of Britain and America in cruiser types and tonnage'.[112] On top of that, the dominance of the naval advisers of both countries over their respective political negotiators 'undoubtedly reduced the possibility of compromise'. McKercher states that whilst the British Admiralty may have pointed out the susceptibility of Britain to blockade in justifying their cruiser demands, they did not mention the fact that 'these same cruisers could be just as effective in enforcing belligerent rights'.[113] He believes that whilst there was great pressure from American naval planners for a powerful cruiser fleet to form the nucleus of the United States navy, the real reason for the failure of the Coolidge Conference was the 'British intention to maintain its ability to enforce maritime belligerent rights versus the American desire to assure neutral trading rights in the event of future war'.[114] America's insistence on 10,000-ton, 8-inch gun cruisers was 'promoted by US naval experts as a means of over-trumping any British advance in heavy cruiser construction'.[115] The General Board insisted that, ship for ship, 'US cruisers had to be as big or bigger' than Britain's, and led American naval experts to adopt a 'doctrinaire insistence' for large cruisers. If, as Cecil maintained, the British were being stubborn in refusing to consider the American point of view, the Americans were equally stubborn in insisting on a parity they did not really require.

Dick Richardson looks at the failure from a different angle; the Conference may have broken down 'primarily on the failure of Britain and the United States to reconcile their differing concepts of limitation', for which he believes Britain should take a large measure of responsibility, but the underlying problem was Japan. Both Britain and America feared Japan more than they feared each other, indeed Britain's naval strategy was based on a possible war with Japan, and each feared that any concession on their part would strengthen their potential enemy. 'There is much truth, therefore', says Richardson, 'in the suggestion that the Geneva Conference broke down, not because of a dispute between Britain and America, but because of an Anglo-American dispute with Japan which never broke the surface at the conference'.[116]

Christopher Hall highlights a number of contributory factors, aside from the central cruiser question, which obstructed agreement. The most obvious, he believes, was the lack of diplomatic preparation by the participating nations. The naval experts had made their plans and drawn up their programmes, but there was no prior consultation, and no political moderation of the experts' views. Hall concludes that '[t]he two naval staffs' requirements, adopted as national policy, became rigid programmes from which, once tabled at the Conference, the negotiators would not be moved'.[117] In the same vein, Salvador de Madariaga, head of the Disarmament Section of the League at the time, maintains that it failed because it addressed the problems left at Washington – Washington succeeded because it left them out![118]

In view of the foregoing analyses of the reasons for the failure of the Conference, it is perhaps relevant to ask whether success could ever have been expected. There was certainly no consensus of aims as there was prior to the Washington Conference; there was no political domination of the naval experts, in fact the naval experts ran the proceedings and refused to make concessions. The Americans themselves recognised this fact; Esmé Howard believed that Coolidge, Kellogg and Hoover were genuinely in favour of reduction of construction and expenditure but were overborne by popular clamour created by the Big Navy party. Hoover confided to Howard: 'I wish they would leave this to be negotiated by civilians. Then I believe we should get an agreement at once'.[119] Also lacking was the ability of each side to make allowances for the other's point of view; Britain recognised that America did not *need* a large navy, but could make little concession to the

Americans' domestic pressures if it meant sacrificing their own position, and, as Howard pointed out, Kellogg had never accepted Britain's reasons for a large fleet of smaller cruisers. Britain's position, however, had changed, without any satisfactory explanation, from a demand for an *absolute* requirement of fifty cruisers at Washington, to seventy at Geneva. There was equally no apparent logic in her adherence to the 6-inch gun at Geneva, when it was she who had put forward the 8-inch gun at Washington. But in persistently professing to see the problem as Anglo-American rivalry, the two main protagonists were tacitly refraining from discussing their *real* fear – Japanese expansionism. The Japanese came to Geneva demanding an increase in their ratio from 60 per cent to 70 per cent, and both Britain and America saw each other's plans in terms of what it would mean for Japan. Britain and America were quite happy *not* to build up to any agreed limit, but the Japanese were reported to have said that 'owing to their national psychology, they would be compelled to build up to any figure that was mentioned as a maximum'.[120] When the Japanese put forward proposals in order to avoid the breakdown of the conference, Britain felt obliged to consider them as the Japanese 'would be seriously hurt at our refusal', but the consideration was not serious, as it would mean 'a very long postponement of the 6-inch gun'.[121] It was quite evident, however, that Britain and America were determined to keep the Japanese figure as low as possible, even though this meant severely damaging their relations with each other.

The aftermath of Geneva

The consequences of the failure of the Geneva Naval Conference were enormous, both for international relations in general and for British policy in particular: a deterioration in Anglo-American relations; a green light to the Big Navy party in America; a feeling in both Boards of Admiralty that they had successfully dominated their respective political masters; and, perhaps worst of all as far as Baldwin personally was concerned, a rift in his carefully crafted Cabinet unity caused by the acrimonious accusations surrounding Cecil's resignation. Internationally, Britain was now almost totally isolated on disarmament. The breach with the United States at the Coolidge Conference compounded the existing breach with France at the Preparatory Commission. The question was how – if at all – the British government could retrieve the position without a fundamental rethinking of policy. In the absence of Cecil, the government's most serious, if idiosyncratic, thinker on disarmament, the likelihood of success was minimal.

In assessing the new situation, Cecil's successor at Geneva, Lord Cushendun, severely criticised the policy of the Admiralty. He was especially disturbed when he discovered that Bridgeman proposed to 'abandon all further attempt to come to agreement on the question of disarmament', believing that such a policy would be disastrous for British interests.[122]

Cushendun pointed out that 'if we arrive at no agreement either with France or the United States, it is not improbable that they may agree together on terms that will leave us isolated at Geneva, and saddled with the odium of the breakdown of the Preparatory Commission'.[123] The Admiralty were aghast. They agreed to look at possible alternatives to Britain's current policies, but suggested that the sole reason for change was that 'according to Lord Cushendun we must agree to a category of cruisers which is not of our choosing, or incur the blame for breaking down not only the Preparatory Commission but "the whole movement for disarmament by international agreement"'.[124]

The grudging concession on the part of the Admiralty to consider alternatives enabled the government to take steps to try to break the deadlock between the French and British positions. Accordingly, in January 1928 Cushendun had discussions with the French Ambassador at London, Aimé de Fleuriau, during which de Fleuriau made it clear that his government 'could not be moved from the position to limit in any way their military trained reserves', to which Cushendun replied 'that we felt at least as strongly that, as regards naval armaments, there must be rigid limitation by classes'.[125] This was one of the key points of the Anglo-French deadlock and, as Joseph Paul-Boncour, Head of the French Delegation at the Preparatory Commission, observed to Chamberlain 'it was useless for the Disarmament Committee to meet again unless Great Britain and France had previously reached agreement'.[126] Paul-Boncour stated to his Foreign Minister, Aristide Briand, that 'the question was now a political one to be settled by the two governments in the light of the higher political considerations involved . . . '.[127]

In June 1928 Chamberlain informed the Cabinet that the French Council of Ministers 'was unanimously of the opinion that an agreement must be reached with us', and that they proposed an agreement on a formula which would 'determine the relative cruiser strength according to the length of lines of communication'.[128] The First Sea Lord immediately objected, saying that there were many interpretations of the meaning of this phrase, and most of them detrimental to Britain. But at least steps had been taken by the French to attempt to reach a solution to the *impasse*.

A further complicating factor now emerged with the attempt by the American Secretary of State, Kellogg, to embellish and widen a plan proposed by Briand, the effect of which would be to outlaw war. Kellogg's move was initially greeted with scepticism by the British government; Chamberlain, indeed, declared to Esmé Howard, Britain's Ambassador at Washington, that 'Kellogg's main thought is not of international peace but of the victory of the Republican Party'.[129] Howard demurred slightly; in his opinion Kellogg was quite sincere. 'The tide of isolation in this country', he declared, 'is ebbing'.[130] In due course, the so-called Kellogg Pact would come to fruition, and be signed by the great majority of countries, including

Britain. However, the effectiveness of the Pact in outlawing war was questionable in that it did not cover wars of 'self-defence', nor did it cover obligations assumed under the Covenant or other treaties, nor provide for sanctions in case of a breach of obligations.[131]

Negotiations for the Pact provided a further excuse for the British Admiralty to try to avoid reaching any compromise with the French. Bridgeman saw the pact as a way out of the disarmament debate. Could we not use the opportunity, he asked, to convince public opinion 'that we are as much opposed to war as any other Nation', and use this moment 'to desist from attempts to devise mathematical tables . . . and having made a public declaration of the will of all the great Nations for peace to leave it to each Nation to make such reductions as their circumstances demand and their need for self-defence will admit?'[132] Cushendun immediately quashed this hope, declaring that the Kellogg Pact would only intensify the pressure in favour of disarmament and that if Britain adopted the line suggested by Bridgeman, 'the only effect would be to cast doubt on our sincerity in signing the Kellogg treaty'.[133]

Chamberlain, also, was furious with the Admiralty; they had taken three months to consider the French proposals on naval disarmament, and only now that progress was being made, were they raising new objections which must have been evident all along. He also expressed his regret that the Cabinet had 'found it impossible to do more than repeat [the] purely negative criticism of the Admiralty' instead of supplying him with 'some positive and constructive suggestions'.[134] Pressure, however, was increasing to try to break the deadlock. The Lord Privy Seal, Salisbury, declared that although there now appeared to be 'only a slender chance that the Preparatory Commission can be saved from shipwreck' Britain must do something to prevent this failure. He pointed out, however, that the suggestions of the French regarding geographical length of lines of communication as a measure of cruiser strength would 'give the British Empire such an advantage as against America that the mere announcement of it might produce an explosion in that Country sufficient to upset the structure of international peace aspirations . . . '.[135]

The need to avoid the 'shipwreck' of the Preparatory Commission eventually drove Britain and France to a compromise. The French went some way towards meeting the British demand for naval limitation by class rather than total tonnage; limitation would be applicable to four classes rather than the nine originally demanded by Britain. In return for this concession, gained in the face of strong opposition by the French Ministry of Marine, the British, who had stood virtually alone against the exclusion of military trained reserves, agreed to withdraw their opposition on the point. Overall, the compromise attempted to break the *impasse* at Geneva and enable the Preparatory Commission to continue with its labours.

Unfortunately, this was not to be. While the general thrust of the compromise – British concessions on land armaments in return for French concessions on naval armaments – was admirable, its specific terms were almost calculated to cause offence in the United States. The naval proposals again ran contrary to American requirements, in that the smaller class of cruiser was left virtually unlimited, whilst the larger cruisers, which the Americans considered more suitable to their needs, were much more tightly controlled. The American Ambassador to London proclaimed that the proposals were 'even more unacceptable than the proposal put forward by the British Delegation at [the Coolidge] conference, not only because it puts the United States at a decided disadvantage, but also because it discards altogether the principle of limitation as applied to important combatant types of vessels'.[136] The situation was compounded by the manner in which the compromise became public knowledge – through leaks in the French press rather than governmental announcement. Accusations of underhand dealings were levelled at the British and French governments, the Italians and Americans being the most affronted at what they saw as a secret naval agreement. Both British and French governments tried desperately to defend their handiwork, maintaining that the initial discussions had been quite open, and that all they had intended to do was to prevent the total failure of the Preparatory Commission. Bridgeman, from whom many of the concessions had been wrung, maintained that it was never more than a draft agenda paper which would have been discussed with the other powers.[137] MacDonald, as Leader of the Labour Opposition, criticised the inept and stupid handling of the affair,[138] and Cecil labelled it 'a thoroughly bad document' which had 'achieved the almost impossible result of combining against itself the opinion of the United States, of Italy, of Germany, and of the great mass of people in this country who take an interest in the subject'.[139] Abroad, the abortive compromise served only to inflame American opinion, and strengthen the hand of the Big Navyites. The Preparatory Commission did not, in fact, collapse, but was adjourned until the air cleared and a way forward could be found. It reconvened again in the spring of 1929, but before any substantial progress could be made the Baldwin government had been defeated at the polls.

Conclusion

In examining how far the Conservative government of 1924–9 contributed to international disarmament, a number of points emerge. The first is that they did not understand the essence of the disarmament problem. Locarno, hailed as the great achievement in security, was meant to achieve disarmament almost as an afterthought. Chamberlain may well have been correct in his assumption that security would lead to disarmament, but Locarno, as the French perceived almost immediately, did not offer real security. The French accepted it because they knew it was as much as any British government would concede to France at the time. But it was not enough to give her the security which would justify a substantial reduction of armaments relative to Germany. The second point is that the *real* problem of German revisionism was never addressed, beyond the intellectual recognition that if the Powers did not make some move towards an international disarmament agreement, Germany would abrogate the Treaty of Versailles. Cecil may well have argued that 'disarmament was no longer within the range of academic talk only',[140] but nothing was *really* done. Locarno admitted Germany back into the international fold, but did not address her grievances.

From 1926 to 1929 the Preparatory Commission stumbled along without any real British commitment. The one committed member of the government was Cecil, who worked furiously to make progress against the apathy of his Cabinet colleagues and the thinly veiled hostility of the Services. Chamberlain espoused a British position – 'a leading part behind the scenes' – which meant nothing, or worse than nothing in that behind the scenes the major sub-committee of the Preparatory Commission – Sub-Committee 'A' – was dominated by the military representatives. Even behind the British scenes, the Reduction and Limitation of Armaments Committee was dominated by the fighting services.

Similarly, the Geneva Naval Conference, was dominated by the Admiralty representatives on all sides. As far as Britain was concerned, there was *no* commitment to reduce armaments, but every commitment to *increase* them. Britain *did* want to retain superiority – not as in the case of the United States, purely to have a 'navy second to none', but because the government's perception of Empire needs *demanded* superiority. The essence of the Admiralty programme – accepted by the Cabinet – was to secure an agreement which would entrench British superiority in a formal treaty.

In their different ways, the Geneva Naval Conference and the Preparatory Commission illustrated the twin *foci* of Britain's security policy: Europe and the Empire. But essentially Britain was looking in the wrong direction to hope ever to solve the question of security; she looked to America, while the real problem – Europe, and specifically Franco-German relations – was all but ignored, at least in the context of disarmament. In this latter respect, good relations with France should have been paramount. In practice, there was little meeting of minds. Cecil was correct in pointing out that France would be averse to separate conferences on land and sea disarmament, since it was natural that France would want to trade concessions on military armaments with concessions by Britain on the naval side – as seen in the abortive 'compromise' of 1928. Yet in the previous year, by attempting to reach a naval agreement with non-European powers at Geneva, Britain effectively reduced the chance of reaching agreement with the European nation whose power she professed to fear most. Moreover, as far as land armaments were concerned, by resting on her own previous unilateral arms reductions, and by refusing to consider any further reductions or commitments, Britain effectively barred any progress towards the international disarmament which was intrinsic to any attempt to meet Germany's grievances.

7

THE LABOUR GOVERNMENT,
1929–31

The General Election of May 1929 brought defeat for Baldwin's Conservatives by a slender margin. They gained 260 seats, whilst the Labour and Liberal parties increased their seats to 288 and 59 respectively. Labour, therefore, was the largest single Party, though still in a minority. Baldwin resigned immediately, and on 5 June Ramsay MacDonald became Prime Minister for a second time, but once again heavily dependent on Liberal support. MacDonald accepted that this time he could not be both Prime Minister and Foreign Secretary; he had decided six months previously that he must 'develop the work of the Prime Minister' in order to co-ordinate the State policy of the various departments which, he believed, had 'never been properly done'.[1] He wished to appoint the veteran trade union leader, Jimmy Thomas, to the Foreign Office but Arthur Henderson declared that he would take no other position. According to MacDonald, he had to threaten to take that post himself, in view of the 'row' over the Foreign Office,[2] but eventually agreed that the Office should go to Henderson. MacDonald was not alone in believing that Thomas would make a better Foreign Secretary. Austen Chamberlain, the former Foreign Secretary, believed that Thomas was 'by far the abler man', whereas he had always thought Henderson 'very stupid and rather afraid of responsibility'.[3] In the event, Henderson proved to be one of the successes of the second Labour government, but the dissension surrounding his appointment left its mark, and the resulting antagonism between MacDonald and his Foreign Secretary continued throughout the period of the Labour administration and beyond.

The foreign policy of the second Labour government, including the conflict between MacDonald and Henderson, has been well documented by David Carlton in his study, *MacDonald Versus Henderson: The Foreign Policy of the Second Labour Government*. However, whilst the present study is concerned primarily with the question of disarmament, one important aspect of the government's overall foreign policy does need to be stressed, and that is the question of the United States of America. MacDonald, in reluctantly handing foreign affairs to Henderson, insisted on retaining control of Anglo-American affairs. This resulted in what one historian has described as the 'two foreign policies' of the Labour government,[4] resulting equally in two approaches to disarmament, Henderson's wide approach via the League and MacDonald's personal approach involving a small number of states with much narrower aims.

The other Cabinet appointments were much less contentious, although MacDonald again agonised over his team; he would rather, he said, 'fight half a dozen elections than make one Cabinet',[5] and confessed he had broken hearts in the process.[6] Snowden was once again Chancellor of the Exchequer, and in lieu of the Foreign Office, Thomas became Lord Privy Seal. Lord Parmoor, who had fought so hard for the acceptance of the Geneva Protocol, was again Lord President of the Council, but only accepted the position after he had received MacDonald's assurance that Henderson would be appointed to the Foreign Office.[7] Secretary of State for War was the pacifist Tom Shaw, while the First Lord of the Admiralty was A.V. Alexander, whose judgement MacDonald repeatedly questioned. Thomson, one of MacDonald's few close friends, was again Secretary of State for Air, until his death in the R101 disaster in October 1930, when he was replaced by Lord Amulree. One of Thomson's first steps was to request a postponement of the completion of the RAF expansion scheme until 1938. This request was readily accepted by the Cabinet, as a means of strengthening Britain's moral position at Geneva, but Thomson was careful to add a *caveat* that there was a need to set some limits to our moderation 'in view of the failure of other Powers to follow our example in limiting our air forces'.[8]

One appointment over which MacDonald had no hesitation was that of Lord Cecil to whom he had suggested some months earlier that he should be one of Britain's representatives at Geneva, should another Labour government come to power. As Cecil felt that he and MacDonald were 'substantially agreed' on League matters, he agreed to accept MacDonald's offer, provided that he was given a room in the Foreign Office.[9] Cecil was optimistic; he felt that '[t]he programme of the Government was cheering', especially as the question of international disarmament was to be 'pushed forward again'.[10]

MacDonald's government came into power with its programme well defined. In 1928 the Party had adopted a document called 'Labour and the Nation', drawn up primarily by Henderson's chief advisers, Hugh Dalton and Philip Noel-Baker. Both were ardent supporters of disarmament, though Dalton had become increasingly anti-German, following a visit to Poland, and began, in his words, to try to shift Labour Party policy 'away from its current anti-French, pro-German mould'.[11] The new manifesto stressed the importance of disarmament and arbitration along with 'pooled security'. Significantly, this security would be looked for within the framework of the League, of which Henderson, Dalton and Noel-Baker were keen supporters. The programme called for the renunciation of war as an instrument of policy, to be achieved by signature of the Optional Clause. The implementation of the General Act for the Peaceful Settlement of

International Disputes was later added to the list of Labour's foreign policy objectives. As in 1924, the principles embodied in the Geneva Protocol – security, arbitration and disarmament – were to be the main thrust of the Labour government's foreign policy.

The Singapore naval base

Again, as in 1924, one of MacDonald's first acts was to turn his attention to the naval base at Singapore. In 1924 he had ordered the suspension of the base, more as an ideological gesture than in the hope of preventing its construction, and on the fall of his government the Conservatives had resumed their programme for its development. Even under the Conservatives, however, this programme had been cut back significantly. In January 1925, for example, Churchill, as Chancellor of the Exchequer, suggested that completion of the whole scheme was not a matter of great urgency, and that he regarded Singapore simply as a link in Britain's chain of Imperial communications.[12] In contrast, in June 1926 the Chiefs of Staff recommended that steps be taken 'as soon as financial considerations permit' to equip Singapore with defences 'on a scale unmistakably sufficient to deter attack'.[13] In October 1927 Worthington-Evans, Secretary of State for War, questioned whether the scale of military defences approved by the CID was not 'unnecessarily lavish', and suggested they be examined afresh to determine whether savings might be effected.[14] By February 1928 even the Chiefs of Staff were prepared to accept that, in view of the CID's assumption that no great war was likely to occur during the next ten years, the development of some of Singapore's defences should be postponed.[15] These decisions were based purely on financial considerations; by July 1928 a summary of the situation, prepared by Hankey, declared that the base 'could not economically be completed before July 1937, and that to hasten the completion date would add disproportionately to the cost'.[16]

If MacDonald were again to call a halt to the construction of the naval base, therefore, it would not be so dramatic a gesture as it had been in 1924. He did immediately institute a report on the status of the base, but the situation had changed a great deal in the intervening five years. The Fighting Services Committee summed up the situation by concluding that 'if the Government's hands had been quite free the right policy on economic and political grounds would have been to abandon the base forthwith' but that because of the money already spent, and the financial penalties of terminating contracts already awarded, whether the base was abandoned or continued would 'make little difference to the expenditure which must be borne by the Exchequer during the next three years'.[17] Eventually, and reluctantly, MacDonald was forced to accept that the financial gain which would result from complete stoppage would, when all obligations were taken into consideration, be comparatively small, and that whilst there was disagreement about defences, the original scheme, suspended by the Conservative government, would remain in that condition.[18] He was not to be completely distracted from his true purpose, however, declaring that whilst, the government would not proceed with any 'hasty scrapping' of the base, as security was found 'stage by stage by the establishment of sure means of peaceful settlement' so military organisation would have to accommodate itself to the new circumstances.[19]

Anglo-American relations

If MacDonald was thwarted in his desire to make a further ideological stand over Singapore, he was not prepared to suffer a similar set-back over naval disarmament. The Coolidge Conference had soured Anglo-American relations, and the abortive Anglo-French Compromise had exacerbated the situation. The need to improve relations had been recognised by Austen Chamberlain before leaving office. In January 1929 Esmé Howard informed Chamberlain that within the American government there was now a 'real atmosphere of willingness to come to reasonable terms and a desire to be friends', and that a naval agreement was considered possible, provided that negotiations were confined to statesmen and not to naval experts.[20] The British government, Howard believed, should send 'some really important statesmen' to establish personal contacts, and warned that any future conference must be preceded by private conversations 'to prepare the ground'.[21] Chamberlain agreed that private conversations were necessary, and that the next step should be the 'despatch of an English Cabinet Minister to Washington' as soon as the forthcoming elections were over.[22]

Whilst the need to improve relations was accepted by all concerned, the Foreign Office were less than optimistic about the prospects of a naval agreement. In a memorandum prepared in November 1928, the Office declared that the incoming President, Herbert Hoover, was 'notoriously difficult to deal with' and that his only public utterance on the naval question had been to the effect that the United States 'must have a navy which removes even the *fear* of attack'.[23] Even the outgoing President, Coolidge, appeared to have come under the influence of the Big Navy party; in his Armistice Day speech he too hinted at the necessity of the United States having the largest fleet in the world.[24] MacDonald therefore had two major tasks ahead of him; first to improve the general state of Anglo-American relations, and second to create a successful naval agreement out of the wreckage of the Coolidge Conference.

The Americans, however, made the first moves. Coolidge's Armistice Day speech in November 1928, in which he furiously attacked the European nations in general, and Britain in particular, on the naval question, caused bitter and unexpected foreign reactions. These reactions in turn created a 'profound impression' in official and public circles in the United States, and the situation began to improve.[25] Further evidence of a more conciliatory attitude on the part of the Americans was evident when the head of the American delegation to the Preparatory Commission, Hugh Gibson, announced in Geneva on 22 April 1929 that Hoover had reconsidered the naval problem and had come to the conclusion that it should be approached from a new angle. '[O]ther factors besides tonnage and gun-power', he declared, 'should be taken into consideration in preparing the way for an agreement which would effectively embody the principle of Anglo-American naval parity, to which the United States' government attach[ed] great importance'.[26] He proposed that a 'yardstick' be defined by which naval strengths might be compared, rather than the quest for mathematical parity which had undermined the Coolidge Conference. This was a break-through upon which MacDonald immediately took steps to capitalise.

MacDonald prided himself on his personal approach to diplomacy, and arranged a private meeting at Forres, near his home in Lossiemouth, with the new American Ambassador to London, General Dawes. Dawes informed MacDonald that the President and his advisers were working on a formula, in accordance with the Gibson declaration at Geneva, by which ships might have different valuations assigned to them, and that the Americans' intention was, if possible, to come to an agreement before the negotiations became official and formal.[27] Dawes also suggested that MacDonald should visit the United States when such agreement had been reached. When MacDonald informed Dawes that he intended to conduct negotiations himself, Dawes observed '[n]ow I can see that with you and the President working together, an agreement will be come to'.[28] This meeting was followed by others at which Gibson also was present, and MacDonald gradually began to prepare the ground both for an informal agreement, and for a personal visit to America.

Initially, progress was slow; in June 1929 the Americans felt that the time was not yet right for a conference, insisting that there must be time for the naval experts to digest the technical questions, and avoid the accusations of lack of preparation which had dogged the Coolidge Conference. As part of the preparation, there was a great deal of compromise between the two powers; Hoover announced the possible postponement of laying down three cruisers in response to the Labour government's decision to do the same. But the Americans still persisted in working on the basis of tonnage, and MacDonald pointed out that unless the 'yardstick' approach was used, the return to total tonnage would result in the same result as occurred in Geneva in 1927. The yardstick' was never actually defined, but in practice the 'yardstick principle' secured a move away from total tonnage and the question of strict mathematical parity which had dogged the Coolidge Conference. Britain, it was decided, would have the superiority she demanded in the smaller cruisers with 6-inch guns, and America would have superiority in the larger 8-inch gun cruisers. MacDonald also succeeded in bringing pressure to bear on the Admiralty to reduce the number of cruisers demanded from 63 to 49[29] – a return to the figure proposed by Beatty at

Washington in 1921 – which in turn enabled the level of parity to be set at a much lower level than would otherwise have been the case.

The voice of the naval experts refused to be totally over-ruled; on 13 August, for example, the Army and Navy Journal published a report that the Prime Minister would not be visiting the United States because negotiations were virtually at a standstill, and emphasised that while Britain might accept parity in principle there was no idea of accepting real parity in cruiser strength.[30] MacDonald, however, insisted to General Dawes that success *could* be achieved if political and not service hands were kept in control.[31] He was sceptical of the Admiralty's supposed concessions over cruiser numbers, and expressed his concern to Alexander:

> Generally, my suspicion is that the Admiralty is getting from us not only 50 ships, which of course is quite a good reduction, but is increasing the fighting efficiency of the navy so that, from that point of view, it is more formidable than it would be if we had more ships with a total efficiency for war purposes of a decidedly lower level than our fleet will be in 1936. Quite obviously this is not a position which we can maintain, and I am afraid that as soon as the experts get to work upon it at the Five-Power Conference we shall find ourselves in awkward corners. I wish you would turn your thoughts to this and see to it that your experts are not controlling you more than you imagine.[32]

On 27 August 1929 MacDonald left for America to conduct his personal diplomacy with the President and Secretary of State, where he 'set the seal' on the improvement in Anglo-American relations.[33] One of the questions which MacDonald had to address was that of belligerent rights, an old favourite of the Americans, but by agreeing to discuss the question with the Americans MacDonald avoided the subject being brought up publicly in open conference.[34] Overall, MacDonald's visit was, in public relations terms at least, a huge success, much of it due to the personality of the Prime Minister himself. As Ronald Campbell of the Foreign Office informed Henderson, 'The figure of the Prime Minister is one which strongly appeals to the American public. Here is a British statesman whom they can admire without reserve. There is no taint of "Toryism" (with its special American significance) which attaches to members of a Conservative government.'[35] At last both MacDonald and the American President felt that sufficient preparatory work had been done for a naval disarmament conference to be called, and an invitation was issued to France, Italy and Japan to meet in London in January 1930.

The London Naval Conference

A week before the conference began, MacDonald again caused consternation at the Admiralty by executing a rapid turn-round on his policy towards capital ships. Having stood firm against Hoover's proposed naval holiday during his visit to America, and endorsing an Admiralty Blue Print along the same lines, he made a statement to journalists on 15 January to the effect that the battleship was now a very doubtful proposition:

> [Britain] would wish to see an agreement by which the battleship would in due time disappear altogether from the fleets of the world. Until that is possible the government would like the Conference to consider whether agreement cannot be reached that no immediate replacements should be made and the life of the existing battleships extended.[36]

The Admiralty were furious and Alexander was totally unaware of the Prime Minister's apparent change of heart. As Dalton commented in his diary, 'what a strange animal is this Prime Minister of ours. It was almost too late, but he has taken at the eleventh hour the simple course!'[37]

Even before the London Conference officially commenced on 23 January, MacDonald was aware that there would be difficulties in at least one quarter: Franco-Italian rivalry. Grandi, the Italian representative, arrived with 'no programme but just a ratio with the "strongest continental power"',[38] and in this instance that meant parity with France. MacDonald again tried the personal approach. During a break for tea on 27 January he 'got Tardieu and Grandi in a corner', and as Tardieu was leaving he commented 'Mr Prime Minister, your tea party may be of historical significance. We (Grandi and he) talked well.'[39] But talking well was not sufficient to bridge the gap between French and Italian ambitions. In practice, the French refused to recognise the Italian claim to parity, and set their own requirements at a level which Britain judged to be unreasonably high (270,000 tons in the smaller cruiser and destroyer group alone). MacDonald complained that the French were simply refusing to react to the improved international situation brought about by the League and the Kellogg Pact. It was, he maintained, a 'military programme' similar to the one to which Britain had stuck so rigidly in 1927. But whereas Britain had recognised the improvement in the international situation, and had reduced her requirement from 70 to 50 cruisers, there was no sign of a corresponding decrease in the French figures.[40] The French reply was always the same: '[e]ither they must retain their present margin over Italy or else have some guarantee of security in its place'.[41] They wanted a Mediterranean Pact; not necessarily a Mediterranean Locarno, but some kind of mutual guarantee which committed the signatories to more than mere consultation in the event of aggression. MacDonald warned against getting into the same position as Sir Edward Grey had got into in 1906 in offering to the French more than consultation. 'Rather than get back to the position of 1906', he declared, he would 'go back to the Admiralty's old programme'.[42] Henderson, however, recognised the French position, having earlier informed Tyrrell, Britain's Ambassador to Paris, that any reduction of armaments would remain impossible for them unless they obtained additional security either under the Covenant or the Kellogg Pact. Tyrrell agreed – and retorted '[t]hat is the price we are paying for the uncompromising turning down of the protocol in November 1924'.[43]

France certainly did not go out of her way to facilitate a Five-Power agreement at the conference. Articles in the French press relating to Anglo-American proposals to go over Grandi's head to facilitate a compromise were calculated to infuriate Mussolini. 'Could this possibly have been the French object?' asked Britain's Ambassador to Rome.[44] There was also evidence of French plotting with the Japanese in order to undermine the conference.[45] MacDonald was forced to conclude that the French had never meant the conference to succeed; France, he believed, was taking steps to enable her to fight Italy, and war was the 'central fact of [her] mind'.[46] When Briand informed him that he could not discuss figures further until the question of security was addressed, MacDonald declared that 'Security has become the most brazen faced word in the language. She is a French strumpet!'[47] It is very significant that attempts to reach a Franco-Italian agreement occupy much more of the proceedings of the conference, official and unofficial, than do the steps to Anglo-American-Japanese agreement.

Whilst at heart many felt that the French were to blame for the Franco-Italian *impasse*, the Foreign Office were against laying the whole blame on France, suggesting that the best course to adopt would be to attribute failure to 'Latin incompatibility'.[48] Vansittart posed the central question of how far Britain could afford to estrange either France or Italy and which of the two would be 'most useful to us for furthering the idealistic policies which we have at heart and for co-operating with us in the everyday problems of post-war Europe'.[49] Perhaps unsurprisingly Vansittart's conclusion was that it would be unwise to denounce France, whose objectives most closely resembled those of Britain, in order to 'whitewash Fascist Italy' who wanted very different things – 'prestige, expansion, [and] troubled waters to fish in'.[50] In practice, therefore, to avoid French displeasure, the blame was shared equally, and Henderson worked hard to facilitate a compromise between the French and Italian positions long after a three-power agreement was reached. He brokered the so-called Franco-Italian Bases of Agreement of 11 March 1931, but even these eventually broke down. He received great appreciation for his tenacious efforts from King George and from the French Prime Minister, but they were to no avail.[51]

If, ultimately, the British and Americans could afford to leave the French and Italians out of negotiations for naval reductions, they could not afford to dismiss the Japanese. As in 1927, the question of Japanese strength was implicit in all their negotiations, so that when the Japanese demanded an increase in the Washington ratios from 60 to 70 per cent, the question could not be ignored. Although the Japanese claimed that this demand was because of the length of their coastline, the large number of their nationals abroad, the necessity for importing food and raw materials, and low ship-building capacity, the British Cabinet Committee set up to prepare for the Conference believed – correctly – that their real reasons were strategic, and that their aim was 'to render the U.S.A. unable to produce a superior fleet in Japanese waters'.[52] In further preparation for the conference, the Cabinet Committee on the London Naval Conference drew up proposals for a reduction in capital ships from 35,000 to 25,000 tons, and of gun calibre from 16 to 12 inches, with an extension of life from twenty to twenty-six years. America, it concluded, would probably object to these reductions, whereas Japan would probably agree to the reduction in size but prefer 14- rather than 12-inch guns. On the question of cruisers, the committee proposed a 'special agreement' as to cruiser strengths with the object of attaining a state of equilibrium in 1936 based on parity between Britain and America. A yardstick would be employed for interpreting parity, and, significantly, British cruiser strength in 1936 would be limited to *fifty* cruisers. Destroyers would have a maximum total tonnage of 200,000, with a maximum individual displacement for destroyer leaders and destroyers of 1,850 and 1,500 tons respectively. Destroyers would also be limited to 5-inch guns and a sixteen-year lifespan. The United States and Japanese were expected to agree to these proposals, although not to a further proposal for the abolition of submarines.

As in 1927, Britain, in outwardly drawing up plans in relation to the strength of the American navy, had her eyes firmly on Japan. The Cabinet Committee on the London Naval Conference pointed out that if the United States were to retain 21 8-inch gun cruisers, the Japanese could clearly not 'rest content' with their present programme of twelve 8-inch gun cruisers, since it would give them only 51 per cent of the American 8-inch gun cruiser tonnage. As Japan demanded a ratio of 70 per cent of American 8-inch cruiser tonnage, she would need to build four more 9,650 ton 8-inch cruisers, which in turn would give her sixteen as against the projected fifteen for the British Empire.[53] America must therefore be induced to reduce the number of their 8-inch gun cruisers from twenty-one to eighteen, giving Japan 67 per cent of American cruiser tonnage in numbers and 60 per cent in tonnage. The committee considered the Japanese demand for a 70 per cent ratio 'embarrassing', because even if an Anglo-American agreement were possible in which each side retained an equal number of 8-inch ships, neither Britain nor the United States could agree willingly to a position which would mean 'a definite accretion of naval strength to Japan'.[54] If Japan were to stick rigidly to her demand for a 70 per cent ratio, Britain was adamant that the projected American cruiser strength must be reduced.

At the conference itself, the capital ship question was settled easily enough.[55] It was agreed that the moratorium on construction would be extended to 1936, with the provision of an 'escalator' clause which would allow any of the signatories to commence further construction should their national security be threatened by new building on the part of a non-signatory to the proposed treaty. Cruisers, as in 1927, were a much more difficult problem to resolve, but on this occasion the painstaking preparatory work and improved working relations between the three major naval powers ensured that a compromise would be reached. The basis of the settlement was an American proposal. The chief American delegate, Colonel Stimson, explained to Craigie, the head of the American Department in the Foreign Office, that he had only been able to persuade Admiral Jones to reduce his demand for large cruisers to eighteen on the understanding that America would be able to build 6-inch gun ships of 10,000 tons.[56] There had been a tremendous struggle to get the demand down from twenty-one to eighteen, and Stimson begged that Britain would not press for a tonnage limit for individual 6-inch cruisers. He emphasised that the proposal was not a 'bargaining one' and that if opposed, it would be withdrawn. For their part, the Japanese were unhappy at being granted only 60 per cent of American strength in 8-inch cruisers, and significantly the problem was once again decided by politicians rather than naval experts. Ambassador Matsudaira and Senator Reed between them reached an understanding that the United States would complete only fifteen out of the allocation of eighteen 8-inch cruisers by the expiry of the agreement in 1936. Whilst some members of the American delegation were prepared to argue over this point, believing that the United States should make no concessions, pressure was brought to bear by the State Department, 'with Hoover breathing down its neck', and a compromise was reached. The compromise had the advantage that it also satisfied the British.[57] The Japanese did, however, hold out successfully for a 70 per cent ratio in light cruisers and destroyers and parity in submarines.

As far as Britain was concerned, there was resistance to the American proposals on the part of the Admiralty. Sir Charles Madden pointed out that the American proposal of 327,000 tons of cruisers fixed a 'yardstick' of 1.36, and that 'this would be perpetuated for ever'.[58] Naval powers, he maintained, only built ships for some specific purpose, and the Americans must have some war plan for which they already knew what would be required. MacDonald felt this was very unlikely. The Americans had in mind, he believed, nothing but parity, the figure of 327,000 tons being arrived at by splitting the difference between 315,000 tons, 'which had been mentioned at one point in the discussion', and the British figure of 339,000 tons. Eventually the compromise figure of 323,000 tons was agreed.

The final terms of the treaty were as follows. Capital ships would remain subject to the naval holiday, with the addition of the escalator clause. The figures for heavy cruisers with 8-inch guns up to 10,000 tons were eighteen for the United States, up to a maximum total tonnage of 180,000 tons, fifteen for Britain, with a maximum of 146,800 tons, and twelve for Japan up to 108,400 tons. The American superiority in the larger class of cruiser was balanced by superiority in the smaller class for Britain; 143,500 tons for the United States, 192,200 tons for Britain and 100,450 for Japan. Destroyers were limited to 150,000 tons each for Britain and America, and 105,500 for Japan, with individual limits set on destroyer leaders and destroyers of 1,850 and 1,500 tons displacement respectively. As regards submarines, a limit of 52,700 tons was allowed to each of the three powers. The treaty, signed on 22 April 1930, was to be coterminous with the Washington Treaty, and would thus expire on 31 December 1936.

The London Naval Conference produced an agreement because, as at Washington, the prerequisites were present. Both political will and political dominance over the naval experts were undeniably present; after the fiasco of Geneva in 1927, both the British Prime Minister and American President were determined to keep the reins of negotiation firmly in their own hands. At the outset of the Labour government, the Admiralty, according to a Treasury memorandum, had requested a building programme estimated to cost £56,000,000, which was larger and more expensive than that carried out by the Conservative government, and anticipated a requirement for seventy cruisers.[59] It was MacDonald who brought the requirement down to fifty, with a consequential reduction in projected expenditure. But not only did he bring the Admiralty into line at national level, at international level it was his undoubted diplomatic skill which, according to many observers, was the deciding factor at the conference itself.[60] According to MacDonald, the Foreign Office took no interest in the Naval Treaty because it was 'not its infant'.[61] President Hoover, for his part, in his 'hope of reducing friction in the world and . . . desire to reduce the great economic burdens of naval armament'[62] exerted similar pressure on his own naval experts. If America had wished to maintain the parity with Britain achieved at Washington, she would have had to commit a further £240,000,000 to naval construction; the pressure to reach agreement was thus very strong. The political need to improve Anglo-American relations, so badly damaged in 1927, was another important factor. But more than this there was an appreciation of the problems involved, both technical and political. The preparatory work carried out by MacDonald and Hoover, and to a slightly lesser extent by the Japanese, ensured a relatively smooth passage. A lot had been learned from the failure at Geneva. Significantly, however, where the preparatory work had not been done, no agreement was reached. This was scarcely the fault of either MacDonald or Hoover; the will to compromise and see the other's point of view did not exist between the French and Italians at this time, and no amount of effort on behalf of Britain or the United States could have bridged the distance between them.

The terms of the treaty did, in fact, involve an increase in the level of armaments in that the Americans would actually have to construct more cruisers if they wished to achieve actual parity. The crucial point, however, was not the level of armaments but the *control* of the levels of both armaments and expenditure by international agreement, a fact appreciated by the political leaders of all three countries. If the ratification of the treaty was less than straightforward, especially in Japan and America, where the respective naval experts were violently opposed to what they saw as infringement of their sovereignty, in practice the politicians were again able to exert their will, and by October 1930 the treaty had been ratified by all three powers. If its success was diluted somewhat by the absence of agreement between France and Italy, it was nevertheless a considerable achievement.

The Preparatory Commission and the Draft Disarmament Convention

One of the main reasons France had given for not attending the Geneva Naval Conference in 1927 was that disarmament should be indivisible: it was impossible to isolate naval from land and air disarmament – which, as Cecil had stressed in the Cabinet at the time, was a very reasonable argument. Thus, whilst accepting the invitation to the London Naval Conference, France still looked to the League in general, and the Preparatory Commission in particular, as the prime means of solving the problem of international arms control. In this respect, Gibson's speech to the Commission on 22 April 1929 showed a more conciliatory American attitude towards France. In addition to the more flexible attitude on the naval question, American acceptance of the French position on the non-limitation of trained reserves appeared to give new hope of breaking the deadlock at the Commission which had existed since 1927.

The more conciliatory American attitude, followed two months later by the accession of the Labour government in Britain, appeared to bode well for international co-operation. At the 10th League Assembly in September 1929, Henderson was able to announce that Britain would sign the Optional Clause of the League Covenant, which called for compulsory arbitration of international legal disputes. Henderson over-ruled the Service Departments' objections to the Clause, claiming that the reservations they wished to attach were the same as those attached by the Conservative government to their signature of the Kellogg Pact, and, in fact, constituted a British Monroe Doctrine.[63] Such a doctrine was, claimed Parmoor, incompatible with Labour policy.[64] Official Labour policy, however, was contested both within the government and Party itself; on sanctions in particular the left and right wings of the Party could not see eye to eye, causing the leaders to concentrate attention on the less contentious issues of arbitration and disarmament.[65] At the 11th Assembly of the League in September 1930 Henderson stated:

security and disarmament are closely interlocked, and nothing can make our peoples truly safe from war until a treaty of general disarmament has been made. We can never fulfil the purpose for which the League has been created unless we are prepared to carry through a scheme of general disarmament by international agreement. The authors of the Covenant never believed that international co-operation could succeed if national armaments should remain unrestricted, and if armament competition should revive.[66]

Henderson emphasised the steps already taken towards international security by the enforced disarmament of the Treaty of Versailles, and by the Locarno Treaties of 1925 and confirmed that His Majesty's government had now ratified the Optional Clause. He also committed the government to signing the General Act for the Pacific Settlement of International Disputes, but this was as far as even the Labour government was prepared to go towards French demands for security.[67]

A number of other factors were tipping the balance in a less than auspicious direction. The Wall Street Crash of October 1929 caused governments to look inwards, to protect their domestic positions, whilst at the same time trying to channel internal tensions on to the international scene. The Young Plan of August 1929 finalised the reparations question once and for all, and the Rhineland was evacuated by the end of June 1930, five years earlier than anticipated in the Treaty of Versailles. However, this did little to alleviate Germany's grievances. Moreover, the deteriorating economic situation helped the Nazi Party to increase its support, and in the September 1930 elections it became the second largest party in the Reichstag. The German government, under Heinrich Brüning, began to press more strongly for equality of rights in armaments to be granted, and in the worsening international situation French fears and insecurity increased. International disarmament now became the major item on Germany's foreign policy agenda.

The widening gap between French and German demands made attempts at compromise both inevitable yet unlikely to succeed. As far as the Labour government was concerned, ministers were presented with a choice of pressing for German equality and accepting the French need to retain superiority. They decided, 'after a long debate and with a heavy heart, to support the French view as the only way of getting any kind of World Disarmament Conference into existence'.[68] The immediate problem was one of procedure. The Preparatory Commission was still in existence and formally committed to the negotiation of a draft convention.

In the circumstances, a sub-committee of the CID was set up in August 1930 to try to define British policy towards the reconvening of the Preparatory Commission and a resumption of negotiations on the Draft Convention. It immediately highlighted the problem of trained reserves, recognising that it would be impossible to persuade continental powers to change their system. The agreed solution was to 'fall back upon the alternative which is an attempt to reduce the efficiency of the reserves and so to curtail the power of aggression'.[69] A further problem was the limitation of land war material, which, to be effective, would involve 'a form of supervision and inspection more drastic than any State could accept'. The Foreign Office had proposed the limitation of tanks and big guns, but the technical difficulties even in these larger categories were very great, and on the whole, the Sub-Committee considered, 'the advantage of limiting them would not be of great importance'.[70] It therefore felt that, if no form of direct limitation on land could be adopted, there should be a limitation of total expenditure on the land forces as well as a specific limitation of expenditure on material. 'Unless material for land armies is limited in some way', the Sub-Committee concluded, 'a disarmament treaty would be a farce. Mechanisation is the fighting policy of the future. . . . '[71] As far as sea and air armaments were concerned, they should be limited both directly by limiting ships and aircraft and indirectly by limiting expenditure.

When the Sub-Committee's report came before the CID on 29 September 1930, the Prime Minister regretted that it could not be accepted as an agreed report, because the Air Ministry representative had 'signed a dissentient note', relating to budgetary and horse-power limitation.[72] In this respect, Lord Thomson pointed out that the Air Ministry were not alone in objecting to budgetary limitation, which, in his opinion, could not be made effective as regards air forces. Britain's air force, based as it was on volunteers, was necessarily expensive, and the fact that it was distributed in different parts of the world added considerably to the cost, making it vastly more expensive than, say, the air forces of France and Italy. Both labour and materials were also more expensive in Britain. More significantly, he added that the air force was 'currently working on an expansion programme, which had been approved by three successive Governments' with the object of completing fifty-two home defence squadrons by 1938.[73] The French, he pointed, out were also expanding. The pacifist War Minister, Shaw, demanded to know whether Thomson was objecting to budgetary limitation because it would leave Britain in an inferior position, or because it was unacceptable in principle to the Air Ministry, but quite acceptable for the other branches of the armed services to be so limited. His own service also had components 'scattered over the world', but the War Office still favoured budgetary limitation.

Henderson remarked that Thomson ought to have voiced his arguments in Cabinet, where it had already been decided that the government would accept the principle of budgetary limitation. It had also been tacitly accepted by His Majesty's government at Geneva, and Britain was thus 'irrevocably committed' to the principle. He failed to see how any disarmament convention could operate without some means of budgetary limitation, but whilst he agreed with Thomson that Britain must not be placed in a position of inferiority, he pointed out that when the air expansion scheme had been considered and approved, there had been no thought of a world disarmament convention taking place. Now, however, the position was 'on a totally different plane' and it was down to the Service Departments to consider how a system of budgetary limitation could be implemented, not to oppose its implementation. Thomson responded that whilst the other two fighting services might have accepted that budgetary limitation was government policy, they felt it was 'valueless in operation' and had 'damned the suggestion with faint praise'.[74] MacDonald closed the discussion by stating that, if the principle of budgetary limitation had been accepted as an essential part of disarmament, the task of the Service Departments should be to ensure the necessary safeguards within the principle, and they should now confer together before reporting to the Cabinet.

In practice, the Air Ministry refused to regard the issue as closed. Although Thomson died before he could see through the task of safeguarding the Ministry's position, when next the question came before the Cabinet, the Air Staff put forward two memoranda prepared from notes left by their former Chief. In the first, they professed themselves in favour of the principle of the limitation of armaments, and pointed out that they had agreed to the imposition of restrictions upon air armaments by means of limitation of personnel by numbers, limitation by numbers of first line strength of aircraft, and limitation by numbers of aircraft in reserve.[75] However, whilst they supported a full measure of budgetary 'publicity' they still objected to restriction by means of budgetary limitation. They claimed that budgetary limitation had been opposed by the United States and China at the Sixth Session of the Preparatory Commission in April 1929, and the resolution had been passed by 22 votes to 2. Moreover, in September 1929 the British representative had tried to re-open the question, but had been met with a general objection against any attempt at going back on the previous resolution. The memorandum offered many other reasons for opposition to the principle, including differences in purchasing power, standard of life, distrust as to good faith, and the risk that if accepted, the result 'might well be the repudiation by other countries of the principle of limitation of material by enumeration'.

The second memorandum tackled the question of horsepower limitation for aircraft which had received provisional assent in the Preparatory Commission in 1927. At that time the British delegate had given his assent subject to the determination of a satisfactory method of estimating horsepower. The Air Ministry memorandum of 14 October 1930 now stated that:

> Due to the intricacies of the problem, the many varying factors which have to be taken into account – for example, the type of fuel used, the altitude at which the engine is to be employed, the

number of revolutions per minute, the degree of 'supercharging' – together with the necessity for evolving a simple method of assessment which could be supplied without the necessity for 'supervision', it has not been found possible to suggest any satisfactory method of determining horsepower.[76]

The Air Ministry recommended that, while Britain should not oppose the application of a horsepower limit, she should not advocate it.

On 15 October 1930, despite the Air Ministry's objections, the Cabinet specifically approved the principle of budgetary limitation, along with the Report of the Sub-Committee on the Reduction and Limitation of Armaments.[77] On 6 November the Cabinet again discussed budgetary limitation, the Treasury noting that no difficulties were anticipated which 'should not be capable of reasonable adjustment at Geneva'.[78] But whilst the Admiralty accepted the principle, subject to the attitude of the other naval powers, and the War Office felt the principle not only feasible but essential, the Air Ministry still declared itself 'unable to recommend that this principle can be applied without detriment to national security'. It also still maintained that the principle of horse-power limitation appeared 'to present grave technical difficulties'. Britain thus went into the final session of the Preparatory Commission without full consensus on her policy towards the Draft Convention. Whilst the government officially supported the principle of budgetary limitation, the Air Ministry were determined to undermine this policy if at all possible, despite MacDonald's over-ruling of their objections.

Three weeks later the Service Departments came up with another problem. The Dutch had put forward proposals to the Preparatory Commission, which involved the disclosure of more information than the Service Departments would like. They maintained they were not afraid of disclosing their strength, but of revealing their weakness. Under the proposals of the Netherlands government more information would have to be given to the public than it was now the practice to lay before Parliament. They then pointed out that

Holland was a country which had, for all practical purposes disarmed herself and that the proposal accordingly involved her in no risk. It was improbable that other countries would send in true returns and the practice would grow up of increasing secret reserves.[79]

Britain also had 'disarmed herself', but since her commitments were far greater than those of Holland, disclosure of her weaknesses would have far greater consequences.

The final session of the Preparatory Commission took place between 6 November and 9 December 1930, and produced a Draft Convention which appeared to raise more questions than it answered, highlighting the major, still unresolved, differences between the parties. The question of trained reserves predominated; the continental powers, with their conscript armies, trained every available man. States with volunteer armies, Britain, the United States and Germany, recognised that they could not impose their system on the other states, but sought to decrease the efficiency of conscripted armies by other means, such as a limitation of the period of service. Another problem concerned the method of limiting war material. Germany and Italy strongly favoured strict limitation of war stock and restriction by enumeration of such equipment. France, however, was opposed to this method and the ensuing vote on the question resulted in a tie, with Cecil abstaining for Britain on the grounds that the scheme was not practicable. As Carlton says, Britain could have cast a decisive vote and 'thereby significantly altered the course of nego-tiations', but whilst this would have pleased the Germans, it is unlikely that the French would have agreed to attend any general disarmament conference if their point of view had been voted down.[80] Cecil favoured a system of budgetary limitation for war material, but this was in turn opposed by the United States, the Soviet Union, Japan and Germany. Aircraft presented another problem: limitation by horsepower and numbers appeared acceptable, though, as pointed out earlier, the British Air Ministry did not like this method. Again, it raised problems as far as Germany was concerned; she was not supposed to have an air force at all, under the terms of the Treaty of Versailles, yet how could the other powers retain their air forces whilst still granting Germany the equality of rights she demanded?

Political expediency dictated that the Preparatory Commission reach a conclusion as soon as possible, but the Draft Convention which it produced scarcely provided a solution. The political problems which underlay the technical questions were avoided; differences over trained reserves, differ-ences over the principle of budgetary limitation versus direct limitation of *matériel*, disagreement over the extent of the powers of the proposed super-visory body, the Permanent Disarmament Commission, as well as the problem of a German air force, were all questions which were left in the air. To make matters worse, the Soviet Union and Germany voted against the adoption of the Draft Convention, on the grounds that it would not bring about any real reduction or limitation of armaments.

The Draft Convention had never been intended to define actual figures; it had always been intended to be a basis for discussion. Even so, it was hardly a satisfactory foundation for the Disarmament Conference's deliberations. As the Foreign Office quite rightly observed, it ignored the real problem, the 'natural legacy of the Peace Treaty', which would inevitably have to be faced sooner or later.

> Let no-one [it said] . . . blame the Preparatory Committee. It has spun out its work for 5 years or more: without that rather

astonishing feat of procrastination, the crisis would have been on us before now.[81]

The contemporary analyst John Wheeler-Bennett put the shortcomings of the Draft Convention more succinctly:

The Draft Convention gave as much satisfaction to a weary and waiting world as did the Red Queen's dry biscuit to a tired and thirsty Alice in Wonderland.[82]

But at least now the *real* discussions for international disarmament could begin.[83]

If the Draft Disarmament Convention was intrinsically a grave disappointment, at least the Labour government could claim credit for helping the Preparatory Commission to end its proceedings without *too* great a loss of face. The government was also successful in another of its projects. Early in its second term a Foreign Office Committee, under Cecil's chairmanship, was set up to consider the General Act for the Peaceful Settlement of International Disputes which had been consolidated at Geneva at the League Assembly in 1928. The aim of the General Act was to submit disputes 'of every kind' between two or more parties, which had proved impossible to settle by means of diplomacy, to a permanent Conciliation Commission.[84] The Admiralty raised the same objections, and reserved the same rights and comments as they had put forward in relation to the Optional Clause,[85] but Henderson was adamant that Britain should sign the Act, in many ways a similar document to the Geneva Protocol of 1924 but without the sanctions clauses. Progress was slow, time being needed to persuade the Dominions to sign, but at the League Assembly in September 1930 he announced that Britain intended to sign. On 21 May 1931, at the 63rd League Council Meeting, Britain and all the Dominions, with the exception of South Africa, who were in favour but wished to have more time to consider their position, acceded to the Act. The Optional Clause and General Act were, in Henderson's opinion, vital preludes to a successful disarmament agreement, and he felt Britain's adoption of them to be a great achievement. He could now move on towards the goal of disarmament itself. In March 1931, Henderson was offered, and accepted, the post of President-elect of the forthcoming Disarmament Conference; a source of pride and satisfaction to himself, and intense chagrin to MacDonald![86]

The Three-Party Committee

The government now set in motion the next steps towards achieving its goal of a general disarmament agreement. The Preparatory Commission finally decided that the long-awaited Disarmament Conference should begin on 2

February 1932, and the Labour government accordingly began to plan its response. At the Cabinet meeting of 4 February 1931, almost exactly 12 months before the projected commencement date, it was suggested that a committee be formed, and that 'representatives of the other political Parties should be invited to associate themselves with this Committee with a view to their taking part in the work of the Conference and bearing their share in the responsibility from the beginning'.[87] There was some discussion as to whether it was actually wise to invite the co-operation of the other parties 'in view of the desire of the government to give a pronounced lead in the matter of disarmament', but it was eventually agreed that representatives of the other parties, and of the Dominions, should be approached with a view to enlisting their support in advising the Cabinet 'as to the policy to be adopted at the coming Disarmament Conference and [directing] in all its aspects the work of preparation'.[88] The other parties agreed to MacDonald's suggestion that they be involved in the formulation of policy. Under the chairmanship of MacDonald, the principal delegates to the sub-committee were Henderson, Austen Chamberlain, Hoare, Eden and Lloyd George.

The conclusions reached by the new sub-committee on 15 July 1931 emphasised the Powers' commitments under the Treaty of Versailles, the League Covenant and the Final Protocol of the Locarno Conference, 'that the maintenance of peace requires the reduction of national armaments to the lowest point consistent with national safety and the enforcement by common action of international obligations'. Britain's delegates to the conference should make a full statement of the reductions already effected by the United Kingdom, and state that 'any further reductions . . . must be part of an international agreement', whilst pointing out that Britain might have to reconsider the low level of her armaments if the other Powers did not agree to similarly reduce their own.[89] In order that nations retained a reasonable security, successive conferences should then be held at intervals 'at each of which a further stage in the reduction of armaments would be reached'. In any case, the military forces of nations, available on the outbreak of war, whether personnel or material, should be limited in such a way as to make it unlikely for an aggressor to succeed with a knock-out blow. The Committee further recommended that in considerations of security, allowances should be made for a nation like France which had been 'twice invaded and once devastated within living memory' and thus was naturally apprehensive about its future security. The system of disarmament adopted in the peace treaties, supplemented by some form of budgetary limitation, would provide the most successful solution. The same methods of disarmament should be applied to all nations alike, and 'should not involve the increase of the fighting strength of the disarmed Powers, but rather the reduction of the armaments of others'. There should be some form of supervision, which would replace the methods of supervision in the peace treaties, and delegates should re-affirm Britain's desire to see conscription abolished, but failing that, 'other methods must be found for the limitation of effective strengths of land and air personnel, and consequently of their reserves'. The Committee concluded:

> delegates should keep in view throughout the idea of gradually leading nations to rely for their security on the obligations undertaken by all the nations of the Conference to renounce war as an instrument of policy and to seek the settlement of disputes by none but peaceful means. Until these engagements are accepted at their face value disarmament can never be complete.[90]

These were the Three-Party Committee's recommendations to the Cabinet in regard to Britain's proposed policy at the forthcoming conference. They amounted to a comprehensive restatement of the ideals which should form part of any disarmament agreement – equality, security and the renunciation of war as an instrument of policy. Equipped with such a positive policy, in line with the broad statement of ideals embodied in the Draft Convention, Britain ought to have been well prepared for a successful outcome. However, in August 1931, before the Cabinet could endorse or reject the proposals, MacDonald's second Labour government fell, amid financial chaos and personal acrimony, and the fate of disarmament passed once again into the hands of a Conservative-dominated administration.

Conclusion

Once again the Labour government had been in office for too short a period, and was too dependent on Liberal support, to make a major impact on British disarmament policy in the longer term. Nevertheless, in the short term, the impact was considerable and it is difficult to see how much more could have been achieved given the prevailing international situation, in particular the Franco-Italian naval divergence. In the longer term, the international financial crisis which had begun with the Wall Street crash in October 1929, had by the end of 1930 undermined still further the political stability necessary to make further progress towards both security and disarmament. The situation worsened in March 1931 when Germany announced that she proposed to institute a Customs Union between herself and Austria. This supposedly purely economic arrangement inevitably increased French fears of a possible *Anschluss*.

At the same time, in some respects the deteriorating international situation provided a more neutral base from which to conduct international relations in general, and disarmament in particular. The major European powers were all under increasing pressure to reach agreement in order to prevent German rearmament, and this could well have made the Labour government's task easier. Be that as it may, despite its problems, and the brevity of its period in office, the Labour government fulfilled almost all of its promises in the area of foreign policy, with the one notable exception of a general disarmament treaty, and this, arguably, through lack of time. Overall, indeed, the two parallel foreign policies had achieved some notable successes. MacDonald had undoubtedly been instrumental in healing the breach with the United States and preventing another naval arms race. Henderson had pushed through the Optional Clause and the General Act, and had raised British prestige on the international scene in general, and at the League of Nations in particular. When Henderson went to Buckingham Palace to hand back his seals of office in 1931, the King said to him: 'Thank you for all you've done at the Foreign Office. Our relations with every country in the world, except Persia, are better now than when you took over. And you're not to blame for Persia.'[91] Both MacDonald and Henderson had shown themselves more willing to stand up to the Service Departments on disarmament and the League. MacDonald, for example, had sharply reminded them that their task was not to undermine the principle of budgetary limitation once it had been accepted by the Cabinet, but to ensure the necessary safeguards within the principle, whilst Henderson had dismissed their proposed reservations over both the Optional Clause and the General Act. This was in marked contrast to the previous Conservative government, which had done little more than accept the Service Departments' reservations and arguments, especially in relation to the Geneva Naval Conference, and allowed them to dictate policy.

Unfortunately, none of these moves had helped bridge the ever-widening gap between France and Germany, which remained the real root of the security and disarmament problems in Europe, whilst the intentions of the Japanese and the Soviet Union cast a shadow over prospects for international stability. Moreover, whilst MacDonald had dominated the Admiralty during the London Naval Conference, this conference had a narrow agenda and was restricted to a narrow group of powers. The negotiations relating to the Draft Disarmament Convention, on the other hand, covered the whole spectrum of armaments and the full international community – and in the Geneva arena the Service Departments were notably less co-operative. Even before the demise of the Labour government, therefore, the prospects of a successful outcome at the Disarmament Conference itself were receding. The replacement of the government by a basically Conservative administration, with MacDonald at its head, reduced those diminished prospects even further.

8

THE NATIONAL GOVERNMENT, 1931–4

In August 1931, MacDonald's minority government fell, as a direct result of the world-wide financial situation. His decision to remain at the head of a National government had grave repercussions for both domestic and foreign policies, including the disarmament question. Henderson, the committed disarmer and President-elect of the Disarmament Conference, was not only out of office, but his already difficult relationship with MacDonald was exacerbated by the sense of betrayal felt by the majority of the Labour Party. The reluctance of former Labour Ministers to serve in the new National government meant that it contained a much greater proportion of Conservatives than of the more pro-disarmament Labour and Liberal members. With the Disarmament Conference now only six months away, any possible cohesion of British disarmament policy appeared to be remote.

Three months after the formation of the first National government, in November 1931, a general election enabled MacDonald to select the Cabinet which was to be responsible for British policy towards the Disarmament Conference. Only three Labour Ministers remained in the government; Snowden[1] became Lord Privy Seal, Sankey[2] was Lord Chancellor, and Thomas became Dominions Secretary. There were two Liberals in the Cabinet, Sir John Simon as Foreign Secretary and Sir Herbert Samuel as Home Secretary, though the latter was to resign in September 1932, to be replaced by the Conservative Sir John Gilmour. With the exception of these five members, and MacDonald as Prime Minister, the remaining Cabinet members were Conservatives: Baldwin became Lord President of the Council, Neville Chamberlain, Chancellor of the Exchequer, and Sir Philip Cunliffe-Lister Colonial Secretary. The armed services were represented by the Marquess of Londonderry, Secretary of State for Air, Lord Hailsham, Secretary of State for War, and Sir Bolton Eyres-Monsell, First Lord of the Admiralty. The choice of personnel did not augur well for the negotiations at Geneva.

The search for a policy

On entering office, the National government had no defined programme or policy on disarmament, other than the recommendations of the Three-Party Committee. At the first Cabinet meeting of the new government MacDonald 'mentioned the question of Disarmament Policy as one on which the Cabinet, before long, would have to settle its procedure' and referred to the work of the Three-Party Committee as a basis for that procedure.[3] But regardless of the recommendations of that Committee, Londonderry soon registered his aims for the forthcoming conference. In Cabinet on 9 December 1931, he maintained 'We are bound to claim at Geneva full theoretical parity with the world's strongest Air Power – leaving it, of course, as an issue of domestic policy to what extent we translate that claim into concrete reality'.[4] The excessive moderation of British air policy, he maintained, had placed Britain in a position of serious disparity, and the only hope of effective air disarmament lay in persuading the French to reduce drastically their present overwhelming air forces.

Less than a week after Londonderry's intervention the Cabinet Committee charged with supervising the remaining work of preparation for the Disarmament Conference asked the Cabinet to consider whether Britain was 'prepared to pay the price which may be the only means of bringing about a reduction in French armaments'.[5] The price which the Committee had in mind was 'some form of guarantee over and above Locarno', for example, a Mediterranean Locarno, or failing that, 'a further alternative proposal of a somewhat shadowy kind, namely the creation of an international force'.[6] Since the most important question posed by the Committee was 'what is to be the British attitude ... in the main controversy which is bound to arise between the German and French positions', a Mediterranean Locarno, which would involve Franco-Italian relations rather than Franco-German relations, was scarcely likely to solve the problem of French security.

Interestingly, at this Cabinet meeting, it was pointed out that, whilst Britain had made substantial reductions in the levels of her armaments, and that as the result of earlier disarmament conferences the navy had been 'diminished to a point beyond which further reduction would be dangerous', there was general agreement that 'the mere recital of the contribution we had already made to Disarmament would not be of assistance in dealing with this question: also that reductions of all armaments must be made on an international relational basis'.[7] Here, then, was proof that the government did, at least privately, recognise the essential difference between arms reductions for domestic/economic purposes, and the further-reaching disarmament by international agreement. It might also mean that the government felt it had few cards to play at Geneva.

As far as French security went, however, MacDonald pointed out that at the Three-Party Committee Lloyd George had pressed the idea that security meant that Germany had as good a right as France to be safe against invasion, and that a memorandum should be prepared which should 'contain an indication of what we meant by "security"'. It was apparent that there would be little sympathy for the French definition. Nevertheless, the question of security was vital to any chance of success for the conference. As Sir Robert Vansittart, no great lover of disarmament, pointed out in a note for Simon on 23 December 1931:

> If His Majesty's Government take the Disarmament Conference seriously, then they must take the question of the security guarantee seriously also. If we are not seriously considering the question of the security pact, then our attitude towards the Disarmament Conference is not wholly sincere. We are giving it lip service only – knowing in our hearts that it is bound to fail.[8]

The Foreign Office, in fact, were adamant that an understanding with France was an essential prerequisite of any agreement. A memorandum produced on 6 December 1931 cited Eyre Crowe's memorandum of January 1907 in which he protested that 'a systematic policy of gratuitous concessions' towards Germany had led 'to the highly disappointing result disclosed by the almost perpetual state of tension existing between the two countries'.[9] Whilst it was not suggested that relations with Germany were 'in all particulars the same in 1931 as . . . in 1907' there were striking similarities. On the other hand, the memorandum pointed out that when MacDonald came to power in 1924 he had immediately decided that the 'aims of British policy in Europe could not be served unless some attempt were made to arrive at an understanding with France' and had not hesitated to 'take the necessary steps to achieve that understanding'.[10] A further memorandum by Sargent underlined Selby's contention that only when Britain and France stood together, denying Germany the chance to divide the two, was progress ever made.[11] It soon became clear, however, that the Cabinet were disinclined to take the advice of the Foreign Office on the matter.

On 8 December 1931 during a discussion on disarmament policy within the Foreign Office, the legality of Germany's claim that the other powers ought to have disarmed was called into question. It was, however, accepted that Germany would seem to have 'quite a strong moral case, even if her legal one [was] invalid'.[12] Nevertheless, whether her claims were legal, moral or both, it '[seemed] difficult to contemplate any attempt to force Germany to remain in her present inferior position *in perpetuo*'. The whole disarmament dilemma was encapsulated in this discussion: if no agreement could be reached and Germany renounced the Treaty of Versailles, France might be provoked into re-entering the Ruhr; and if it were found that under Locarno, Britain had some moral or legal obligation to take action, 'it would obviously be desirable to take such a factor into consideration in framing [British] policy *vis-à-vis* France and Germany'.[13] Whilst Britain could neither further reduce her forces nor undertake further international obligations, if agreement was to be reached it would be necessary to pay the French price of a specific guarantee:

> not an indefinite obligation as in Locarno – but rather a categorical undertaking to come to her assistance under certain conditions in accordance with a pre-arranged plan. . . . [I]t will obviously be necessary to consider carefully the price demanded and to decide whether we would be willing to pay it or whether it is too heavy.[14]

The dilemma was obvious: pay the price demanded by the French for any agreement to reduce her armaments further, or refuse to pay the price and bring about German renunciation of the Versailles Treaty with consequent international *re*-armament! But as Vansittart had pointed out, there was little point in going to Geneva unless Britain *was* prepared to pay France's price.

Although discussions on British policy went on in Cabinet until the beginning of the Disarmament Conference, perhaps unsurprisingly no real policy emerged. What, in fact, happened was that an *ad hoc* policy evolved in response to events at Geneva. In the main, as the following discussion will show, it was a catalogue of negative reactions to proposals put forward by others. Not until March *1933* did the government accept the need to lead by positive example, and even this acceptance was forced upon them by the 'men on the ground' in Geneva.

At the Cabinet meeting on 15 December 1931 it was suggested that 'it would be inadvisable at the outset for [Britain] to take any active initiative' and that in any conversations with the French and German governments it was important to avoid committing herself to one side or the other. MacDonald's attitude was simple, if not simplistic:

> We need at Geneva a policy quietly pursued without turning off our way to right or left.[15]

He did not believe that a negative policy – based on little more than reciting the unilateral arms reductions undertaken by Britain since 1919 – would be ineffective; rather he saw positive benefits from the standpoint of public opinion. As he stated in the Cabinet immediately prior to the opening of the Disarmament Conference:

> [Our policy] might be lacking in positive new proposals, but the sentiment and the intention behind were excellent. The Delegation ought to emphasise the fact that we had not waited for the Disarmament Conference to begin disarming, and to describe the

situation which had been reached as the result of our efforts. In this respect we had a magnificent case. Whether other nations believed us or not was not very material, provided that the whole case were put and reached our own public.[16]

In practice, however, the policy would turn out to be completely *in*effective, a point which began to be recognised by certain members of the Cabinet as the Conference progressed. Even so, the government's attitude would remain essentially the same throughout the conference. Britain would offer no further arms reductions without an international agreement, yet no commitments which would enable France to make such an agreement.

The Conference for the Reduction and Limitation of Armaments

In examining British policy in relation to the Disarmament Conference,[17] it is necessary to omit a great deal of material on both policy discussions and conference proceedings simply because of the vast amount of primary information available. It is also difficult to divide policy decisions from chronological events at Geneva, as they are very closely inter-woven. For these reasons the present work will examine the three major proposals presented during the Conference – the Brüning, Hoover and MacDonald Plans – and, inter-woven with these proposals, the policy responses of the British government. It is not the purpose of this study to attempt to assess the reasons for the failure of the Disarmament Conference *per se*: there were many such reasons, though it can be argued that the failure of the other nations to respond positively to Germany's claim for equality was one of the main factors. Indubitably, however, each nation was anxious that the blame for its failure should fall on the shoulders of others. Britain was no exception.[18]

The Disarmament Conference finally commenced on 2 February 1932, and the Draft Convention which had occupied the Preparatory Commission for six years, was virtually ignored. At the opening session, delayed because the League Council had first to consider Japanese bombings in Manchuria, the major powers each put forward their own disarmament plans, and these were debated 'one after the other in no logical order'.[19] For Britain, Simon put forward a proposal for qualitative disarmament, under which all aggressive weapons should be abolished. This proposal received widespread approval, but the difficult question of the definition of aggressive weapons led to the formation of a sub-committee, which in turn led to the slowing down of all progress on Simon's suggestion. By 21 March Simon was complaining to the new Ministerial Committee on the Disarmament Conference that 'so far there had been a good deal of posturing but very little effective work accomplished'.[20] He felt that whilst Britain ought not to rush into the discussions, she must have a definite line on which to work. Hoare was for pressing on with the qualitative disarmament line, and advocated restricting just those arms which were restricted to Germany. Thomas felt that the disarmament question rested squarely on the issue of sanctions, and 'sanctions were barren without the co-operation of the United States', a point with which Simon was inclined to agree: 'it must be remembered', he said, 'neither of us are European States' thus, at best, Britain 'might be able to undertake to exhibit . . . "benevolent neutrality" '.[21]

Within the Ministerial Committee, the practical issues of arms limitation were relegated to a secondary position while the question of sanctions and security was debated. There was a discussion at the meeting on 21 March of the abolition of tanks and bombing from the air, but the overriding opinion was that 'if we were prohibited from using all bombing machines and all tanks we should also prevent ourselves from using these weapons for the maintenance of peace and order in places like Iraq, the North-West Frontier of India etc.'.[22] Only MacDonald dissented from this view, claiming that 'it might possibly be difficult to say, in effect, that we were horrified at the idea of bombing, but that while we would agree not to bomb others we must still reserve the right to bomb our own people'. Hailsham maintained that this was a different issue: the gas bomb was perhaps 'the most humane weapon' provided that it was filled with tear gas, presumably in contrast to bombing designed to destroy enemy lives and property.

At this meeting the question of French security again predominated. It was pointed out that when the conference re-assembled after Easter a discussion would take place on the respective French and German proposals, and it would be necessary for Britain to make a general statement of policy. Simon reminded his colleagues that the French and German theses would be strongly contrasted; Germany would press her claim for equality and France would deny that Germany had any case at all for claiming to be released from Part V of the Treaty of Versailles. More significantly, France would state that she was perfectly ready to disarm given the right terms, and that these terms were contained in such theses as the creation of a super-state at Geneva, and the definition of an aggressor. 'It seemed hardly possible that we should be able to keep aloof from this violent clash of ideals when the time came.'[23] A super-state was perhaps an exaggeration of the French demands, but security was always going to be at the top of her agenda. Nevertheless, throughout much of the conference France was willing to accept rather less in the way of compensation than a super-state, or even an Anglo-French alliance or a military back-up to Locarno, providing the provisions for verification in the disarmament convention were tight enough.[24] Londonderry appeared to be one of the few who recognised this possibility, suggesting that too much importance was being attached to the super-state proposal:

He was quite certain that France would much rather have a guarantee from us than from anybody else, and what we wanted to know was what guarantee would satisfy France . . . and it was his opinion that it would be very much less than we were disposed to think. He thought if the whole of our present commitments were resolved down to hard facts, it might be found possible to diminish greatly France's pertinacity, particularly if we could suggest something to which we were already committed although we might perhaps wrap up any suggestion so as not to make this fact too obvious. He thought that under such conditions France might be found to be more reasonable than we supposed.[25]

There was little justification to continually blame the French for their inability to state exactly what their security requirements were; they could not define them until they knew what exactly it was that Germany wanted. The Germans, however, followed a policy of reacting to other powers' proposals rather than putting forward proposals themselves. Both diplomatically and militarily, it was more advantageous to them to say 'not enough' to the proposals of other powers than to formulate a defined position. They wanted always to ask for 'more'. Germany, in fact, attempted to use the Conference as a cover for the pursuit of her rearmament.[26] At only one point during the conference did the Germans put forward a specific proposal for an overall settlement. This was in April 1932, when the Chancellor, Heinrich Brüning, endeavoured to gain a disarmament settlement at Geneva to preserve his precarious position at home. The Nazis had just made considerable gains at provincial elections in Prussia, Bavaria, Württemberg, Anhalt and Hamburg, and he determined to outflank them by returning to Berlin with an agreement securing equality of rights.

The Brüning Plan

On 26 April 1932, Brüning put forward his proposals in conversation with MacDonald and the American Secretary of State, Henry Stimson, preparatory to a further meeting on 29 April which would include the French Prime Minister, André Tardieu. In private, at Stimson's villa at Bessinge, he insisted that he would be satisfied with a reduction in the period of service of the Reichswehr from twelve years to six and a reduction in the armed forces of France – though not to the German level – through the abolition or restriction of 'particularly aggressive' weapons. Equality of rights would be secured through the transfer of Germany's disarmament obligations from Part V of the Treaty of Versailles to the proposed disarmament convention, which might last for ten years. In return, Brüning was willing to consider an agreement along the lines of Tardieu's plan for an international force, with the ultimate objective of abolishing the weapons under its control.[27]

In the circumstances, the Brüning Plan appeared to be very moderate. It satisfied Germany's claim for equality – temporarily at least – whilst assuring France of military superiority in Europe for a period of ten years. MacDonald and Stimson, while not specifically accepting the plan, agreed that the discussions of 26 April had helped 'towards immediately clearing away some of the fundamental obstacles towards ultimate agreement'.[28] Success, however, depended on the negotiations with the French scheduled for 29 April; and in practice, these discussions did not take place. Tardieu was unable to journey to Geneva because of an attack of laryngitis (real or diplomatic, depending on the source). Two days later his government was defeated in the first round of the French general elections, and any chance of agreement simply melted away.

Opinions vary as to the possibility of an agreement based on the Brüning Plan. Many who were close to the personnel involved, for example the political commentator John Wheeler-Bennett[29] and the military adviser to the British delegation, A. C. Temperley, believe the Bessinge conversations were a lost opportunity. Both attack MacDonald and Stimson for their failure to press Tardieu into attending the 29 April meeting.[30] It is perhaps difficult to see how the hard-line Tardieu could have accepted a compromise in the middle of an election campaign, but the French Premier was well aware that Brüning's failure to reach agreement might result in his replacement by a more aggressive nationalist, and there had been earlier indications that Tardieu was ready to make concessions.[31] As far as Britain was concerned, however, there is no record at all of the Bessinge meeting in any official papers. It is possible that MacDonald preferred to let the chance die with Tardieu's defeat rather than face the question of French security demands, which, even pitched at a lower level than a month previously, might still be higher than those which the Cabinet had only recently rejected. If this is so, it casts grave doubt on MacDonald's professed commitment to disarmament,[32] although interestingly MacDonald notes in his diary in June 1934, when he met Brüning again in England, that Brüning 'regretted that [the] French prevented the negotiations Stimson and I began with him'.[33] Brüning himself, at least as far as MacDonald was concerned, appeared to place no blame on MacDonald for the failure of his Plan.

Further policy discussions

From the standpoint of British policy, the 'April episode' is extremely informative. Whilst ostensibly acting as mediator between France and Germany, Britain deliberately shunned this role. The explanation is simple. Any realistic proposal would raise the question of taking on a security commitment to equate French security with German equality, and Britain was unwilling to accept such a commitment. Another possible factor in MacDonald's apparent lack of commitment to the Brüning Plan is that he did not yet believe that Germany was as grave a threat as France obviously did. In a letter to Simon dated 31 May 1932, MacDonald commented:

> From this distance Brüning's resignation is very disquieting, although I cannot imagine any German Government which will not be reasonable at the present time. It is all very well to make high-falutin' speeches with a dummy pistol in your hand, but when you have not only got the real pistol but also the responsibility of leadership of a battle, nature makes your feet cold and grace keeps your head cool.[34]

This lack of urgency was to characterise Britain's attitude towards the Disarmament Conference for another 10 months, and arguably more, which was not to say that the subject of disarmament did not occupy a great deal of the thoughts of the policy-making élite. These thoughts, however, were piecemeal and uncoordinated, and discussion on the subject was to remain, for the moment, purely reactive. One of the most prominent discussions at Geneva concerned the abolition of bombing. On this question, Hankey declared that '[t]he form of armaments that most imposes the element of fear on the population of Europe is aviation . . . [c]ompared with bombing aeroplanes, the public interest in such matters as heavy guns, tanks, or whether a battleship should be of 35,000 or 25,000 tons, is almost negligible'.[35] Hankey pursued this argument further; abolition of military aviation would in turn lead to a significant reduction in the size of battleships and level of anti-aircraft artillery, thus effecting great savings. Londonderry, on the other hand, regretted that it had been 'most unfortunate' that he had had to 'appear to stand in the way of [Simon's] valiant efforts to make some contribution worthy of Great Britain at the Disarmament Conference' by opposing the abolition of bombing.[36] He believed, however, that the abolition of bombing was a 'Utopian picture'[37] which would not solve a problem which was essentially one of human nature:

> so long as we maintain national sovereignty, so long shall we find war the last resort, and as we, for one, are not proposing to sacrifice our sovereignty, we are compelled to maintain our position as a great power by those means which impress other nations equally determined to maintain their sovereignty.[38]

This attitude irritated MacDonald, who pointed out that the Service Departments must realise that nothing would be signed by Britain that would not be signed by everyone else. He was concerned that 'public opinion might become restive if [Britain] adopted a purely negative attitude to the one form of disarmament which might actually affect the man in the street in this country', whilst recognising that any agreement must be 'completely safeguarded at every turn'.[39] In the end, however, no firm conclusion was reached. Prevarication prevailed. When a telegram arrived from Simon, on 13 April, requesting definite authorisation to propose prohibition of bombing, Allen Leeper records that the Cabinet had come to *no* conclusion except to 'remit the matter to U.K. Delegation at Geneva!'[40]

The Cabinet still refused to give any lead to the Conference as a whole, or even to Britain's delegates to the Conference. At a Cabinet meeting on 2 May 1932 it was decided that the delegates themselves should be given discretion on both budgetary limitation, which the Cabinet's Budgetary Limitation Committee had agreed presented 'great practical difficulties in application', and on the restrictions on bombing from the air.[41] The latter point was one which aroused a great deal of controversy within the Cabinet. It was recognised that there was an urgent need for Britain to declare its policy on air disarmament, as nearly every other nation had done so, but whereas Baldwin declared that if nations were serious on the question of disarmament they ought to agree to scrap all military and naval aviation, to which 'no objection in principle was raised' by the other members of the Cabinet, Londonderry argued that it was useless to try to ban the act of bombing. Once a war began, bombs would be used 'whether they were fired from land or from air [and] if they once plunged into the theory of bombing, the Conference would sit for ever'.[42] Rather strangely, the question was referred to the Coast Defence Sub-Committee.

On 11 May, the Cabinet considered a report by the CID Sub-Committee on Air Disarmament which had concluded that the prohibition of bombing 'on the territory and shipping of another sovereign State possess[ed] considerable disadvantages from the point of view of imperial defence generally, and decisive disadvantages from that of the defence of London and other objectives to air attack in the United Kingdom'.[43] The report recommended that the British delegation at Geneva should not be authorised to make a proposal for the prohibition of bombing, but went on to suggest the restriction of aircraft, other than civilian aircraft, to a weight of 11,000 pounds unloaded weight.[44] The Cabinet expressed 'considerable disappointment' at this suggestion, since it did not involve any serious reduction in air armaments. Discussion then reverted to Baldwin's proposals in favour of the 'entire suppression of military and naval air forces', which, he pointed out, as Hankey had done, would have other repercussions on various forms of disarmament. The size of capital ships, for instance, depended to a great extent on the necessity for protecting them against submarines and air bombers, and if by abolishing military and naval aircraft it was possible to get an agreement from the other powers to abolish submarines, 'great results might be achieved'.[45] The Cabinet, however, whilst willing to allow Baldwin to pursue his proposals in a personal capacity, essentially decided to continue the policy of prevarication. The Delegates in Geneva were given discretion on the question of budgetary limitation, but instructed *not* to make proposals for the prohibition of bombing.

The Hoover Plan

By June 1932, with new governments in France and Germany, no decisions had been reached in Geneva. The Land, Sea and Air Commissions wrangled interminably over the definition of 'aggressive' weapons, all apparently choosing to ignore the fact that this definition had been clearly stated in the Treaty of Versailles – 'aggressive' weapons were those which were forbidden to Germany! On 13 May Baldwin discussed his ideas relating to the abolition of capital ships, and the consequent possibilities for reduction and/or abolition of other weapons, with Andrew Mellon, the American Ambassador in London. Although the proposals by no means represented official government policy, they did cause sufficient consternation in the United States to give impetus to the formulation of an American scheme. Presented to the conference on 22 June 1932 by Hugh Gibson, this was known as the Hoover Plan.

In the opening sentence President Hoover clearly set out the intention to 'adopt some broad and definite method of reducing the overwhelming burden of armament which now lies upon the toilers of the world'.[46] His Plan embodied five main principles. The first was the concept of non-aggression, based on the Briand-Kellogg Pact of 1928, whose signatories had agreed to use their arms solely for defence. The second was the concept of broad general cuts which would increase defensive power by 'decreases in the power of the attack'. The third was that the relative level of armaments among states should be preserved in making reductions. The fourth consideration was that reductions must be real and effective enough to effect economic relief, while finally it was to be accepted that land, air and naval forces were inter-connected and that reductions should take place simultaneously in all three areas. 'Based on these principles', declared Hoover, 'I propose that the arms of the world should be reduced by nearly one-third'.[47]

In order to reduce the offensive character of land armaments, the Plan proposed the abolition of all tanks and large mobile guns and the prohibition of chemical warfare. The strength of land armies would be reduced by one third, over and above a 'police' component, by which was meant the necessary force to maintain internal order. It was suggested that this 'police' component be fixed in the ratio to which Germany was limited under the Versailles Treaty; 100,000 troops per 65 million people. All bombing planes were to be abolished, and all air bombardment prohibited. The number and tonnage of battleships were to be reduced by one third, aircraft carriers, cruisers and destroyers by one quarter, and submarines by one third, with no nation retaining a submarine tonnage greater than 35,000 tons. Relative naval strengths were to be those agreed by the London Naval Treaty of

1930, with the French and Italian figures fixed in line with this Treaty. The proposals involved the United States scrapping over 300,000 tons of existing ships and forgoing the right to build over 50,000 tons.

> These proposals are simple and direct. They call upon all nations to contribute something. The contribution here proposed will be relative and mutual. I know of nothing that would give more hope for humanity today than the acceptance of such a programme with such minor changes as might be necessary.[48]

But the changes which Britain was to propose were far from minor. In the subsequent debate in Geneva, the smaller powers accepted the Plan enthusiastically. They were tired of the succession of closed conversations held by the major powers, and felt that at last here was something simple, effective and apparently fair to all concerned. Italy accepted the Plan in its entirety, and the USSR greeted it with guarded approval as it contained many aspects of their own policy of proportional disarmament. Germany felt it did not go far enough towards disarming the other nations, but in general welcomed the Plan as a basis for discussion. The Japanese were, in Temperley's words, 'very reserved'; they had agreed to the London Naval Treaty limits only because they were to end in 1936. France, not unnaturally, could not accept a scheme which 'committed the deadly sin of not mentioning "security" at all'.[49]

Admittedly Japan posed a problem which might have proved insoluble, but amongst the rest of the nations only France was hostile, and that hostility was based not so much on the Plan itself, which still offered her a clear superiority over Germany in armaments for the duration of the convention, but on the lack of security compensations for the diminution of her superiority. Thus if the Hoover Plan was to form the basis of a disarmament treaty, it would be necessary for Britain both to support the arms proposals in principle and to make concessions to the French on security.

After a brief debate, the Disarmament Conference postponed further discussion of the Hoover Plan until delegates had had time to consider its implications. Britain used this time to undermine the Plan. Simon returned from Geneva expressing a certain irritation at the way in which the Plan had been presented; first it was 'distinctly disturbing' to the private and detailed discussions which had been taking place, one topic at a time, in endeavouring to find some common ground between the major powers, and second he objected to the lack of notice given to the other powers.[50] He further emphasised that the Hoover Plan 'did not allow sufficiently for the varied responsibilities of different naval powers'.[51] The fundamental problem, however, seemed to be one of public relations. As the Foreign Secretary explained:

Britain must not lag behind America in zeal for disarmament. We have in fact now assembled a better set of proposals and a far more practical set.[52]

But unfortunately,

the general impression throughout the world was that Mr Hoover had at all events produced a scheme, and that Great Britain was in danger of missing a great opportunity. He [Simon] attached the greatest importance to the production, as soon as possible, by the United Kingdom Delegation at Geneva, of a British Disarmament plan, which would not be open to the obvious objections and drawbacks of the Hoover plan.[53]

From the British point of view, naval reductions had to be framed along very different lines from those advocated by Hoover. In due course, therefore, the First Lord put forward some figures in which the total tonnage reductions actually exceeded those in the Hoover Plan but which were tailored to meet British requirements. For example, he proposed that Britain should cease building 8-inch cruisers, a policy advocated consistently since the disastrous Coolidge Conference, and suggested a further reduction in the size of capital ships. In other respects, however, the British figures anticipated arms increases rather than arms reduction. The Admiralty's figures for cruiser numbers had risen since MacDonald had exerted pressure on them in 1930; they again spoke of 70 cruisers, 60 under age and 10 over age, compared with the 50 agreed at the London Naval Conference just two years previously.[54] Ignoring the fact that the Admiralty had again increased their demands, Simon informed the Cabinet that 'Japan would be much more likely to agree to proposals on the Admiralty basis, than to those on the Hoover basis'.[55]

But it was not only on the question of naval reductions that the Cabinet criticised the Hoover Plan. They were also unhappy about the 'police' and 'defence' components of the army in case they did not provide an adequate 'police' force to cover Imperial commitments. They stressed that the British army was as small as it could possibly be. At the same time, according to Hugh Gibson, 'both the British and American armies [had been] given minus values under a "defence component" heading'.[56] In other words, there would, in practice, be no question of reducing Britain's army under the Hoover scheme.

Britain was now faced with a problem; she had been presented with a plan which every other country except Japan was prepared to consider favourably, but which went against everything she hoped to achieve. It reduced the number of cruisers she needed to safeguard her trade routes, yet failed to abolish the submarines which were a direct threat to those routes. It would prohibit the tanks, bombers and bombing which were considered necessary to police the Empire. But outright rejection of the Hoover Plan was impossible if Britain wished to remain a credible supporter of disarmament. The Cabinet therefore decided that a declaration of British policy should be put forward, though without the 'somewhat theatrical procedure' with which the Hoover declaration had been published.[57] It was felt that Britain 'had been treated very badly by the Americans' in the matter of the Hoover declaration, and it was 'difficult to see what claim they had to any consideration'. Consequently – and perhaps not surprisingly in the circumstances – during the time the Cabinet took to draw up its response to the Hoover Plan, it sought, and gained, Japanese support against the American President's naval proposals.[58]

In the event, in an attempt to avoid incurring the criticism of those states who supported the Hoover Plan, Britain put forward her own proposals as though they were a constructive plan based on Hoover's ideas. Significantly, they were made public by Simon, not in Geneva, but in a 'Statement of Views' to the House of Commons on 7 July 1932. The Foreign Secretary welcomed the Hoover Plan as 'a contribution to an agreed programme' and added, as had been agreed by the Cabinet, that the proposals he was to put forward on behalf of the British Empire 'while they differ in some important respects as to method or measure [from those in the Hoover Plan] are inspired by the same purpose, and a comparison will show that already there is a substantial area of common ground'.[59] Simon openly asserted that his 'Statement of Views' was deliberately framed by the Cabinet 'to remove any ground for the suggestion that the document contained anything savouring of disparagement of President Hoover's proposals',[60] but in essence, the Statement was a negation of the Hoover Plan rather than proposals for implementing its principles. Rather than adopting the quantitative naval cuts envisaged by Hoover, Britain proposed a qualitative reduction, under which cuts would be made in size not quantity, which would enable her to maintain her Imperial obligations.[61] The abolition of submarines was called for, rather than the reduction proposed by the American President, while the proposal to abolish tanks was rejected on the grounds that light tanks of 20 tons and under could not be classed as offensive weapons. (The largest tank in the British army at the time was 16 tons.) Similarly, the proposals to abolish bombing planes and air bombardment were also rejected, on the grounds that it was desirable to retain both in order to police outlying regions. The real reason was that, as with tanks, retention of bombers was considered necessary for the maintenance of Britain's Imperial commitments.[62]

There was thus little 'area of common ground' between the British and American proposals. In fact, the abolition of chemical and biological warfare (already accepted in 1925) and the abolition of heavy mobile guns were all that the proposals had in common. Moreover, Britain's proposals failed to address the major problem faced by the Disarmament Conference – equating Germany's claim for equality of rights with the French claim for security. Although the Hoover Plan made no provision for increased security guarantees, it did at least have the merit of winning the basic approval of the majority of the other countries at the Conference, including Germany. It might also have been possible to graft security proposals on to it – perhaps along the lines which the French delegate Joseph Paul-Boncour was to suggest in his plan of November 1932.[63] In contrast, the British disarmament proposals were so weak and so tied to a static and blinkered perception of British security requirements that they were unacceptable to any of the other major powers.

There was much contemporary criticism of Britain's decision to undermine the Hoover Plan. Noel-Baker, Henderson's secretary at Geneva, subsequently condemned Simon for his inability to stand up to the 'hawks' in his own government, and for failing to push through the demands for qualitative disarmament which he had previously advocated strongly. He placed the blame for the failure of the Plan squarely on Simon's shoulders, and believed that Paul-Boncour's 'sincere' welcome for the Plan in all respects but that of security was not given the consideration it should have had.[64] Partly this is true. Simon possessed neither the personality, ability, nor 'political clout' to stand up to the likes of Hailsham, Eyres-Monsell and Londonderry. But the problem does not seem to lie so much with Simon's inability, or unwillingness, to persuade the 'hawks' of the Cabinet to accept the Hoover Plan as a firm basis for negotiation, rather the Plan conflicted totally with Britain's own requirements as perceived by the Service Departments and the majority of the Cabinet. Once again Britain had failed to address the problem of French security versus German equality. Instead, the government had chosen to tailor its plans to suit Britain's own demands, specifically those of the Empire, without any real thought for the wider and longer-term implications. It could be argued that the Hoover Plan itself did not address the central issue of French/German relations, in that the proposed reductions applied equally to everyone, but by reducing everyone's armaments Germany would have been less inferior and France – relatively – less secure. Germany would achieve complete equality as far as bombers and bombing were concerned, while her domestic 'police' component would have been equal to that of every other nation. At the same time, while the Hoover Plan can be considered far more objective than the British plan, it suffered from what Salvador de Madariaga – chief Spanish Delegate to the Disarmament Conference at the time – described as being too elementary. In other words, it overlooked the primacy of politics over armaments. 'What was then necessary', he declared, 'was not physically to disarm the French but morally to disarm the Germans'.[65]

In practice, in the wake of Britain's rejection of the Hoover Plan, the delegates at Geneva concocted a tripartite resolution which, to quote

Temperley, was 'a masterpiece of drafting'[66] in that it said nothing concrete, allowed everyone to interpret it as they chose, and avoided the main issues. Germany and the Soviet Union voted against its acceptance, eight other states abstained, and the German delegate announced that 'as there was no reference to equality of rights in the resolution, Germany would be compelled to leave the Conference until it had been conceded'.[67] Effectively, Simon's 'Statement of Views' of 7 July not only 'killed the Hoover plan',[68] but ended discussions at Geneva – at least temporarily. Indirectly it led to the German walk-out from the conference on 23 July 1932.

Equality of rights for Germany

The British Cabinet reacted to the German withdrawal with some consternation. At a Cabinet meeting on 30 September 1932 they agreed that the principle of equality of rights should be approved, and that 'British policy should be directed towards securing the return of Germany to the Disarmament Conference'.[69] The seriousness of the situation caused them to re-think their position; it might, for instance, be 'unavoidable' to agree to Germany possessing some of the weapons prohibited by the Treaty of Versailles, and supervision by the proposed Permanent Disarmament Commission should be accepted, though 'on the distinct understanding that [it] must not have the right to act as a roving Commission'.[70] By mid-October the Cabinet was prepared to agree 'to adopt and apply the principle of equality of rights . . . if all other governments will do the like' in respect of Germany's armaments, and, more significantly, to 'content ourselves with those kinds of arms to which Germany is now limited'.[71] By the end of October, the Cabinet decided that they were prepared to make a 'moral gesture of a declaration of German equality' in return for a German undertaking that they would 'do nothing that would be a new cause of unsettlement in Europe'.[72] This equality, however, would not mean that everyone had to come down to Germany's level of armaments, rather that Germany should be allowed other weapons 'subject to there being no increase in her fighting strength or in her expenditure for defence'.[73] Significantly, at the Cabinet meeting on 31 October it was suggested that it was desirable to get away from such phrases as 'the principle of no re-armament' and that it would be wiser to use other phrases 'such as the Prime Minister's suggestion of "measures to secure the peace of the world"'. It was now being tacitly accepted that if disarmament meant a *reduction* in the level of armaments, disarmament was unattainable. Perhaps more significantly, however, it was being accepted that a *reduction* in the level of armaments was not necessarily the way to secure the peace of the world.

The question of Germany's intentions preoccupied the Cabinet at this time; Neville Chamberlain pointed out that the fear of France and of those countries that had gained by the territorial settlement of Versailles was unlikely to be abolished by any reassurance that was obtained from Germany. 'Everyone was afraid of reducing their armaments', he declared, 'without some security that Germany was not re-arming while they disarmed'.[74] All proposals based on immediate disarmament within a very short time, therefore, appeared to those nations to be 'a gamble of their security on German good faith'. For that reason he suggested that a policy of 'one step at a time' which should never diminish the sense of security would be the best, if not the only, way to achieve any significant measure of disarmament. Chamberlain recognised that it was not only France who would refuse to disarm without first obtaining a sense of security. A further point which he somewhat optimistically put forward in support of his approach was that 'by giving notice of the various stages of the gradual abandonment of armaments, the armaments manufacturers would receive a warning and would refrain from embarking capital in special weapons and thus avoid their becoming opponents of the abolition of these weapons'.[75] Simon, however, dismissed Chamberlain's suggestion of a gradual approach to the problem, claiming it was doubtful whether Germany would undertake not to re-arm merely in response to such a scheme. It was generally accepted that there was no alternative but to bring Germany back to the Conference, and to search for a swift solution.[76]

In a speech to the House of Commons on 10 November 1932, Simon addressed the question of Germany's claim to the principle of equality, and suggested that the European States 'should join in a solemn affirmation that they [would] not in any circumstances attempt to resolve any present or future differences between themselves by resorting to force'. In return for Germany's acceptance of the same obligation, His Majesty's government, and the governments of other nations, were prepared to acknowledge the moral right of Germany to parity of treatment.[77] Following this statement, the five major powers, Britain, the United States, France, Italy and Germany had several meetings in Geneva, culminating in an announcement on 11 December which declared that:

> The Governments of the United Kingdom, France and Italy have declared that one of the principles that should guide the Conference on Disarmament should be the grant to Germany, and to the other Powers disarmed by treaty, of equality of rights in a system which would provide security for all nations.[78]

On the basis of this declaration Germany declared herself willing to return to the Conference. At the same time the European states declared that they would not in any circumstances attempt to resolve any present or future differences by resort to force, and the five major powers resolved to co-operate in the Conference 'to work out a convention which shall effect a substantial reduction and limitation of armaments with provision for future revision with a view to further reduction'. Reduction was thus apparently back on the agenda, and the Conference was able to re-open on 2 February 1933.

Return to the Conference

Prior to the re-opening, Simon informed the Cabinet that the impetus which the Conference had received from the return of Germany would quickly die unless 'a new direction and an effective lead' could be given.[79] But procedural wrangling at Geneva ensured that no immediate progress was made, and at the beginning of March the Foreign Secretary warned the Cabinet that the international situation in Europe was deteriorating very fast and that there was 'a real danger that the Disarmament Conference might break down within the next ten days or fortnight'.[80] He expected to receive proposals from Anthony Eden, the Parliamentary Under-Secretary recently appointed as day-to-day leader of the British delegation at Geneva 'with a view to averting a breakdown'. It had taken Eden and his colleagues, Cadogan and Temperley, a considerable amount of time and frustration to impress upon Simon the real gravity of the situation. Simon's own apparent aversion to the proceedings at Geneva was a constant source of irritation to his juniors; Cadogan at one stage commented that Simon was 'in his usual state of complete spiritual collapse which always visits him on his arrival in Geneva',[81] and that on another occasion Simon had 'only brought one dress shirt and means to bolt away'.[82] Whilst many of Cadogan's observations on Simon's state of mind are somewhat cynical, they do highlight the Foreign Secretary's attitude. Arriving by plane one day, Simon complained that he 'had suffered from his goggles, which tickled his nose. He had tried to persuade himself to disregard it, and has tried to make himself believe that it was "psychological – like the disarmament Conference" '.[83] In view of the lack of guidance which Cadogan and Eden received, the former was inclined to suppose that the government did not want disarmament. Indeed, the chief Foreign Office representative at Geneva wrote in his diary, 'Simon doesn't [want disarmament] because he, like I, suspects that the P.M. doesn't'.[84]

Simon was, as far as his juniors were concerned, a disaster both as Foreign Secretary and British delegate to the Conference.[85] The diaries and correspondence of both Eden and Cadogan are strewn with complaints about the Foreign Secretary's attitude towards his task. Even Cadogan's humour began to wear thin:

> I only write you this plaint to show you that we are drifting to disaster. To navigate difficult seas you must have both a chart and a Captain. I had hoped to get the latter, but you know the difficulties that have arisen there. I thought at least we were going to get a

chart, but wven [*sic*] that seems doubtdul [*sic*]. You know that through a good many months I have kept up a ridiculous optimism, but I am bound to tell you that I can't do that much longer.[86]

Cadogan was well aware of what was needed:

> This blessed Conference will fail unless it is taken properly in hand. We are the people who ought to do that. The French won't: if the Italians did, the French wouldn't follow: the Germans would wreck everything: the Americans talk very big when there is nothing doing, but old Norman Davis is the direct spiritual descendant of the Duke of Plaza Toro. We are the only people who could make it a success.[87]

Eden and Cadogan, therefore, in conjunction with Temperley, began to draw up a plan for what they saw as a last ditch attempt to save the Conference. At this point MacDonald was prepared to lend his support, being 'angry at no policy having been prepared', his remarks apparently meant for Simon.[88] But the junior delegates, as usual, received little or no help from their Service colleagues, except Temperley. The Air Ministry proved to be the worst culprits, Cadogan declaring the airmen to be 'disastrously witless'[89] both in their approach to the Air Committee and in their reluctance to draft the air section of the proposed British Draft Convention. Eden eventually informed them that if they were not prepared to supply the information required, he would have to do it for them, to which the air delegates strongly objected, and 'suggested something futile and without meaning'.[90]

A draft proposal was eventually presented to the Ministerial Committee for approval. In putting forward his proposals, Eden commented that any Convention 'must provide sufficient disarmament to meet to a reasonable extent the German claim for equality, and equally to meet the French claim that they could not tolerate any re-armament of Germany'.[91] As far as naval disarmament was concerned, Eden proposed only that 'others should do what we had already done', which had the advantage of including other countries in the London Naval Treaty. In order to meet the German claim for equality, it was proposed that there should be no construction of tanks for the period of the Convention, a truce being the only way to compromise between Britain's refusal to accept a policy of limitation of numbers of tanks, and Germany's claim to equality. The air section had proved difficult since the decisions of the Cabinet Committee were not known in Geneva. The progressive reductions proposed would not meet the German claim for parity, and further work would need to be done on this area. 'In only two cases', Eden stated, 'had any departure been made from Cabinet conclusions. The first was in the case of tanks, and the second concerned the consultative pact; acceptance of the latter must depend on the United States of America.'[92]

Whilst MacDonald agreed that something must be done to save the Conference, there was dissent in the Ministerial Committee over both the content of the Convention, and the advisability of presenting it at Geneva.[93] The first point of contention was that of security, provided for in Part I of the proposal; Hailsham and Cunliffe-Lister both made the point that Britain would be 'deluding France into the belief that we were giving her security which, in fact, we had no intention of providing', while Simon added that any document must certainly contain something for France, but it must be made equally plain that 'we could never accept any further commitments in Europe'.[94] Three days later the Committee moved on to consider Part II, which covered the armaments side of the proposals. The kernel was the inclusion of actual figures for effectives of the major European powers, including Britain. Hailsham was quick to point out that the inclusion of figures, as far as Britain was concerned, should be avoided as they would show 'a considerable increase on our existing establishment' and he was unsure what the effect on public opinion would be 'if and when this came to light'.[95] Hailsham also insisted that there was no scope for reduction of tanks, as 'tanks were definitely a substitute for men in [Britain's] army', and the abolition of bombing created problems for both the Colonial Office and Air Ministry.[96] The Committee finally concluded that the total abolition of military air forces was not practicable, and suggested that the United Kingdom delegates should instead propose the abolition of bombing aircraft and bombing from the air 'apart from the use of such machines as are necessary for police purposes'. Each country would be allowed to retain a 'sanctions' force of aircraft 'to combat the possible misuse in time of war . . . of civil aircraft as bombers', but there would be a quantitative reduction in all air forces.[97]

When the proposed Draft Convention was submitted to the Cabinet, three major problems remained. The first was the abolition of bombing from the air, since, in contradiction of the Ministerial Committee's conclusions of 8 March, the Cabinet had earlier expressed support for the 'entire abolition of military and naval aircraft'.[98] Needless to say, Londonderry had objected strongly to this suggestion.[99] The second problem remained that of tanks: as justification for the War Office's demand to retain an unlimited number of tanks not exceeding 16 tons, Hailsham presented the Cabinet with a statement which 'was of so secret a character that it had not been recorded in detail in the Minutes of the Ministerial Committee'.[100] This statement showed that the substitution of tanks for men in the British army 'was a policy which [Britain] had initiated, partly as a result of the enormous reductions in personnel which had been effected after the war'.[101] In other words, the War Office argued that, having evolved a strategy which had enabled them to meet the reductions demanded by the Treasury on grounds of economy since 1919, there was absolutely no further room for manoeuvre on grounds of international disarmament.

The final problem which Britain found unacceptable in any disarmament convention was the question of verification. This question acted as a touchstone for the seriousness with which delegations approached the disarmament problem, and Eden and Cadogan included a provision for on-site verification of specific allegations of non-compliance if agreed by a two-thirds majority within the proposed Permanent Disarmament Commission. Without proper verification provisions, there was no way of ensuring that a convention was being adhered to; no way of exposing a party which infringed the convention; no way, if necessary, of applying sanctions against a recalcitrant party. The French, throughout the Disarmament Conference, pressed for the tightest verification provisions as a means of ensuring their security against Germany. During the summer of 1933, there were indications from both Paris and Geneva that France would relax her demands for formal security guarantees if the verification procedures were adequate, by which they meant permanent, automatic and continuous supervision of the convention's provisions. Lord Tyrrell, ambassador at Paris, suggested in a despatch of 7 June 1933 that verification was perhaps the key to an agreement at Geneva, with the French reducing their demands on other points of contention if the question of supervision was resolved to their satisfaction.[102] In Geneva, Eden reached a similar conclusion, hence the proposal in his draft convention that Britain make concessions to the French point of view.[103] As might be expected, however, the Service Departments vehemently opposed Eden's ideas, even though they went only a short way towards meeting the demands of the French. The Admiralty declared that '[i]f countries act in good faith, supervision is unnecessary – if not, it is useless'.[104] Other objections included infringement of national sovereignty, the revelation of the lack of reserves and essential defence preparations, the undermining of the Official Secrets Act, and even (according to Eyres-Monsell) the 'fact' that verification would be 'rather degrading'.[105]

Despite these major reservations on the most critical issues, Cadogan and Eden's proposals were eventually accepted by the Cabinet, though Hailsham declared that 'No British Secretary of State for War could possibly accept this plan.' (This latter remark caused Cadogan some surprise, as apart from one provision about tanks, the military portion had actually been drafted by the War Office.[106]) However, the over-riding view in London was that the plan should not be produced at Geneva if it could possibly be avoided; only if the Conference looked certain to fail would MacDonald agree to submit it for consideration.

Cadogan, for one, felt that 'after 24 hours in Geneva' MacDonald would 'realise that it's the only thing to do'.[107] He therefore pressed the Prime Minister to go to Geneva, with the plan in his pocket. Eventually, both MacDonald and Simon agreed to go and, as Cadogan had predicted, they soon realised that the situation there was desperate. MacDonald still, however, hoped to avoid presenting Britain's proposals, especially as an invitation had just been received from Mussolini to go to Rome to discuss the possibility of a Four-Power Pact, which he found a much more attractive proposition. Eden, however, pointed out that Mussolini would want to talk about revision of treaties, at which 'the French would be scared stiff', and eventually MacDonald agreed to stay in Geneva and present the proposals.[108] Even then, a last-minute hitch occurred as an argument arose as to the advisability of including actual figures in the Draft Convention. Cadogan insisted that without them 'the more important parts of the convention [would] mean nothing'[109] There was also further disagreement over the air proposals; Cadogan commented '[h]e [MacDonald] doesn't want to disarm – particularly in the air (Londonderry air). Without tanks, or a decent air Chapter, the Convention will be heavily riddled.'[110]

The MacDonald Plan

On 16 March 1933, MacDonald finally presented the British Draft Convention, or MacDonald Plan as it became known, to the Disarmament Conference. Part I of the Convention dealt with security and included a consultative pact which laid down procedures to be followed in the event of a breach of the Kellogg Pact. These included an 'exchange of views for the purpose of preserving the peace and averting a conflict', or, in the event of a breach of the pact taking place, the use of 'good offices for the restoration of Peace' and failing this, measures 'to determine which party or parties to the dispute [were] to be held responsible'. Part II dealt with disarmament and included, for the first time, tables of actual figures of effectives, guns, tanks, ships and planes. Armies on the European continent were to be standardised on the basis of 8 months' service, and each country was allocated a number of 'average daily effectives' – figures being given separately for forces at home and overseas. Germany was to be allowed a total of 200,000, France 400,000 (200,000 metropolitan and 200,000 abroad), Italy 250,000 (200,000 metropolitan and 50,000 abroad), and the USSR 500,000. No figures were given for Britain. Mobile land guns were to be 105 mm maximum, though existing guns up to 155 mm could be retained, and the maximum size of coastal defence guns would be 406 mm. Tanks over 16 tons were to be prohibited, and all weapons over these limits destroyed within three years of the Convention coming into force. The Washington and London Naval Treaties were to remain in force until 1935 when a further naval conference was planned, although Italy would be allowed to lay down one more capital ship in response to one already begun by France. Germany would be freed from the naval limitations imposed by the Treaty of Versailles, but allowed to build only replacements until the expiry of the Washington and London Treaties.

Bombing from the air was prohibited, except for police purposes in outlying regions, and military planes would be restricted in number, each of the Great Powers being allowed 500, until the Permanent Disarmament Commission could prepare a scheme for the complete abolition of military aviation and the effective supervision of civil aviation. Failure to agree on such a scheme of supervision would mean that the Commission would determine the minimum number of machines required by each of the contracting parties. All warplanes, with the exception of troop-carriers and flying-boats, would be limited to an unladen weight of three tons, and at least 50 per cent of those aircraft which exceeded the qualitative and quantitative restrictions would be destroyed by 30 June 1936. Germany and the other states who were not allowed military aviation would not be permitted warplanes during the period of the Convention. Chemical, incendiary and biological warfare were prohibited, as already accepted by the Conference, and a Permanent Disarmament Commission would be set up to monitor the operation of the Convention. The Convention would replace the Peace Treaties and would last for five years, after which time it would be replaced by a new one.[111]

The MacDonald Plan went a long way towards meeting the German demands for equality of rights. Continental armies were to be standardised, which would give Germany the same number of domestic effectives as France, and she would eventually be able to build up her material to that of France, except in the air. But having apparently addressed one side of the problem, it ignored the other – the French demand for security. There were no effective provisions for compliance; the consultative pact was much weaker than that suggested by Paul-Boncour in November 1932, and the verification organ, the Permanent Disarmament Commission, had provision only to investigate, report and recommend, rather than enforce any action.

Nevertheless, the MacDonald Plan was generally well received as a basis for further discussion, and, according to some contemporary observers, could have been successful. Temperley felt that '[t]he presentation of the British Draft Convention was . . . the psychological moment for saving the Conference'.[112] With forceful presentation, and emphasis on the vital importance of reaching agreement before the political climate deteriorated further, he thought that the mood of the conference was such that, had MacDonald emphasised that this was the last chance of saving the Conference, the delegates would have accepted the plan with only minor alterations. Madariaga thought the Plan was 'remarkable in that it was concrete, precise and built on the balanced inclusion of every one of the *sine qua non* requirements of each of the important powers. It was as good a racehorse as ever had run the Disarmament stakes . . . but it had started twelve months too late.'[113]

However, a number of factors, domestic and international, were against its chances of success. One of these factors was the attitude of MacDonald and the Cabinet towards the Plan. Although finally recognising that a grand gesture was needed to prevent the collapse of the Conference, and that this must necessarily come from Britain, in MacDonald's eyes it was never more than a gesture. Five days before presenting the plan, MacDonald had received a visit from the German delegate, Nadolny, who made a 'rather strong and intransigeant statement' of the German case, following which, according to Cadogan, the Prime Minister cheered up and said 'Well, *that* shows that this Conference can't succeed'.[114] This underlines the fact that the real reason for presenting the Plan, in the eyes of government ministers at any rate, was to avoid Britain being blamed for the failure of the conference. As MacDonald himself admitted in a letter to the King, three days before presenting the plan at Geneva:

> The British plan was a stop-gap, designed not to achieve disarmament, but to prop up a conference which everyone knew to be disintegrating.[115]

The government's lack of belief in disarmament in general, and the British Draft Convention in particular, was further underlined on the day following its presentation, 17 March. Instead of staying in Geneva to push forward the convention, MacDonald and Simon departed for Rome for talks with Mussolini on his proposal for a Four-Power Pact. Wheeler-Bennett declared that:

> [I]n the early days of the London Foundling Hospital . . . unwanted children were placed in a basket hung outside the gates, the depositor rang the bell and left hastily. Mr Ramsay MacDonald treated the new British Disarmament plan in much the same way.[116]

Negotiating for position – spring and summer 1933

Following MacDonald's and Simon's departure from Geneva, Eden and Cadogan were left to push for the acceptance of the British Draft Convention. Discussion on Part I, the consultative agreement, was soon adjourned 'for the reason that the Americans were not ready to consider it',[117] and little progress was made initially on Part II because the Germans rejected the proposals for the standardisation of continental armies, to which the French attached the utmost importance. In spite of these problems, however, the general feeling at the Conference was that the MacDonald Plan would at least form the basis of discussions, and amendments were invited to be submitted by 20 April, following the Easter recess. In the meantime, however, conditions in Germany deteriorated rapidly. The excesses of the new Nazi régime caused consternation in many states who had previously felt that the terms of the Treaty of Versailles were harsh. Even in England there was a rise in anti-German sentiment.

The Cabinet felt that Germany was now 'clearly manœuvring for position' and sent the following instructions to Eden in an attempt to ensure that Britain maintained control of the Geneva agenda:

> It is essential that we should keep the discussions on the broad issues on which public opinion is united against Germany and avoid being driven into details about guns, tanks, aeroplanes, etc. on which opinion would be muddled and divided. You should therefore try to concentrate on effectives, and persuade French to agree to this. Public opinion here is united in opposition to German attitude. If you cannot avoid question of material being raised, you should refuse to discuss details until principles are settled. You should therefore refuse to formulate or discuss any detailed figures, until Germany has accepted the principle that equality must be reached by stages, and until principles are settled accordingly. German's attitude (e.g. Neurath's speech) makes this vital.[118]

The problem was that, now the other Powers were prepared to use the MacDonald Plan as the basis of discussion, it was sensible to move on to the discussion of particular questions. But this placed the British Cabinet in a difficult position since they were not prepared to make the compromises on bombing, tanks or verification which might have brought about general agreement, except perhaps for the Japanese. Paradoxically, the nearer the Disarmament Conference came to success on the most important technical questions, the greater became the gap between the necessities of an international convention and the politico-military assumptions of the British government.[119]

Certainly, by the summer of 1933, the government was increasingly isolated at Geneva on the crucial issues of tanks, air disarmament and verification. The majority of the powers, with the exception of Japan and France, would be happy to see tanks abolished altogether, and even the French attitude towards tanks was neither immovable nor illogical; if tanks were to be retained, the French would prefer to see them as part of a League contingent, and therefore a threat only to an aggressor. The problem was that, once having declared tanks to be a substitute for men in the British army, the War Office were immovable. But if tanks under 16-tons were to be retained, Germany would have to be allowed them, in accordance with the principle of equality. On the question of air disarmament, Britain again found herself in isolation – with the exception of Japan. On the question of the retention of bombing, Britain's position was simply one of self-interest. She preferred to retain the right to bomb 'outlying regions' rather than to secure an agreement in Europe. Britain was also increasingly isolated over her position on verification. The other powers who had initially opposed on-the-spot investigation becoming continuous and automatic – including the Americans, Italians and Germans – gradually realised that such verification was essential if any disarmament agreement was to be reached. The British Service Departments, however, remained adamant that continuous and automatic verification be opposed.

During the summer recess of the Disarmament Conference, the Cabinet's fears concerning Britain's isolation at Geneva on technical questions were compounded by renewed fears of French demands for security compensations in return for reducing their military superiority over Germany, in line with the requirements of the MacDonald Plan. In particular, they were anxious that French demands for more stringent measures of verification at Geneva would simply be the precursor for further British concessions. The French now believed that the evidence of German re-armament 'was so strong that when it came to light no-one could ask France to do very much in the way of disarmament'.[120] But in the opinion of the Cabinet, if concessions were made to France on one point, she would 'merely produce a further point as soon as she had extracted a concession from us'. France's policy of 'continual nibbling' made Britain's position extremely difficult.[121]

In the light of further Nazi excesses, the Ministerial Committee advised the Cabinet to 'consider very seriously' whether it would be justified in attempting to make France reduce her armaments down to the level suggested in the British Draft Convention. The Committee maintained that, from a legal point of view, if no convention emerged from Geneva, Germany would continue to be bound by the Treaty of Versailles.[122] There were only two alternatives: if the Convention could be achieved it might be the means of ensuring stability for a period of years by holding Germany back and reducing the armaments of France and other countries. Alternatively, if no convention was achieved, Germany would presumably go straight ahead and re-arm. Interestingly, however, without specifying it as such, the Committee defined a third alternative: Germany might go ahead and re-arm even if she did sign a convention.

> It was felt to be extremely difficult under these conditions to insist that France would be safer after having reduced her forces and got a Convention than she would be if the situation remained as it was now.[123]

Basically, the government could see no way forward. The kind of re-orientation of policy which might still have produced an agreement – making concessions on technical issues and/or giving France additional guarantees of security – was not even considered at this time. The dilemma of British disarmament policy was heightened.

The French amendments to the MacDonald Plan

Ultimately the Cabinet would be rescued from the corner into which they had pinned themselves by the French, who, fully aware that the MacDonald

Plan gave them no real security compensations in return for a diminution of their power in relation to Germany, produced their own disarmament plan, disguised as amendments to the MacDonald Plan. In effect, the five-year convention envisaged by the MacDonald Plan was converted into an eight-year convention divided into two equal parts. The first stage of the convention would constitute a four-year 'trial period' during which stringent verification procedures would be tested for effectiveness. It was only after these procedures had been declared acceptable that France would start reducing her armaments in order to facilitate equality of rights for Germany.[124] During the 'trial period' France would stop all construction of *matériel* over 155 mm calibre, limit her tanks to a global tonnage of 3,000 (25 per cent of the present figure), and reduce her naval and military aircraft by 50 per cent. These measures were conditional on agreement being reached on budgetary control, the abolition or strict supervision of the private manufacture and trade in arms, and the application of sanctions should the convention be violated.[125] Supervision would be continuous and automatic, and if it proved satisfactory, France would then agree to either destroy her prohibited *matériel* or hand it over to the League, during the second four-year period.

Despite being agreed in principle as early as May, the French released details of their amendments to the MacDonald Plan only in September following a visit by Eden to Paris. The junior minister concluded that 'the French Government did want a Disarmament Convention', and in the subsequent Cabinet discussions Simon commented that 'for the first time . . . the French [had] said what they were prepared to do and it was something quite substantial'.[126] He added that there appeared to be only two alternatives: no convention at all, with the resulting German re-armament, or to enter into this convention 'in two parts' which the Germans 'might be brought to accept' although part of their price would be permission to have specimens of weapons forbidden to them under the Treaty of Versailles. He recognised that this would be in breach of the expectations of many advocates of disarmament, but only by accepting this point, as well as the Franco-Italian plan of inspection and control, might it be possible to get a Convention. In reality, however, the French would never allow the Germans to have 'samples' which would certainly be used as a blueprint for mass-produced weapons – unless, of course, they received concrete guarantees of security which Britain was not prepared to give. Moreover, if Germany violated a convention the French would wish to know what action Britain would take and Britain 'of course did not intend to take any action'.[127] In any eventuality France could not accept the original MacDonald Plan; she had to have the increased security set forth in her amendments. The British government might well claim that their Draft Convention still held the floor at Geneva, but it was obvious that France, in view of the continuing increase in German re-armament, would *never* accept it as it stood.

During separate conversations with the French during September 1933, the Americans and Italians accepted the French amendments. The idea was to present a united front to Germany: either accept the agreed plan or assume responsibility for breaking up the Disarmament Conference. Would the British government follow suit? Ministers had a choice. On the one hand, they could continue with the MacDonald Plan and allow equality of rights for Germany in five years; make concessions on the technical issues where Britain was isolated; face demands by the French for security compensations; and ultimately, having turned down the French security demands, allow France to incur the blame for the failure of the conference. Alternatively, ministers could accept the French amendments in the knowledge that the Germans would reject them, except on terms that the French would find impossible to accept. In this case, the Germans would incur responsibility for the breakdown of the conference. Eden reported from Geneva that, given American support for the idea of a united front, 'he felt confident that a demand that some such offer should be made would grow in the next day or two' and that it was most likely to be effective if it could be made jointly by the four Powers.[128] Even without the anticipated American pressure, the British decision was never in doubt. The French amendments not only freed the Cabinet from its dilemma of being isolated at Geneva on the most important technical questions, but from having to make additional concessions on the security issue. Britain could go along with France, Italy and the United States in a united front on the principle of the four-year 'trial period' whilst maintaining reservations on the exact nature of the verification procedure and individual technical issues.

The Cabinet made a virtue of necessity. On 3 October, Simon produced a 'compromise' which was not, he stressed, in any way preferred to the original Draft Convention, but rather 'an honest effort by the party to the Conference which is in the best position to do it, to mark out the necessary middle course' if there was to be any chance of obtaining a Convention.[129] In producing this compromise, Simon hoped that the majority of states at Geneva would recognise that Britain was once again 'making a final effort to save the Conference from shipwreck' – in other words, again taking the initiative! However, within this suggested compromise it was stated clearly that

[t]he Convention, though signed as one document and binding as one document, should provide for two periods of four years each.[130]

And, within the first of these two periods, continental armies would be transformed – as provided for in the original Draft Convention. Also during the first period, the signatories would undertake not to *increase* the present levels of their armaments, and Germany 'would be limited to the armaments she is now entitled to possess'. Only during the second period would there be a gradual reduction of armaments, as set out in the Draft Convention. The details of such disarmament as set out in the document were largely irrelevant: the most relevant change was that, in accepting *two* periods of four years each, Simon had effectively accepted the French amendments. In fairness, as noted earlier, the British government was under pressure from the Americans to adopt just such a course,[131] but the actual importance attached by the Cabinet to this gesture appears to be negligible. On 9 October, after a long discussion on the appropriate action to be taken, the Cabinet, extraordinarily weakly, 'registered no decision' other than that Simon, in consultation with MacDonald, should 'use his judgement' as to the action to be taken.[132]

This 'tacit approval' of Simon's 'compromise' was the closest the Cabinet came to a formal acceptance of the French amendments. But in practice the decision had been made to accept them. The British Cabinet decision had enormous implications. On 14 October, Simon put forward at Geneva, on behalf of Britain, France, Italy and the United States, a revised scheme, based on the French amendments, which would effectively have put the Germans on probation, with no control over whether or not they had fulfilled their requirements at the end of four years.[133] As a result, faced with a united front on a system which moved equality of rights further from their grasp, the German delegation voiced its disapproval by walking out not only of the Disarmament Conference but the League of Nations. They had good reason to do so. In July 1932, Hitler's conservative predecessors had withdrawn from the Conference because little or no progress had been made in some five months of discussion. In October 1933, Hitler could justifiably complain that the Western Powers, Britain in particular, had gone back on their word regarding equality of rights.[134]

The final stages

The German withdrawal from the Disarmament Conference was not the end of negotiations. Attempts at agreement were to continue through alternative channels. On 24 October Hitler put forward specific proposals to the British and French Ambassadors at Berlin, and to the Italian government;[135] these proposals were re-submitted in revised form on 11 December.[136] The blame for failure of the Disarmament Conference was laid firmly at Britain's door for 'having led other Powers to substitute a second draft of the Disarmament Convention for the first draft which Germany had herself accepted'.[137] As a consequence, Hitler declared that Germany would refuse to take part in any disarmament conference pending the recognition of her *actual* equality of rights, stating that Germany alone had executed the disarmament clauses of the Treaty of Versailles.[138] The German government no longer believed that the highly armed States really intended to disarm.

Hitler proposed a new way forward. In return for an agreement by the highly armed States not to increase their present armaments, Germany would content herself with a short-service army of 300,000 men with no offensive weapons – such as tanks over 6 tons, heavy artillery over 150 mm, and bombers. Germany would also give a 'general pledge to conduct war humanely and abandon use of certain weapons against civilians' and offer ten-year non-aggression pacts with all states surrounding Germany. She asked for equal, periodic and automatic supervision for all, and for the retention of the SA and SS, whose non-military character would be verified by the aforementioned supervision. Hitler finally declared that 'if other countries decide on full disarmament, Germany will do the same'. This was the first time since the Brüning Plan that Germany had put forward any real proposals of her own. She had hitherto been presented with plans by the other Powers, which had aimed to keep her armaments at a low level, whilst suiting the needs of those putting forward the plans.

Britain was again confronted with the old dilemma. Germany apparently had not given up hope of reaching a disarmament agreement, but had merely decided to copy the Allies in putting forward a plan which, temporarily at least, matched her own requirements. To accept Hitler's proposals would, admittedly, mean accepting German re-armament, but Britain had already implicitly accepted that this was the most likely outcome, without explicitly adapting her own policy to cover this eventuality. Acceptance of Germany's plan had the advantage of removing her alleged grievances against the disarmament provisions of Versailles and against the dictatorial attitude of the powers, whilst ensuring that at least *some* basis could be found to control the level of international armaments. It would almost certainly, however, involve some level of British commitment to France, who, although allowed to retain her present level of armaments, would be expected to agree to an *increase* in German armaments. To reject the German proposals out of hand would mean that Britain would incur the blame for failure of negotiations, which in turn would lead to global rearmament. Britain's own public opinion, in spite of growing Nazi excesses and reduced sympathy for the German position, was still firmly behind a disarmament agreement.[139] To further complicate matters, the French government had taken up a policy of 'No re-armament by Germany' and should Germany be allowed to re-arm by agreement, was likely to demand considerable security guarantees from Britain.[140]

On 7 December a telegram was despatched to Britain's Ambassador at Berlin, Sir Eric Phipps, containing 'preliminary observations' on the new German scheme, an attempt having first been made to allay French fears that Britain was actually 'contemplating an agreement which would involve some German re-armament'.[141] The Cabinet recorded their agreement with Hitler's view that 'the achievement of a disarmament agreement would be immensely facilitated if it were accompanied by political assurances calculated to improve and consolidate good relations between Germany and her neighbours',[142] but doubts were expressed as to the means of achieving these good relations. As far as the technical aspects of Hitler's proposals were concerned, Phipps was instructed to inform the Chancellor that the proposed increase in the German army to 300,000 men would certainly be considered excessive, while the suggestions in respect of guns and aircraft appeared 'very formidable'. The Cabinet also requested assurances that the SA and the SS would be absorbed into the new army, and that the Reichswehr would disappear. The telegram finished by pointing out that 'His Majesty's Government earnestly desire to use the present opportunity to hammer out without delay in co-operation with Germany and other States, a practical basis for agreement for limitation of world armaments . . . .'[143]

To Corbin, the French Ambassador at London, Simon was keen to stress that whilst regarding Hitler's proposals as a real offer, and giving them careful consideration, their idea was 'to keep Chancellor Hitler in play while avoiding any language which could be misconstrued as either accepting his proposals or seeking to develop any special Anglo-German bargain'.[144] Simon also pointed out that Britain was firmly convinced that 'the achievement of a disarmament agreement would be immensely facilitated if it were accompanied by political assurances calculated to improve and consolidate good relations between Germany and her neighbours', and that he had stressed this point in his reply to the German Chancellor. Corbin's guarded reaction was that it seemed to him that Britain's reply to Hitler 'might be taken as surrendering the position that rearmament was to be resisted at all costs' and 'admitting as the basis of negotiation proposals for the positive increase of armaments'. Simon's reply summed up, in a few words, the way in which the British Cabinet viewed the current situation. There were, he said, three possibilities:

1   That the heavily-armed States would come down to the level and list permitted to Germany by the Treaty of Versailles;
2   that a level should be fixed by agreement intermediate between this level and the present level of the highly armed Powers; and
3   that there should be no agreement at all, with the result that an unlimited race of armaments would follow.[145]

There was, he believed, 'no fourth possibility', such as Germany being permitted to change her armaments while the other powers retained theirs. There was equally no possibility that a joint Anglo-French declaration that Germany should not re-arm would have the 'necessary compulsory effect'.

In practice, Hitler's proposals of 24 October had re-opened the differences between Britain and France that had been papered over by Britain's acceptance of the French amendments to the MacDonald Plan. He had called Britain's and France's bluff. No effective action had been taken in support of the united proposals put forward by Simon on 14 October. The question now, as far as Hitler was concerned, was to widen the Anglo-French breach, taking advantage of the fact that the British government still dreamed of the conclusion of a disarmament convention along lines which favoured Britain – if only for fear of the possible alternative – while the French, debilitated by the revelations surrounding the Stavisky scandal in domestic politics, found it difficult even to define a policy.

On 29 January 1934, the British government came up with a new scheme based on a combination of French disarmament and German re-armament. Under the proposed scheme, effectives would be limited according to the original MacDonald Plan, but the period of service in the short-term continental armies would be open to negotiation, as would the number of effectives should the proposed 200,000 prove inadequate. There would be considerable reduction in French overseas forces, and para-military training was prohibited; however, provided that the SA and SS were proved to be of non-military character, they could be retained. Germany would be allowed anti-aircraft guns, 155 mm mobile guns and tanks of six tons, as Hitler had demanded, and the other powers would destroy all tanks over 16 tons within five years and *matériel* over 155 mm within seven years. Pending the formulation of a successful scheme for the complete abolition of military and naval aviation, and supervision of civil aviation, military aircraft would be limited to their present level. In the event of failure to formulate an effective scheme of supervision, all countries would be permitted to retain military aviation, with Germany achieving parity within ten years. Construction or acquisition of the types of weapons to be destroyed during the convention would be prohibited, and the convention would be enforced by a system of permanent and automatic supervision. On the security side there was provision for consultation in the event of violation of the convention, and Hitler's offer of ten-year non-aggression pacts with Germany's neighbours was accepted as a means of strengthening security, along with her return to the League.[146]

Once again, however, Britain had produced a scheme which was unlikely to bridge the Franco-German divide. Whilst it admittedly meant that France would retain superiority in *matériel,* the land proposals were more favourable to Germany than Hitler's own had been, and the security offered to France was unlikely to be considered adequate. Moreover, as Germany had already begun re-arming in the air, she was unlikely to accept Britain's air proposals. The question now was whether the French would accept the new British plan. The answer, in an official note dated 19 March 1934, was an emphatic 'no'. France refused to disarm whilst Germany was re-arming without much stronger guarantees of security. In her search for security France again desired the full implementation of the League Covenant and Germany's return to the League, rather than a mere restatement of the Locarno guarantees and the consultative scheme proposed by Britain. In practical terms, the French would accept no agreements involving German rearmament without compensatory security guarantees – and these guarantees would now be pitched at a higher level than in the summer of 1933.

As far as Britain was concerned, the situation was serious. Indeed, even before the French *démarche* of 19 March, Simon had suggested to the Cabinet that, rather than face a complete breakdown of the conference, with the possibility of a return to pre-war conditions of competitive re-armament, it might be necessary to examine whether, 'by further concession and additional undertakings' on security there would be any means of bringing about agreement.[147] He did not conceal his own view that 'this could only be done by meeting, *more fully than we had yet done*, French demands for security'.[148]

On the same day as the French *démarche*, 19 March, the Cabinet found itself being asked to approve the idea that 'we take Germany as the ultimate potential enemy against whom our "long-range" Defence policy must be directed'.[149] The reasons for putting Germany in the position of the 'ultimate potential enemy' were discussed for some time, before Baldwin asked how the Cabinet could possibly discuss the question without also discussing the Disarmament Conference. In that connection, he pointed out, the question 'to which attention was constantly being directed' was whether we were prepared to undertake a guarantee to France. 'It might even be a choice between a guarantee and losing the friendship of France . . . .' The Cabinet appeared reluctant to be dragged into a discussion of a possible guarantee, preferring to return to the reasoning for adopting Germany as 'ultimate potential enemy', but eventually they had to confront the question. Ministers were in a renewed dilemma. They opposed taking on any further commitments, but recognised that failure to do so could cost very much more in terms of financing a heavy re-armament programme, especially in the air. Once again they prevaricated, holding over a final decision.

At a Cabinet meeting held on 22 March to consider the questions of security and sanctions, Simon summarised the results of the recent negotiations on disarmament to the following effect:

> Germany is unwilling to remain disarmed below a certain minimum, and is not likely to be moved therefrom: France cannot agree to the German minimum unless she receives some satisfaction on security: consequently if we still contemplate an agreement we must consider whether we can find some way to meet the difficulty by means of a guarantee.[150]

Faced with this stark choice, there was no unity in the Cabinet. Simon pointed out that he referred to a European guarantee rather than one involving the Far East or South America, for example, whereby some practical guarantee would be given that if a breach of the Disarmament Convention was made by any of the principal European states, 'the others should contemplate the exercise of certain restraints'. This would obviate the need for Dominion assent, which Thomas assured his colleagues would not be forthcoming.[151]

Eventually, the Cabinet put into words the implications of a guarantee to France. France would not be satisfied with mere economic sanctions; in any event these would be impractical without the co-operation of the United States, and this co-operation was a 'very dubious assumption'. France, it was pointed out, would only be satisfied if Britain was prepared to offer a guarantee of armed intervention in a war, and '[g]iven the conditions in France today, to ally ourselves to France was a terrible responsibility'. Britain's main concerns in Europe were first, the defence of London against air attack 'which many people would probably prefer to provide by our own forces', and, second, Belgium. France, however, would no doubt maintain that her own air force was adequate to meet air defence requirements, and would prefer Britain to have a larger army. 'In any event some expenditure would have to be incurred in this country on armaments, but in this latter form the expenditure was less favourable to us than any other.'[152] Here was the problem: if Britain *must* re-arm she obviously wanted to do it in areas which she felt to be important to her own security, and not specifically to that of France. In view of this, it was decided that Hitler's proposals be given further consideration, as this appeared to be the only method to obtain a limitation of German armament. It might well be argued that by now a limitation of German armament was a forlorn hope, but, and here was the *real* point, '[a]greement with France . . . was only possible on conditions of a guarantee which the nation would not accept'.[153] Having discussed the question of a guarantee on a number of occasions, and refused to discuss it on even more occasions, whilst recognising that it was possibly the *only* answer to the problem, the Cabinet dismissed it on the grounds that the 'nation' would not accept it![154]

Even having made this decision, the Cabinet's course of action was not clear to them. If they accepted Hitler's proposals for a measure of German re-armament, it would have to be done *immediately*, as in a few months Hitler would be unlikely to accept concessions merely in order to legalise a measure of re-armament which had already taken place. But if that course of action was taken, the French would 'become very embittered' and accuse Britain of perfidy. In such circumstances, France would become a 'formidable and immediate risk'. She would also take measures which would provoke counter-measures in Germany and compel Britain to re-arm. It was thus essential to maintain good relations with France.[155]

Cabinet discussions went round and round in circles; there was certainly no lack of awareness of the problems, but a solution to these problems was quite another matter.

It was suggested that to adopt a policy designed specifically to keep us out of all war in Europe or the Far East was to adopt too narrow a view. If we could secure the pacification of Europe and the removal of all risk of aggression, it would be the greatest possible boon to this country. . . . Our policy . . . ought to be directed towards the restoration of international peace and confidence. We could not do this by backing out of Europe and leaving others to take the consequences. We should recognise that France was justified in refusing to disarm without satisfactory assurances of security. At any rate, we should recognise that France would not disarm without security.[156]

In the end, the Cabinet was unable to reach a decision, and decided to refer the problem to the Ministerial Committee on Disarmament.

The Ministerial Committee, unsurprisingly, had as much difficulty as the Cabinet in attempting to formulate a policy. Simon hoped Britain would not, at this stage, formulate anything definite to the French government because they 'would be most likely to sniff at it and then ask for more'.[157] Meanwhile, figures now published showed very large increases in the level of German armaments. Once again, ministers focused on France's reluctance to say what she actually wanted. Cunliffe-Lister remarked that the situation was deteriorating so badly that no one in Britain would say she was justified in taking on any kind of commitment.[158] Hailsham agreed that it was quite clear that Germany intended to re-arm 'and that nothing would stop her except a preventive war which France was not prepared to undertake'. There was, therefore 'no point in bothering about security'. Sir Bolton Eyres-Monsell then raised the subject of an isolationist policy for Britain; was the theory that Britain must be drawn into any continental war now somewhat out of date? Eventually, it was agreed that the British Ambassador at Paris, Lord Tyrrell, should ask Louis Barthou, the Foreign Minister in the new, hard-line, French National government, whether France would accept a convention based on the British proposals of 29 January if Britain gave France guarantees regarding the execution of the convention.[159] On 17 April the government received the French reply, which avoided the specific question posed, but declared that France would not be justified in proceeding with a conference which effectively legalised German rearmament. The French government felt that it had waited long enough, and on the same day as the French Note was despatched, Barthou declared that France would, from now on, look after her own security. The Cabinet and Ministerial Committee had taken far too long to formulate an acceptable policy, and France had finally accepted that she was on her own. Since the Germans walked out of the Disarmament Conference in October 1933, Britain and France had circled warily round each other, each afraid to make concessions without some commitment from the other, and time had now run out.

To all intents and purposes, the Disarmament Conference was over, and British delegates at the forthcoming meeting of the General Commission on

29 May were instructed to 'recall our efforts in the cause of disarmament, emphasising the importance of the British Draft Convention', and if the French chose to reject the Convention and concentrate instead on the question of security, the British delegates should agree to such discussions, provided that the French delegation took the lead.[160] Should France require some re-affirmation of British commitments under Locarno, this should be given, but it should be pointed out that Britain was 'unable to enter into any further commitments of that character'. This was, undeniably, the very thing against which Vansittart had warned in December 1931 – Britain paying lip-service to the question of a security pact rather than treating it seriously. In effect, British policy had once again reverted to merely reacting to the suggestions of others. The final touch was provided by Barthou, speaking to the General Commission on 30 May. In dispelling any hopes that a convention might be obtained he not only condemned Germany but, in a fitting touch of irony regarding British policy, referred to Simon as 'mon cher collègue et presque ami'.[161] On 11 June the Disarmament Conference adjourned *sine die*.

Conclusion

Britain's policy towards the Disarmament Conference can be summed up in one word – reactive. Ministers reacted not only to events at Geneva, to each set of proposals as they occurred, but also to events on the international scene. In some respects the government cannot be criticised for this approach; international events, especially the increasing assertiveness and impatience of Germany, could not be left out of the equation. It might be debatable whether a more positive and convincing stance at the beginning of the Conference could have affected the outcome, but the fact remains that Britain did not even try. She based her policy on the premise that Britain had already reduced her armaments unilaterally to the lowest point consistent with national safety – failing to recognise that the other powers had done exactly the same and that the need was for concessions by *all* in the general interest. Britain's moralisation of her own position and unwillingness to mediate between France and Germany represented a constant obstacle to agreement at Geneva.

Disarmament *per se*, however, was not at the top of Britain's agenda, whether within or outside the Geneva Conference. The Cabinet's real priority was to avoid a further commitment to France: the question of security predominated all early discussions. The link between French security and French disarmament was clear – as Vansittart pointed out before the Conference began – yet Britain continued to insist that the guarantees given under the Locarno Treaties were sufficient, even though privately she was determined that, should Germany break her agreement under Locarno, she would do nothing.[162] Fear of French demands was undoubtedly the major reason for MacDonald not pressing the apparent advantage offered by the Brüning Plan. Equally, one of Britain's prime reasons for rejecting the Hoover Plan – apart from the fact that it did not meet Imperial defence requirements as conceived by the Service Departments – was that it would have necessitated additional security guarantees to the French if it was to have had any chance of being accepted. The problem was that any hope of agreement at Geneva depended on Britain giving an enhanced commitment to France – a commitment which the government was consistently unwilling to give.

Even Britain's one positive proposal – the MacDonald Plan – was essentially reactive, in this case to the urgings of Britain's (junior) representatives in Geneva. Primarily, it was put forward not in any spirit of hope for disarmament, but in an effort to avoid blame for failure of the Conference. The Plan may have given a sense of direction to the Conference for a time, but it was still so intertwined with Britain's own perceived security requirements that it would have required considerable modification for international acceptance. As a result, during the summer of 1933, Britain became isolated on the major technical provisions of her own Convention. To have brought about an agreement, she would have had to accept conditions which she found totally unacceptable. This included a reduction in – or even the abolition of – tanks, which would have led to an *increase* in manpower, and a system of verification which the Cabinet was convinced would actually *reduce* France's feelings of security by highlighting Britain's inability to honour her Locarno commitments.[163] The government was only released from this dilemma by the tabling of the French amendments – Britain's acceptance of them was a further example of the reactive policy.

Over-shadowing the whole of the Disarmament Conference was the question of Germany. But only gradually did the British Cabinet recognise what the French had known for a long time; that in spite of Germany's apparently reasonable offers at the outset, she was determined to re-arm. Her demands increased every time they were met, thus French insecurity increased with every new German demand. That is not to say that Germany did not want a disarmament agreement, even under Hitler, as it was better to re-arm with the *consent* of the other powers than in opposition to them.[164] At the same time, the price of agreement demanded by Germany tended to increase the further time progressed and the further Britain and France drew apart on the security question.

Following Barthou's speech of 30 May, even Eden, the architect of Britain's only significant attempt to reach agreement, found himself echoing Eyres-Monsell's view on isolationism:

> Barthou's speech is only intelligible if the French want to break up the Conference. It will be grand material for our own isolationists at home, and almost converted me into one. Certainly I believe that it

would now be in the interests of world peace if Britain drew herself back a little from Europe, re-armed in the air, and watched events.[165]

For his part, MacDonald observed that:

The nations seem bent on war and are in no mood to negotiate and agree upon anything.[166]

Whatever his previous convictions MacDonald had reached the conclusion that the political situation had deteriorated to such an extent that any search for peace via a reduction in armaments was a waste of time. To return to his earlier analogy, he felt that the world was 'up against realities which cannot be shelved when the international weather seems for a time set foul'.[167] Even so, it can be said that during the Disarmament Conference the British government contributed significantly to the foulness of the weather and was unable, if not unwilling, to steer a fair-weather course.

9

CONCLUSION

Having analysed the detail of Britain's approach to the dilemma of confronting the disarmament problem, the study has shown that the method chosen by successive British governments was, as a general rule, merely to *react* to events and proposals instigated by other powers. The two minority Labour governments did, at least, try to impose their own ideology on their conduct of foreign policy, including the pursuit of disarmament, but their success was restricted by factors largely outside their control. Overall, however, Britain took refuge behind the twin myths that her own unilateral arms reductions had been undertaken to bring about agreement at the League – and so absolved her from making further reductions – and that her own reductions in armaments after 1919 were on a different level and scale from any other power. Accordingly, she left others to make the running at Geneva. With one or two exceptions, the result was a purely reactive policy, with a considerable element of procrastination thrown in for good measure.[1]

The Lloyd George Coalition government presided over what was arguably one of the most successful examples of disarmament in the period under review – the Washington Naval Conference. The Coalition was also responsible for initiating policy in regard to the *international* quest for disarmament under the auspices of the League. In this respect, it should be emphasised that the unilateral arms reductions undertaken by the Coalition – upon which Britain was to base her credentials in successive negotiations at Geneva – were brought about by the need to channel the vast expenditure on armaments of 1914–18 into the social and domestic areas, not by any wish to meet the 'obligation' to pursue multilateral disarmament enshrined in the Versailles Treaty and League of Nations Covenant. Significantly, priority was given to the Washington Conference which had nothing to do with the League's attempts to formulate a plan; no help was given to Esher in the preparation of his plan at the Temporary Mixed Commission.

After the first flood of enthusiasm for arms reductions had passed, and the signatories to the League had reduced the level of their armaments in line with immediate postwar requirements, the more pro-disarmament members of the international community began to press for progress in the League's search for a plan. In Britain, the search was led by Lord Robert Cecil, acting independently as a member of the Temporary Mixed Commission, though latterly a member of the Baldwin administration of 1923 as well. With help from his French counterpart, Colonel Réquin, he drafted a scheme – the Treaty of Mutual Assistance – which approached the disarmament question in an indirect manner in that it sought to establish a system of security which would enable disarmament to be implemented. Significantly, Cecil received no support whatsoever for his work from his Conservative colleagues in the first Baldwin administration. Similarly, his colleagues made no effort to resuscitate his initiative on their return to power after the minority Labour government of 1924. The Labour government itself rejected Cecil's plan, but in turning it down at least put forward a more comprehensive plan, the Geneva Protocol for the Pacific Settlement of Disputes. This too aimed at achieving disarmament indirectly, by increasing the perceived level of security even more than Cecil's plan had done. But the Conservatives turned the Protocol down, fearing a substantial increase in commitments to military action on behalf of the League.

Unusually, insofar as Britain was concerned, these indirect attempts at disarmament – the Treaty of Mutual Assistance and the Geneva Protocol – were based on a real belief in disarmament as a means of promoting international peace and stability. There was no element of mere reaction in them. In addition, both Cecil's promotion of the TMA and MacDonald's sponsorship of the Protocol demonstrated a recognition of France's need for increased security commitments. It must be stressed, however, that the initiatives in both cases were personal – a fact which illustrates the importance of individuals in disarmament negotiations. The difference was that MacDonald was backed by his Labour colleagues, whilst Cecil was almost unique amongst his Conservative colleagues in that he was completely committed to the idea of disarmament through the League.

Ideology was an important factor in the admittedly limited steps which the first Labour government was able to take. MacDonald himself believed in disarmament as a by-product of peace and stability, and his first term in office was devoted to achieving that stability. His decision to over-rule the Admiralty, and all other official opposition, in abandoning the proposed Singapore naval base can have been little more than an ideological gesture, knowing that his administration would not be in power long enough to enforce the decision. But it was a significant attempt towards improving the international situation by encouraging a feeling of trust, which, as Madariaga has pointed out, is a vital necessity in the search for disarmament. MacDonald devoted almost the whole of his first administration to the search for stability in Europe, and his successful steering of the London Conference on reparations was an important step along that road.

Any advances achieved by MacDonald's first Labour administration were soon lost by Baldwin's second Conservative government of 1924–9. Whilst, like MacDonald, the Conservatives believed in security first, unlike MacDonald they showed no inclination to follow up their security achievements with any measure of disarmament. They merely reverted to a policy of reacting to external stimuli. Even Austen Chamberlain's triumph at Locarno stemmed from his recognition that, having refused to accept the Geneva Protocol, Britain was compelled to offer some kind of security agreement to France. In practice, the Conservative administration's attitude towards the League's attempts to formulate a disarmament plan via the Preparatory Commission, was to stand on Britain's record of unilateral arms reductions and, in Chamberlain's words, to take a leading part behind the scenes. The Sub-Committee set up to advise on British policy towards the Preparatory Commission, ironically headed by Cecil, adopted a course of responding to events at Geneva and highlighting problems rather than putting forward positive proposals. By refusing to allow senior ministers or officials to attend the Preparatory Commission in Geneva, and refusing to over-rule the numerous interferences by the Service Departments, the government clearly demonstrated its commitment to the policy of not taking a leading part in the formulation of an international disarmament agreement.

The conduct of the second Baldwin government at the abortive Geneva Naval Conference of 1927 could be said to indicate the Conservative ministers' lack of understanding of the politics of disarmament negotiations, though equally it might be interpreted as a lack of desire to reach an agreement in the first place. Once more responding to an American initiative, the government decided to try to take the lead in announcing their proposals at the beginning of the conference, without considering the effect which their programme would have on the Americans. Moreover, whilst publicly claiming that they would be satisfied with parity with the Americans in auxiliary vessels, the real objective of Britain's proposals was to secure superiority. The initial programme put forward at Geneva exceeded both the current building programme and Britain's existing number of ships! Despite Cecil's arguments and pleas, the Admiralty refused to reconsider their fundamental objectives and bring the British proposals in line with both the building programme and international realities. The resentment which followed the failure of the conference was exacerbated by the government's decidedly undiplomatic attempt to reach a compromise with the French over the questions of military trained reserves and naval limitation by class of vessel. The government's mishandling of this attempted compromise not only set back the attempt to reach agreement at the Preparatory Commission but placed a great strain on Anglo-American relations. This deterioration had barely been halted when MacDonald returned to power in 1929.

The second Labour government was able to achieve more in the disarmament field than in its previous term of office, although its twin approach to the problem was more a result of the split between MacDonald and

Henderson than of any defined policy. MacDonald stuck to the direct, personal approach in mending relations with the United States and steering the London Naval Conference to a successful conclusion, thanks in great measure to his handling of the Admiralty and the insistence of both the Americans and the British that careful preparations must be made in order to ensure a successful outcome. Henderson, on the other hand, worked to achieve measures of trust and security through the mechanism of the League, pushing through the Optional Clause and General Act – both key aspects of Labour's foreign policy – and bringing the negotiations for a draft convention at the Preparatory Commission to a conclusion. Even if a number of powers were, to say the least, not entirely happy with the document, as it papered over many cracks, the very conclusion of the draft convention was significant. In particular, it showed that Henderson, as President-elect of the Disarmament Conference, was aware of the need to take France's security position into consideration, and that this might entail additional, though unspecified, concessions on the part of the British government. In all, the uneasy combination of MacDonald and Henderson did at least ensure that disarmament was tackled from both sides, direct and indirect. Certainly the second Labour government contributed significantly to an improvement in international trust and stability. Equally, on the domestic front the Labour government was assiduous in preparing the ground for successful disarmament negotiations; MacDonald insisted that representatives of all three major political parties should form a committee to attempt to draw up a *British* policy towards the forthcoming Disarmament Conference.

It was left to the Conservative-dominated National government, under a leader who had lost the credibility and the support of his own Party, to tackle the last-ditch attempt to achieve disarmament at Geneva between 1932 and 1934. But the MacDonald of 1932–4 was not the same leader as that of 1929–31. The Prime Minister not only suffered the loss of faith of his former colleagues, his physical and mental powers were declining. His commitment to disarmament was also called into question both by his former colleagues like Henderson, and by junior politicians and officials like Eden and Cadogan. At the same time, it can be argued that MacDonald was never committed to disarmament *per se*. He had always maintained that disarmament must be tackled from the security end, and that multinational general conferences were unlikely to achieve anything significant. Certainly he preferred to tackle more specific questions on a much smaller scale. In this type of diplomacy he was undoubtedly a master. But although MacDonald had proved his ability on previous occasions to over-rule those who he felt stood in the way of success, during his premiership of the National government he was reluctant to over-rule – or even attempt to over-rule – either his Conservative colleagues or his Service advisers. There are two explanations for this reluctance. First, he was not strong enough, either politically or mentally to deal with the opposition, and second, he was not committed to the Conference itself. It went against all of MacDonald's instincts to hope for success from such a large venture during a period of international instability and insecurity.

The National government, therefore, was virtually leaderless as far as its policy towards the Disarmament Conference was concerned. It retreated into a reactive role. It was only fear of being blamed for the Conference's ultimate failure that finally drove it into taking the lead, and then only at the instigation of the government's junior advisers in Geneva a whole year after the Conference had opened. It is difficult to estimate whether Britain would have taken a more pro-active role had the Labour government remained in power, but it is much more likely to have done so given that Henderson, the President of the Disarmament Conference, would have retained international prestige, and that the pro-disarmament ideology of the Labour Party would have been firmly behind MacDonald. He may then have felt it worthwhile to attempt to take the lead; his undoubted vanity and desire for prestige may even have been enough to persuade him to overcome his instinctive distrust of large-scale conferences. But MacDonald was now a spent force, and fear of failure was not enough to persuade the Conservative majority in the National government that sacrifices and commitments must be made. They would avoid confronting the dilemma as long as they possibly could, and when they eventually were forced to confront it, seized gratefully on the opportunity to relinquish their initiative when faced with the French 'amendments' to the MacDonald Plan.

Throughout the changes in government runs the thread of the non-elected officials – the Foreign Office, Cabinet secretariat and Service advisers for example – whose influence cannot be overlooked. It is impossible to define the exact influence exerted by the permanent advisers to the governments in question, but policy was inevitably influenced by their advice, and, with one or two exceptions, these advisers were sceptical about the benefits of disarmament. Crowe and Hankey, for instance, strongly advised against acceptance of the Treaty of Mutual Assistance, the latter's approach being consistently in favour of military strength as a means of maintaining peace. Vansittart, whilst warning that French demands for security would have to be met, was not a believer in the concept of disarmament. Only certain junior members of the Foreign Office – Cadogan and Leeper, for instance – came to accept that a pro-disarmament policy *must* be pursued, and pursued in good faith.

In summarising the approaches taken by individual governments to the disarmament question, the overall impression is one of lip-service being paid to a problem which, if ignored, would hopefully go away. In general, in resting on the extent of her own unilateral disarmament, Britain preached a policy of 'follow my lead' and refused to admit that the obligations inherent in the Treaty of Versailles and the League Covenant would require *British* reductions as well as reductions by other powers, notably France. There was a constant desire to prove that there was no legal obligation to disarm, merely a moral one, and an equally constant assertion that France had sufficient security and was paranoid as far as Germany's intentions were concerned. There were, of course, exceptions to this general rule. Lloyd George was arguably sincere in his recognition that a general reduction in the level of armaments was desirable; but the rush to reduce armaments in the aftermath of the Great War removed the immediacy of the international obligation, and the Washington Naval Conference did not come into the scheme of arms reduction laid down by the League Covenant. MacDonald and Henderson, each following his individual beliefs, worked to achieve a measure of disarmament and security, but were hampered by the international situation in which they found themselves, and by the tenuous hold which each of the Labour administrations had on power. Conservative achievements in the disarmament field were non-existent; they persistently refused to recognise that the international obligation to reduce the level of their armaments was an entirely different question from the reductions which they had carried out on a unilateral basis in order to meet the demands of the Treasury. The attempts they did make – at the Geneva Naval Conference, for example – were conducted with an arrogance and inability to accommodate the views of others which were bound to lead not just to failure, but to a distinct worsening of the situation.

The conclusion reached by the present study is thus two-fold. First, there was a complete absence of a positive policy to address the disarmament obligations laid down in the Treaty of Versailles and the League Covenant. Perhaps the main reason for this lies in the second conclusion; that there was no real understanding of the nature of these obligations. Consciously or unconsciously, most members of the policy-making élite, certainly during the long periods of Conservative or Conservative-dominated government, came to believe that disarmament meant that Britain would have to reduce the level of her armaments *below* that perceived necessary for her own and Imperial security. In essence this was wrong. Certainly military experts such as Temperley believed that multilateral disarmament on terms 'available' at the Disarmament Conference could have improved rather than reduced British security.[2] In practice, however, British governments would base their policy on Britain's unilateral force reductions and refuse to consider any concessions towards the requirements of the other powers involved. If, in some circles, there was a recognition that France's chronic feelings of insecurity could only be alleviated by a firm guarantee from Britain, the bottom line as far as the British government was concerned was that such a guarantee would involve a structuring of Britain's forces so as to answer the needs of France rather than Britain. The reality, of course, was that such a restructuring might enable France to make the reductions which were essential not only to fulfil the international obligations to which all the signatories of the Treaty of Versailles and Covenant of the League of Nations were committed, but to bring about an international disarmament agreement which Germany would freely sign.

In essence, British ministers were unable to make the mental adjustment necessary to transform a short-term policy of national self-interest into a long-term prospect of a stable and disarmed community of nations with a common interest. It is not suggested that Britain alone was responsible for the collapse of the disarmament provisions of the Versailles Treaty and League Covenant as, in the final analysis, the majority of the major powers at the Disarmament Conference of 1932–4 were more concerned with avoiding blame for the anticipated failure of the conference than with trying to ensure its success. However, Britain must certainly bear a great deal of the responsibility for failing to achieve European stability by refusing to recognise the need to align her policy with that of France in order to address the problem of the resurgence of Germany.

The purpose of this study has been to analyse successive British governments' response to the disarmament obligations imposed by the Treaty of Versailles and the Covenant of the League of Nations. The approach taken has been to look at the problem of disarmament as a dilemma – a logical or actual position presenting only a choice between equally unwelcome alternatives – and these alternatives have been examined from Britain's point of view. The question of whether the search for an international disarmament agreement was a logical or viable position for any of the powers to have adopted during the inter-war period is not the point at issue. Their commitment to adopt such a policy was firmly laid down for them in the aftermath of the Great War. The contention which *is* put forward is that, in her reluctance to accept any of the unwelcome alternatives perceived to be before her, Britain consistently refused to take the one step which could conceivably have helped to create a situation in which a policy of international disarmament was *not* illogical – the offer of a meaningful guarantee to France.

It is not argued that such a guarantee would have solved wider international problems such as Japanese expansionism or the international financial crisis. Even with the benefit of hindsight it is impossible to say what effect such a guarantee would have had, but it is logical to assume that the legitimacy of Germany's claim to re-arm would have been severely undermined by France's adherence to an international disarmament agreement which even an anti-disarmer like Sir Eyre Crowe believed would follow from a guarantee by Britain. By refusing to face the disarmament dilemma openly and honestly, Britain merely ensured that international events would force unwelcome decisions upon her. A commitment to France, undertaken voluntarily in the early part of the period under review, could conceivably have avoided an involuntary commitment to France in 1939. Had Britain worked towards an 'improvement in the weather', to use Ramsay MacDonald's analogy, it is *just* conceivable that the storm-clouds of war could have been averted.

NOTES

1 INTRODUCTION

1 The former is in Dick Richardson and Glyn Stone (eds) *Decisions and Diplomacy*, and the latter in P. Catterall and C.J. Morris (eds) *Britain and the Threat to Stability in Europe, 1918–45*. Other works have tackled disarmament indirectly as part of a more general study, for example Brian Bond's *British Military Policy between the Two World Wars*, and Brian McKercher's *The Second Baldwin Government and the United States, 1924–1929*.

2 This volume also contains articles by K. Hovi on 'Security before Disarmament, or Hegemony? The French Alliance Policy 1917–1927', and Maurice Vaïsse on 'Security and Disarmament: Problems in the Development of the Disarmament Debates 1919–1934'. Vaïsse's monumental study of French policy at the World Disarmament Conference of 1932–34, *Sécurité D'Abord,* should also be noted here.

3 B.J.C. McKercher (ed.) *Arms Limitation and Disarmament: Restraints on War, 1899–1939*.

4 Chaput, *Disarmament in British Foreign Policy*, p. 13.

5 *Ibid.*, p. 363.

6 For example, during the negotiations to persuade the Germans to return to the negotiating table at Geneva in the autumn of 1932, Foreign Office officials spent a considerable amount of time in drawing up possible plans and strategies in the event of these negotiations proving successful. It is not, however, feasible to include all these discussions in the present study, and in the main they merely formed part of the overall policy which emerged once the Germans had agreed to return, and which is discussed in detail herein.

7 For discussion on these questions, see, for example, John Underwood's study of British policy at the World Disarmament Conference.

8 For an analysis of Britain's early position on an Anglo-French agreement see Anne Orde, *Great Britain and International Security, 1920–1926*.

2 THE CONCEPT AND CONTEXT OF DISARMAMENT, 1919–34

1 For a detailed analysis of the disarmament versus arms control debate, see Dick Richardson, *A History of Disarmament and Arms Control*, Chapter 1.

2 See Dick Richardson, *The Evolution of British Disarmament Policy in the 1920s*, Chapters 2 and 13.

3 CAB27/505, DC(M)(32), 18th Meeting of the Ministerial Committee, 23 November 1933.
4 P.J. Noel-Baker, *Disarmament*, p. 7. Italics added.
5 *Ibid.*, p. 10.
6 S. de Madariaga, *Disarmament*, p. 5.
7 *Ibid.*, p. 6. Amongst the many who disagreed with this theory was Sir Maurice Hankey, who, as will be shown later, firmly believed that the decline of empires could definitely be traced to the decline of the military spirit.
8 Viscount Grey of Fallodon, *Twenty-Five Years*, pp. 160–2.
9 H.J. Morgenthau, *Politics Among Nations*, p. 398.
10 S. de Madariaga, *Morning Without Noon*, p. 48.
11 See, for example, a lecture given by Allen Leeper of the Foreign Office to the Imperial Services College at the end of 1932, in which he categorically states that '[t]he British point of view all along has been that disarmament in itself brings about an increase of security. If countries are less well equipped for war they are less likely to indulge in it' *(Leeper Papers*, LEEP 4/1).
12 Madariaga, *Morning Without Noon*, p. 56.
13 *Ibid.*, p. 72.
14 *Ibid.*, p. 48.
15 *Ibid.*, p. 323.
16 Richardson, *A History of Disarmament and Arms Control*, Chapter 2.
17 For a detailed discussion on these factors, see *ibid.*, Chapter 6.
18 See, for example, A. Lentin, *Lloyd George, Woodrow Wilson and the Guilt of Germany*, J. Headlam-Morley, *A Memoir of the Paris Peace Conference*, M.L. Dockrill and J.D. Goold, *Peace Without Promise: Britain and the Peace Conferences 1919–23*.
19 L. Jaffe, *The Decision to Disarm Germany*, p. 28.
20 Reply of the Allied and Associated Powers to the Observations of the German Delegation on the Conditions of Peace (16 June 1919), *Papers Relating to the Foreign Relations of the United States, Diplomatic Papers* (hereafter cited as *FRUS*), Paris Peace Conference 1919, Vol. 6, p. 954.
21 The Treaty of Peace, 28 June 1919, *Parliamentary Papers*, Cmd. 153 of 1919.
22 Viscount Cecil, *A Great Experiment*, p. 123.
23 See, for example, A. Lentin, 'The Treaty that Never Was: Lloyd George and the Abortive Anglo-French Alliance of 1919', in J. Loades (ed.) *The Life and Times of David Lloyd George*.
24 H. Kissinger, *Diplomacy*, p. 256.
25 Tardieu letter to House, 22 March, 1919, in André Tardieu, *The Truth About the Treaty*, p. 136 cited in H. Kissinger, *Diplomacy*.
26 *Ibid.*, p. 251.
27 The question of a guarantee to France runs through Cabinet deliberations on defence/disarmament policy throughout the whole of the period under review. The reasons for its rejection are always the same: it would mean rearmament (i.e. armament configurations not in accord with Britain's perceived requirements) and a commitment to Europe, which *must* be avoided. The question of public opinion also enters into the question of a guarantee to France, although the part played by public opinion in the formulation of British disarmament policy is a moot point. Certainly in the immediate post-war period, public opinion was firmly behind such a policy to such an extent that it is scarcely referred to in Cabinet discussions, being taken for granted by Cabinet Ministers. It was not until the end of the period that public opinion showed any sign of changing. In his study of the part played by public opinion in the

formulation of British Defence policy in the period 1931–5, Patrick Kyba concludes that 'for most of the period majority sentiment in the country opposed rearmament' (P. Kyba, *Covenants without the Sword*, p. 199), and that it was not until the Abyssinian crisis of 1935 that opinion began to change. However, it could be argued that had Britain adopted a long-term strategy, as advocated by Kissinger, and accepted the need for a guarantee to France, public opinion *could* have been swayed towards the acceptance that such a guarantee, with consequent armaments restructuring, was the best way to ensure that the events of 1914–18 were never repeated.

28 See, for example, R. Henig, *The Origins of the Second World War*, M. Kitchen, *Europe between the Wars*, A.J.P. Taylor, *The Origins of the Second World War*.

29 R. Henig, *The Origins of the Second World War*, p. 5.

30 *Ibid.*, p. 7.

31 Dockrill and Goold, *op. cit.*, p. 63.

32 See R. Higham, *Armed Forces in Peacetime*, pp. 325–7; Memorandum by M. Jakobsen (Secretary of the Committee of Experts on Budgetary Questions at the Preparatory Commission for the Disarmament Conference), 26 March 1927, *Cecil Papers*, ADD51099; W.P. Coates, *U.S.S.R. and Disarmament*, p. 82. The quote is taken from Richardson, *The Evolution of British Disarmament Policy*, p. 214, footnote 6.

3 THE HUMAN ELEMENT

1 L. Jaffe, *The Decision to Disarm Germany*, p. 67.

2 *Ibid*, p. 35.

3 T. Jones, *Lloyd George*, p. 170.

4 D.J. Shorney, *Britain and Disarmament 1916–1931*, p. 74.

5 K.O. Morgan, *Consensus and Disunity: The Lloyd George Coalition Government, 1918–22*, p. 133.

6 M.L. Dockrill and J.D. Goold, *Peace without Promise: Britain and the Peace Conferences, 1919–23*, p. 28.

7 D. Lloyd George, *The Truth about the Peace Treaties*, p. 609.

8 *Ibid.*, pp. 410–11.

9 A. Lentin, *Guilt at Versailles: Lloyd George and the Pre-history of Appeasement*, p. 47.

10 Morgan, *op. cit.*, p. 133.

11 Dockrill and Goold, *op. cit.*, pp. 82–3.

12 *Hankey Papers*, HNKY 1/5, diary entry 29 December 1920.

13 Riddell, *Lord Riddell's Intimate Diary of the Peace Conference and After 1918–1923*, p. 255.

14 Viscount Cecil, *A Great Experiment*, p. 132.

15 John Simon, Foreign Secretary, 1931–5.

16 *Cecil Papers*, ADD51101, Cecil to H. St George Saunders, 18 July 1932.

17 Lord Avon, *Facing the Dictators*, p. 28.

18 D. Dutton, *Simon: A Political Biography of Sir John Simon*, p. 337.

19 *MacDonald Papers*, PRO30/69/1753/1, diary entry, 2 June 1934.

20 P.J. Noel-Baker, *The First World Disarmament Conference*, p. 77.

21 Cadogan reports that when Cecil heard Simon described as 'the worst Secretary of State we have had for 50 years', he asked 'Why 50?' (*Cadogan Papers*, Diary 5 February 1933).

22 Viscount Simon, *A Retrospect*, p. 185.

23 A.J.P. Taylor (ed.) *Off the Record*, p. 143, cited in Dutton, *op. cit.*, p. 332.

24 Noel-Baker, *op. cit.*, p. 77.
25 Sir Herbert Samuel, Home Secretary 1931–2.
26 J. Bowle, *Viscount Samuel*, p. 283.
27 Stanley Baldwin, Chancellor of the Exchequer in Bonar Law's Conservative Cabinet, Prime Minister May 1923 to January 1924, and November 1924 to June 1929, Lord President August 1931 to June 1935.
28 L.S. Amery, *My Political Life*, Vol. 2, p. 480.
29 *Cecil Papers*, ADD51078, 20 May 1926.
30 *Bridgeman Papers, Political Notes,* Vol. II, p. 181.
31 *Hankey Papers,* HNKY 5/1, diary entry 9 December 1923.
32 *Templewood Papers*, TEM XIX:5.
33 A.J.P. Taylor, *English History 1914–1945,* p. 265.
34 Ivone Kirkpatrick, *The Inner Circle*, p. 38.
35 *Baldwin Papers*, Vol. 130, 10 March 1927.
36 N. Rostow, *Anglo-French Relations 1934–36*, p. 247.
37 B. Ranft (ed.) *The Beatty Papers*, p. 350.
38 *Cecil Papers*, ADD51108, Cecil to Noel-Baker, 26 November 1933.
39 *Ibid.*, ADD51101, 12 May 1933.
40 Cecil, *op. cit.*, p. 146.
41 K. Young, *Stanley Baldwin*, p. 27.
42 A.J. Balfour (created Earl 1922), Lord President in Lloyd George's Coalition Cabinet, and in Baldwin's second Cabinet from April 1925.
43 K. Young, *Arthur James Balfour*, p. 418.
44 *Ibid.*
45 R.F. Mackay, *Balfour: Intellectual Statesman*, p. 346.
46 *Hankey Papers*, HNKY 1/5, diary entry 30 October 1918.
47 CAB 2/4, Minutes of 205th Meeting of CID, 17 November 1925.
48 Lord Robert Cecil, Lord Privy Seal, 1923, Chancellor of the Duchy of Lancaster, 1924–7.
49 G. Clemenceau, *Grandeur and Misery of Victory*, 138.
50 CAB 2/4, CID Paper No. 733-B, 3 November 1926.
51 CAB 2/4, 195th Meeting of CID, 13 February 1925.
52 *Ibid.*
53 *Hankey Papers*, HNKY 5/1, diary entry 11 November 1923.
54 *Ibid.*, 20 December 1920.
55 *Bridgeman Papers, Political Notes*, Vol. II.
56 L.S. Amery, *My Political Life,* Vol. 2, p. 475.
57 B.J.C. McKercher, *The Second Baldwin Government and the United States, 1924–1929*, p. 77.
58 *Cecil Papers*, ADD51073, 26 July 1927.
59 *Ibid.*, ADD51080, 9 August 1927.
60 *Ibid.*, ADD51073, 19 March 1929.
61 *Ibid.*, ADD51081, 21 June 1929.
62 *Ibid.*, 21 January 1924.
63 Baron Cushendun, formerly Ronald McNeill, Parliamentary Under-Secretary at the Foreign Office, November 1924 to November 1925, Chancellor of the Duchy of Lancaster 1927–9.
64 *Cecil Papers*, ADD51107, 2 April 1928.
65 *Bridgeman Papers, Political Notes*, Vol. II, p. 199.
66 *Ibid.*
67 *Cushendun Papers*, FO800/228, 13 June 1928.

68 Austen Chamberlain, Chancellor of the Exchequer 1919–22, Foreign Secretary 1924–9.
69 CAB24/174, Cabinet Memoranda, CP357(25), Memorandum by Chamberlain, 16 July 1925.
70 *Ibid.*
71 *Austen Chamberlain Papers*, AC54/77, Chamberlain to Cecil, 11 April 1927.
72 *Ibid.*, AC54/94, Chamberlain to Cecil, 14 August 1927.
73 Cecil, *op. cit.*, p. 163.
74 Winston Churchill, Secretary of State for War 1919–21, Dominions Secretary 1921–2, Chancellor of the Exchequer 1924–9.
75 *Bridgeman Papers*, *Political Notes*, Vol. II, p. 213.
76 *Ibid.*
77 *Hankey Papers*, HNKY 5/1, diary entry 31 December 1920.
78 CAB24/171, Cabinet Memoranda, CP118(25), Memorandum by Chancellor of the Exchequer, 24 February 1925.
79 *Austen Chamberlain Papers*, AC52/156, rough notes by Churchill on proposed pact, undated.
80 CAB2/4, 193rd Meeting of the CID, 5 January 1925.
81 *Bridgeman Papers*, *Political Papers*, Vol. II, p. 109.
82 *Hankey Papers*, HNKY 5/1, diary entry 25 August 1919.
83 A.J.P. Taylor (ed.) *Lloyd George: A Diary by Frances Stevenson*, 5 April 1919.
84 *Cecil Papers*, ADD51079, Cecil to Austen Chamberlain, 15 August 1927.
85 *Bridgeman Papers*, *Political Notes*, Vol. II, p. 105.
86 CAB2/4, 215th Meeting of the CID, 22 July 1926.
87 *Ibid.*, 190th Meeting of the CID, 4 December 1924.
88 *Cecil Papers*, ADD51073, 20 January 1925.
89 CAB27/355, 3rd Meeting of Further Limitation of Naval Armaments Committee, 19 July 1927.
90 Sir Samuel Hoare, Secretary of State for Air 1923 and 1924–9, Secretary of State for India 1931–5, created Viscount Templewood in 1944.
91 *Templewood Papers*, TEM V:5, Speech on Disarmament and the Church, Albert Hall, 4 July 1928. See also TEM XIX:6, and TEM Pam. 2.
92 *Ibid.*, TEM V:5, Speech at Guildhall Banquet, 9 November 1925.
93 *Ibid.*, TEM V:5, Speech on Disarmament and the Church, Albert Hall, 4 July 1928.
94 *Ibid.*, TEM XIX:6, Notes on Disarmament 1931–2.
95 *Ibid.*
96 *Ibid.*, TEM V:5, Speech at Cambridge Union, 29 November 1927.
97 *Ibid.*, TEM V:5, Speech on Disarmament and the Church, Albert Hall, 4 July 1928.
98 *Ibid.*, TEM V:5, Speech at Cambridge Union, 29 November 1927.
99 *Ibid.*, TEM XIX:6, Notes on Disarmament 1931–2.
100 L.S. Amery, First Lord of the Admiralty, 1923, Colonial Secretary 1924–5, Colonial and Dominions Secretary 1925–9.
101 Amery, *op. cit.*, Vol. 3, p. 145.
102 J. Barnes and D. Nicholson (eds) *The Empire at Bay – The Leo Amery Diaries, 1929–1945*, p. 273.
103 *Ibid.*
104 Amery, *op. cit.*, Vol. 3, p.145.
105 Amery, *op. cit.*, Vol. 2, p. 254.
106 *Ibid.*, p. 300.
107 Amery, *op. cit.*, Vol. 3, p. 152.

108 William Bridgeman, Home Secretary 1922–3, First Lord of the Admiralty 1924–9.

109 *Bridgeman Papers, Political Notes*, Vol. II. pp. 167 and 201.

110 *Ibid.*, p. 107.

111 *Ibid.*, p. 111.

112 *Ibid.*, p. 113.

113 CAB24/229, Cabinet Memoranda CP119(32), Notes on meeting of Ministerial Committee relating to Attitude to be adopted by the United Kingdom Delegation on the General Commission, March 1932.

114 Noel-Baker, *op. cit.*, p. 105.

115 *Ibid.*

116 *Cecil Papers*, ADD51108, Cecil to Noel-Baker, 4 May 1933.

117 Avon, *op. cit.*, p. 26.

118 *Ibid.*, p. 14.

119 *Ibid.*, p. 31.

120 *Ibid.*, p. 28.

121 *Avon Papers*, AP20/1/12, diary entry 7 March 1933.

122 James Ramsay MacDonald, Leader of the Labour Party 1923–31, Prime Minister and Foreign Secretary 1924, Prime Minister of Labour Government 1929–31, Prime Minister of National Government 1931–5.

123 *House of Commons Debates*, Vol. 167, Col. 83, 23 July 1923.

124 *MacDonald Papers*, PRO30/69/1753/1, diary entry 1 May 1923.

125 J.R. MacDonald, *National Defence: A Study in Militarism*, p. 12.

126 *Cecil Papers*, ADD51081, MacDonald to Cecil, 25 February 1924.

127 *MacDonald Papers*, PRO30/69/1753/1, diary entry 14 September 1927.

128 A number of observers , including some in his own party, questioned whether MacDonald was, in fact, a socialist. See, for example, Templewood Papers XIX:5 and MacDonald Diary 22 June 1926.

129 *Cecil Papers*, ADD51081, MacDonald to Cecil, 5 March 1934.

130 *Ibid.*, 22 February 1923.

131 *MacDonald Papers*, PRO30/69/1753/1, diary entry 12 February 1930.

132 *Ibid.*, 7 April 1930.

133 *Ibid.*, 22 February 1931.

134 Viscount Esher, *Journals and Letters of Reginald, Viscount Esher*, diary entry 21 March 1923, Templewood XIX:6, Cecil Papers, ADD51164, Parmoor, *A Retrospect*, p. 187.

135 This antipathy is well-documented in David Carlton's *MacDonald Versus Henderson: The Foreign Policy of the Second Labour Government*.

136 This warmth was apparently reciprocated, as demonstrated by Aristide Briand laying a wreath on the grave of Henderson's son, in response to which Henderson declared that 'this act of friendship and affection' would never be forgotten.

137 See, for example, A.J.P. Taylor, *The Trouble Makers*, p. 153.

138 Philip Snowden, Chancellor of the Exchequer 1924 and 1929–31, Lord Privy Seal 1931–2, created Viscount 1931.

139 C. Cross *Philip Snowden*, p. 223.

140 *Ibid.*, p. 203.

141 *Baldwin Papers*, Vol. 129, Snowden to Baldwin, 27 May 1932.

142 *MacDonald Papers*, PRO30/69/1753/1, diary entries 12 August 1924 and 13 August 1924, *MacDonald Diary Papers*, PRO30/69/1753/4, 14 August 1924.

143 Lord President of the Council 1924 and 1929–31.

144 M.A. Hamilton, *Arthur Henderson*, p. 245.

145 Lord Parmoor, *op. cit.*, p. 197.

146 *Ibid.*, p. 192.

147 *Ibid.*

148 J.H. Thomas, Colonial Secretary 1924, Lord Privy Seal 1929–31, Dominions Secretary November 1931–5.

149 *Cecil Papers*, ADD51131, diary entry 26 January 1919.

150 D.N. Dilks (ed.) *The Diaries of Sir Alexander Cadogan 1938–1945*, p. 7.

151 *Ibid.*

152 *Ibid.*

153 Thomas' lack of interest in the disarmament question is perhaps demonstrated by the fact that his biographer, Gregory Blaxland, devotes six lines to Thomas' participation in the Disarmament Conference, followed by two paragraphs on the controversy in which Thomas was involved in relation to the Australian cricket tour of 1932–3 (Blaxland, *J.H. Thomas: A Life for Unity*, pp. 263–4).

154 *MacDonald Papers*, PRO30/69/1753/1, diary entry 28 April 1924.

155 Carlton, *op. cit.*, p. 17.

156 *Alexander Papers*, AVA 5/2/5 MacDonald to Alexander, 17 September 1929.

157 *Ibid.*, AVA 5/2/7, MacDonald to Alexander (undated 1929).

158 Thomas Shaw, Minister of Labour, 1924, Secretary of State for War, 1929–31.

159 A.C. Temperley, *The Whispering Gallery of Europe*, pp. 118–19.

160 Carlton, *op. cit.*, p. 17.

161 Clemenceau, *op. cit.*, p. 141.

162 *Hankey Papers*, HNKY 1/6, diary entry 31 October 1918.

163 *Ibid.*, Vol. 1/5 20 December 1920.

164 *Ibid.*, 15 April 1919.

165 CAB 63/37, 6 August 1925.

166 *Crowe Papers,* FO800/243, 25 June 1923.

167 *Ibid.*, 24 June 1923.

168 *Ibid.*

169 Memorandum written by Sir Eyre Crowe in 1916, FO371/3082, cited in Ruth B. Henig (ed.) *The League of Nations*, p. 68.

170 *Crowe Papers,* FO800/243, 24 June 1923.

171 *Ibid.*, Memorandum dated 24 May 1923.

172 Lord Vansittart, *Bones of Contention*, p. 84.

173 *Ibid.*

174 N. Rose, *Vansittart: Study of a Diplomat,* p. 93.

175 CAB24/189, Cabinet Memoranda, CP256(27), Memorandum by Sir Alexander Cadogan, 26 October 1927.

176 *Ibid.*

177 *Cadogan Papers*, ACAD/1/1, 27 January 1933.

178 *Ibid.*, 3 February 1933.

179 *Ibid.*

180 *Ibid.*, 17 March 1933.

181 *Cecil Papers*, ADD51164, 22 February 1924. See also Richardson, *The Evolution of British Disarmament Policy*, pp. 20–7.

182 See, for example, Cabinet Memoranda CAB24/174, CP357(25), Memorandum by Chamberlain, 16 July 1925, CAB24/192, CP190(28), Memorandum by the First Lord of the Admiralty, 11 May 1928 and CAB2/4, Minutes of 205th Meeting of CID, 17 November 1925.

4 THE LLOYD GEORGE COALITION GOVERNMENT, 1918–22

1 Lloyd George's speech at Wolverhampton, 23 November 1918, cited in K.O. Morgan, *Consensus and Disunity; The Lloyd George Coalition Government 1918–1922*, p. 81.

2 *Ibid.*, p. 118.

3 CAB24/107, Cabinet Memoranda, CP1467(20), Memorandum by Churchill on British Military Liabilities, 11 June 1920.

4 *Ibid.*

5 *Hankey Papers,* HNKY 1/5, diary entry 25 August 1919.

6 *Lloyd George Papers,* F/33/2/26, Long to Lloyd George, 13 March 1919.

7 *Hankey Papers,* HNKY 1/5, diary entry 25 August 1919. The corresponding figure for 1914 was £47.4 million and for 1919, £148 million.

8 CAB 24/98, Cabinet Memoranda, CP645(20), Memorandum by the Board of Admiralty, 13 February 1920.

9 J.H. Maurer, 'Arms Control and the Washington Conference', in E. Goldstein and J.H. Maurer (eds) *The Washington Conference, 1921–22*, p. 269.

10 CAB24/109, Cabinet Memoranda, CP1677(20), Memorandum on Naval Construction by the First Lord of the Admiralty, 23 July 1920.

11 CAB2/3, Minutes of the 134th Meeting of the CID, 14 December 1920.

12 CAB23/36, Cabinet Conclusions, S.47, 21 February 1922.

13 CAB24/109, Cabinet Memoranda, CP2274(20), Memorandum by Churchill on Military Expenditure, 9 December 1920.

14 *Hankey Papers,* HNKY 1/5, diary entry 20 December 1920.

15 CAB2/3, Minutes of the 134th Meeting of the Committee of Imperial Defence, 14 December 1920.

16 *Ibid.*

17 CAB32/2, Imperial Conference, 4th Meeting, 22 June 1921.

18 *Documents on British Foreign Policy* [hereafter *DBFP*], Ser. I, Vol. 1, No. 522, 7 October 1919.

19 *Ibid.*

20 CAB32/2, Imperial Conference, 8th Meeting, 28 June 1921.

21 American feeling against the Alliance came, in fact, more from the press and public opinion than from the State Department, where it was regarded more as a 'source of irritation' than anything more serious. (CAB32/2, Imperial Conference, 8th Meeting, 28 June 1921).

22 E. Goldstein, 'The Evolution of British Diplomatic Strategy for the Washington Conference', in E. Goldstein and J.H. Maurer, *op. cit.*, p. 13.

23 CAB2/3, Minutes of 134th Meeting of the CID, 14 December 1920.

24 FO371/5617, A5489/18/45, Curzon to Geddes, 27 July 1921.

25 *Ibid.*, miscellaneous correspondence between Curzon and Geddes. Geddes maintained that Hughes 'in his own mind [was] fighting the British Foreign Office for prestige' and had 'no intention of giving way'.

26 Goldstein, *op. cit.*, p. 23.

27 CAB63/34, Hankey to Lloyd George, 2 December 1921.

28 *Ibid.* Hankey certainly respected Lloyd George's reason for remaining in London, and insisted that 'we have never got to a point here where I could honestly telegraph that a good settlement would not be reached unless you came . . . and . . . until a day ago you were well nigh indispensable at home'. When a settlement of the Irish question was reached he conveyed to the Prime Minister the many 'tributes to your extraordinary skill in extricating a settle-

ment from what appeared to be a hopeless tangle'. The Irish settlement improved relations with the Americans, and even the French 'crowded round with tributes of admiration', although Hankey did observe that 'unfortunately Sinn Fein does not react on our Oriental colleagues and we are unable therefore to speed matters up'.

29 *Lloyd George Papers* F/143, Balfour to Foreign Office, 24 November 1921.
30 *Lloyd George Papers* F/60/4/22, Geddes to Lloyd George, 11 December 1921.
31 CAB63/34, Hankey to Lloyd George, 14 November 1921.
32 *Lloyd George Papers* F/143.
33 Goldstein, *op. cit.*, p. 23.
34 CAB23/26, Cabinet Conclusions 67(21)3, 15 August 1921.
35 CAB4/7, CID Paper No. 280-B, The Washington Conference on Limitation of Armaments, 24 October 1921.
36 *Ibid.*
37 CAB24/125, Cabinet Memoranda, CP3039, Memorandum by Hankey on Singapore: Development as a Naval Base, 13 June 1921.
38 *Ibid.*
39 CAB2/3, Minutes of 146th Meeting of CID, 21 October 1921.
40 *Ibid.*, Minutes of 147th Meeting of CID, 31 October 1921.
41 CAB4/7, CID Paper No 280-B, 24 October 1921.
42 CAB63/34, Hankey to Lloyd George, 11 November 1921.
43 *Ibid.*
44 *Ibid.*
45 *Ibid.*, 2 December 1921.
46 *Ibid.*, 17 November 1921.
47 *Lloyd George Papers* F/61/1/2, Balfour to Lloyd George, 14 November 1921, Despatch No. 2.
48 CAB21/218, CID Paper on the Washington Conference, Opening Address by Mr Hughes, 12 November 1921.
49 *Ibid.*
50 *Ibid.*
51 *Ibid.*
52 *Ibid.*
53 CAB4/7, Telegram from Balfour to CID, CID Paper No. 283-B, 14 November 1921.
54 *Ibid.*
55 CAB63/34, Hankey to Lloyd George, 17 November 1921.
56 *Ibid.*
57 *Ibid.*, 25 November 1921.
58 *Lloyd George Papers* F/143, Lloyd George to Balfour, Telegram No. 101, 9 December 1921.
59 *Ibid.*
60 *Ibid.*
61 *Ibid.*, Telegram No. 66, 1 December 1921.
62 CAB63/34, Hankey to Lloyd George, 12 December 1921, and CAB30, Balfour to Curzon 28 November 1921.
63 CAB63/34, Hankey to Lloyd George, 2 December 1921.
64 CAB30/31, Sir Maurice Hankey's draft of a conversation between Balfour, Hughes and Kato, 2 December 1921.
65 *Ibid.*
66 *Ibid.*
67 *Ibid.*

68 *Ibid.*
69 *Ibid.*
70 *Ibid.*
71 *Lloyd George Papers* F/61/1/12, Balfour to Lloyd George, 18 December 1921.
72 CAB30/1A, 62nd Conference of the British Empire Delegation, 20 December 1921.
73 CAB63/34, Hankey to Lloyd George, 12 December 1921.
74 CAB30/1A, 1st Conference of the British Empire Delegation, 13 November 1921.
75 *Ibid.*
76 CAB30/1A, Balfour to Curzon, 28 November 1921.
77 See, for instance, Joel Blatt, 'France and the Washington Conference', in Goldstein and Maurer, *op. cit.*, p. 203.
78 *Lloyd George Papers* F/61/1/15, 2nd Meeting of Committee on Limitation of Armament and Sub-committee on Limitation of Naval Armament, Washington Conference (no date).
79 *Ibid.*
80 *Ibid.*
81 CAB4/7, CID Paper No. 280-B, 24 October 1921.
82 *Ibid.*
83 CAB4/7, CID Paper No. 279-B, 1 October 1921.
84 *Ibid.*, CID Paper No. 280-B, 24 October 1921.
85 *Lloyd George Papers* F/61/1/8, Balfour to Lloyd George, 29 November 1921.
86 *Ibid.*, F/143, Balfour to Lloyd George, 24 November 1921.
87 *Ibid.*, Foreign Office to Balfour, 23 November 1921.
88 *Ibid.*
89 CAB2/3, Minutes of 150th Meeting of CID, 23 November 1921.
90 *Ibid.*
91 CAB30/1A, Balfour to Curzon, December 1921.
92 *Ibid.*
93 *Ibid.*
94 CAB30/1A, 56th Conference of British Empire Delegation, 1 December 1921.
95 CAB63/34, Hankey to Lloyd George, 9 December 1921.
96 *Lloyd George Papers* F/61/1/10, Balfour to Lloyd George, 9 December 1921.
97 CAB63/34, Hankey to Lloyd George, 9 December 1921.
98 *Lloyd George Papers* F/61/3/7, Balfour to Lloyd George, 6 February 1922.
99 *Ibid.*
100 CAB63/34, Hankey to Lloyd George, 12 December 1921.
101 CAB23/27, Cabinet Conclusions 83(21)(2), 1 November 1921.
102 *Crowe Papers,* FO800/243, 'Notes respecting the possible conclusion of an Anglo-French Alliance', 26 December 1921.
103 Viscount d'Abernon, *An Ambassador of Peace*, Vol. I., p. 247.
104 CAB23/29, Cabinet Conclusions 1(22), 10 January 1922.
105 d'Abernon, *loc. cit.*.
106 CAB23/29, Cabinet Conclusions 1(22), 10 January 1922.
107 CAB24/132, Cabinet Memoranda, CP3612, Notes on a conversation held at the British Embassy, Paris, 14 January 1922.
108 Cecil, *A Great Experiment*, p. 79.
109 *Cecil Papers*, ADD51103, ff. 3–23, 6 June 1923.
110 *Noel-Baker Papers*, NBKR 4X/65, Report of TMC, 8 January 1924, cited in P. Towle, 'British Security and Disarmament Policy', in R. Ahmann, A. M. Birke

and M. Howard (eds) *The Quest for Stability: Problems of West European Security, 1918–1957*, p. 132.
111 Cecil, *op. cit.*, p. 95.
112 Esher, *Journals and Letters of Reginald, Viscount Esher*, Esher to Cecil, 1 August 1922.
113 CAB24/128, Cabinet Memoranda, CP3388, Resolutions of the League Assembly, 1 October 1921.
114 Esher, *op. cit.*, Esher to Sir Douglas Haig, 3 January 1919.
115 *Ibid.*, Esher to Hankey, 14 September 1919.
116 *Ibid.*, Esher to Maurice Brett, 21 February 1922.
117 *Ibid.*, Esher to Oliver Brett, March 1922.
118 *Ibid.*, Esher to Cecil, 1 August 1922.
119 *Lloyd George Papers* F/16/7/82, 24 February 1922.
120 *Ibid.*
121 CAB4/8, CID Paper No. 339-B, 3 April 1922.
122 *Ibid.*
123 *Lloyd George Papers* F/16/7/81, Esher to Fisher, 21 February 1922.
124 CAB4/8, CID Paper No. 341-B, 6 May 1922.
125 CAB2/3, Minutes of 171st Meeting of CID, 11 April 1923.
126 Towle, *op. cit.*, p. 133.
127 CAB4/8, CID Paper No. 339-B, 3 April 1942.
128 Esher, *op. cit.*, Esher to MacDonald, 25 August 1924.
129 *Ibid.*, 3 March 1922 .
130 Towle, *op cit.*, p. 135.
131 S. de Madariaga, *Disarmament*, p. 102.
132 *Ibid.*, p. 103.
133 Esher, *op. cit.*, Esher to MacDonald, 25 August 1924.
134 *Ibid.*
135 Towle, *op. cit.*, p. 135.

5 THE CONSERVATIVE GOVERNMENTS, 1922–3, AND THE FIRST LABOUR GOVERNMENT, 1924

1 A.J.P. Taylor, *English History, 1914–1915*, p. 254.
2 With the additions of Sir Samuel Hoare as Secretary of State for Air, and Lord Robert Cecil as Lord Privy Seal.
3 CAB23/45, Cabinet Conclusions, 11(23)1, 21 February 1923.
4 CAB23/46, Cabinet Conclusions, 31(23)9, 13 June 1923.
5 CAB24/159, Cabinet Memoranda, CP200(23), Memorandum by the Secretary of State for War on the Future Size of the Regular Army, 17 April 1923.
6 *Ibid.*
7 CAB24/160, Cabinet Memoranda, CP248(23), Memorandum by the Chancellor of the Exchequer, 17 May 1923.
8 CAB23/45, Cabinet Conclusions, 25(23)1, 9 May 1923.
9 CAB23/46, Cabinet Conclusions, 32(23)1, 20 June 1923.
10 *Ibid.*
11 CAB24/158, Cabinet Memoranda, CP88(23), Memorandum by the Secretary of State for Air, February 1923.
12 *Ibid.*, Appendix I, Note by Lord Balfour on the Air Menace.
13 CAB24/160, Cabinet Memoranda, CP294(23), Memorandum by the Secretary of State for War, 15 June 1923.
14 CAB4/9, CID Paper No. 393-B, Memorandum by Cecil, 5 January 1923.

15 CAB4/8, League of Nations Resolution No. CL119,1922.IX, CID Paper No. 377-B, Letter from the President of the Council of the League of Nations, 23 October 1922.
16 *Ibid.*
17 *Ibid.*
18 CAB4/8, CID Paper No. 383-B, Memorandum by Lord Robert Cecil, 21 December 1922.
19 *Ibid.*
20 Cecil, *A Great Experiment*, p. 152.
21 *Ibid.*
22 *Ibid.*
23 *Crowe Papers,* FO800/243, Memorandum by Crowe, 24 May 1923.
24 CAB4/8, CID Paper No. 381-B, Memorandum by the Admiralty, 12 December 1922.
25 *Ibid.*
26 CAB4/9, CID Paper No. 406-B, Memorandum by the Admiralty, 15 February 1923.
27 *Ibid.*
28 *Ibid.*
29 The interesting point to note here is that, in the final document, the Council's role was to define the party which was the 'object of aggression' rather than the party which was the aggressor. Presumably if only two states were involved, by a process of elimination the state which was not the 'object of aggression' was the aggressor, but there was no more explicit definition envisaged by the final version of the Treaty, and in the event of more states being involved, the issue became less clear. However, Cecil's draft treaty, which was the object of discussion by Cabinet and CID, did contain the provision for the League to identify the aggressor, within four days.
30 CAB4/9, CID Paper No. 395-B, Memorandum by the General Staff, War Office, January 1923.
31 *Ibid.*
32 *Ibid.*
33 *Ibid.*
34 *Ibid.*
35 CAB2/3, Minutes of 171st Meeting of CID, 11 April 1923.
36 *Ibid.*
37 CAB24/161, Cabinet Memoranda, CP311(23), Memorandum by Amery, 4 July 1923.
38 *Ibid.*
39 *Ibid.*
40 *Ibid.*
41 *Ibid.*
42 CAB24/164, Cabinet Memoranda, CP18(24), Memorandum by the Secretary of State for India, 11 January 1924.
43 CAB4/9, CID Paper 420-B, Note by Lord Salisbury, 7 May 1923.
44 *Ibid.*
45 *Ibid.*
46 Ivone Kirkpatrick, *The Inner Circle*, p. 39. See also, on this point, Richardson, *The Evolution of British Disarmament Policy*, p. 20.
47 *Crowe Papers,* FO800/243, Memorandum by Eyre Crowe, 24 May 1923.
48 FO371/10568, W637/1334/98, Memorandum by Campbell, 25 January 1924.
49 *Ibid.*

50 FO371/10568, W3066/G, Note by E.W. Orde on draft CID minutes relating to Treaty of Mutual Assistance, 14 April 1924.
51 *Ibid.*
52 FO371/10568, W3508/1334/98, Letter from Hankey to Tyrrell, 29 April 1924, covering document dated 20 March 1924.
53 *Ibid.*
54 *Cecil Papers*, ADD51081, ff. 36–9, 23 June 1924.
55 British Delegate to the League of Nations under the first Labour Government.
56 *Cecil Papers*, ADD51081, ff. 36–9, Memorandum by Cecil to MacDonald, 23 June 1924.
57 *Ibid.*, ff. 1–3, MacDonald to Cecil, 22 February 1923.
58 *Ibid.*, f. 18, MacDonald to Cecil, 25 February 1924.
59 *Ibid.*
60 CAB23/48, Cabinet Conclusions, 35(24), 30 May 1924.
61 A. J. P. Taylor, *English History 1914–1945*, p. 291.
62 CAB23/46, Cabinet Conclusions, 5(24)4, 17 January 1924.
63 CAB23/47, Cabinet Conclusions, 14(24)6, 18 February 1924.
64 *MacDonald Papers*, PRO30/69/1753/1, diary entry 9 December 1923.
65 Unpublished biographical notes on William Leach, prepared by S. Bradfield, a freelance journalist, in the possession of Leach's grandson, Richard Leach.
66 *MacDonald Papers*, PRO30691753/1, diary entry 28 April 1924.
67 *Ibid.*, 1 July 1924.
68 MacDonald was, in fact, accused of being unduly influenced by both Crowe (*Cecil Papers*, ADD 51106, f 219) and Hankey, though Hankey for one was a great admirer of MacDonald's abilities (see, for example, *Hankey Papers*, HNKY 1/5, diary entry 11 October 1924).
69 *Ibid.*
70 *MacDonald Papers*, PRO/30/69/1753/1, diary entry 22 January 1924.
71 *Hankey Papers*, HNKY 1/5, diary entry 11 October 1924.
72 Unpublished biographical notes of William Leach.
73 *Ibid.*
74 *Hankey Papers*, HNKY /15, diary entry 11 October 1924.
75 *MacDonald Papers*, PRO30/69/1753/1, diary entry 3 February 1924.
76 *Ibid.*
77 *Ibid.*
78 *Ibid.*
79 *Ibid,* FO800/218, MacDonald to Poincaré, 26 January 1924.
80 *Ibid,* Poincaré to MacDonald, 28 January 1924.
81 *Ibid.*, FO800/219 Foreign Office, MacDonald to Mussolini, 1 April 1924.
82 *Hankey Papers*, HNKY 5/1, diary entry 11 October 1924.
83 *MacDonald Papers*, PRO30/69/1753/1, diary entry 9 October 1924.
84 CAB2/3, Minutes of 137th Meeting of the CID, 6 May 1921.
85 CAB2/3, Minutes of 140th Meeting of the CID, 10 June 1921.
86 *Ibid.*
87 CAB2/3, Minutes of 145th Meeting of the CID, 13 October 1921.
88 *Ibid.*, Minutes of 168th Meeting of the CID, 14 December 1922.
89 CAB23/47, Cabinet Conclusions, 18(24)1, 5 March 1924.
90 *Ibid.*, 21(24), 17 March 1924.
91 *Ibid.*
92 *Ibid.*
93 *Ibid.*
94 B. Ranft (ed.) *The Beatty Papers*, Vol. II, No. 208, 27 February 1924.

95 *Ibid.*, No. 203, 19 February 1923.
96 CAB27/236, R.S.(24), 1st Minutes, 27 February 1924.
97 *Ibid.*, 2nd Minutes, 3 March 1924.
98 *Ibid.*, 3rd Minutes, 5 March 1924.
99 Ranft, *op. cit.*, p.392.
100 CAB23/48, Cabinet Conclusions, 35(24), 30 May 1924.
101 Parmoor, *A Retrospect*, p. 251.
102 *Ibid.*, p. 254.
103 M.A. Hamilton, *Arthur Henderson*, p. 249.
104 CAB2/4, Minutes of 190th Meeting of the CID, 4 December 1924.
105 *Ibid.*
106 *Ibid.*
107 CAB16/56, Sub-Committee of the CID on the Protocol for Pacific Settlement of International Disputes, GP(24), 1st meeting, 18 December 1924.
108 CAB24/169, Cabinet Memoranda, CP538(24), telegram from the Secretary of State (Austen Chamberlain) to Prime Minister and Sir Eyre Crowe, 10 December 1924.
109 CAB23/49, Cabinet Conclusions, 7(25)20, 11 February 1925.
110 Parmoor, *op. cit.*, p. 236.
111 *Ibid.*, p. 238.
112 *Ibid.*, p. 239.
113 *Ibid.*, p. 254.
114 *Ibid.*
115 Hamilton, *op. cit.*, p. 247.
116 *Cecil Papers*, ADD51078, Chamberlain to Cecil, 19 June 1925.
117 *Ibid.*, 19 November 1924.
118 Ramsay MacDonald, *Protocol or Pact*.
119 *Ibid.*
120 Cecil, *op. cit.*, pp. 159–60.
121 See for example, Richardson, *The Evolution of British Disarmament Policy*, pp. 29–35.
122 CAB23/49, Cabinet Conclusions, 12(25)1, 2 March 1925.
123 Parmoor, *op. cit.*, p. 227.
124 *Cecil Papers*, ADD51174, Cecil to Gertrude Bell, 22 February 1924.

6 THE CONSERVATIVE GOVERNMENT, 1924–9

1 Taylor, *English History, 1914–1945*, p. 283.
2 CAB23/49, Cabinet Conclusions, 16(25)3, 18 March 1925.
3 CAB23/50, Cabinet Conclusions, 24(25)3, 6 April 1925. For Bridgeman's support see CAB23/47 2(25)6, 15 January 1925, and for Churchill's endorsement see CAB2/4, Minutes of 193rd Meeting of the CID, 5 January 1925.
4 CAB24/171, Cabinet Memoranda, CP38(25), Memorandum by Bridgeman, 27 January 1925.
5 *Ibid.*
6 *Ibid.*
7 CAB2/4, Minutes of 195th Meeting of the CID, 13 February 1925.
8 CAB24/168, Cabinet Memoranda, CP481(24), 9 November 1924, Foreign Office Memorandum C16913/3048/18.
9 CAB2/4, Minutes of 195th Meeting of the CID, 13 February 1925.
10 *Ibid.*

11 CAB24/172, Cabinet Memoranda, CP116(25), Memorandum by General Staff, 26 February 1925.

12 *Ibid.*

13 *Ibid.*

14 *Ibid.*

15 CAB24/172, Cabinet Memoranda, CP122(25), Memorandum by Chamberlain, 4 March 1925.

16 *Ibid.*, CP118(25), Memorandum by Churchill, 24 February 1925.

17 *Ibid.*, CP121(25), Memorandum by Hoare, 27 February 1925.

18 *Ibid.*, Cabinet Memoranda, CP105(25), Memorandum by Curzon, 19 February 1925.

19 *Ibid.*, Cabinet Memoranda, CP106(25), Memorandum by Harold Nicolson, 20 February 1925.

20 *Ibid.*

21 CAB23/49, Cabinet Conclusions, 12(25)1, 2 March 1925.

22 *Ibid.*

23 See Richardson, *The Evolution of British Disarmament Policy*, pp. 39–41.

24 *Austen Chamberlain Papers*, AC52/238, Chamberlain to Crowe, 8 March 1925.

25 CAB23/49, Cabinet Conclusions, 26(25)2, 20 March 1925.

26 CAB24/174, Cabinet Memoranda, CP329(25), Memorandum by Cecil, 6 July 1925.

27 *Austen Chamberlain Papers*, AC52/109b, Chamberlain to Briand, 24 July 1925.

28 CAB24/174, Cabinet Memoranda, CP357(25), Memorandum by Chamberlain, 16 July 1925.

29 *Ibid.*

30 *Ibid.*, CP365(25), Memorandum by Hankey, July 1925.

31 *Ibid.*

32 *Ibid.*, CP312(25), Memorandum by Chamberlain, 26 June 1925.

33 *Ibid.*, CP256(25), Translation of Memorandum by French Government, 18 May 1925, and CP317(25), Memorandum on the proposed Security Settlement on Germany's Western Frontier, 18 June 1925.

34 *Austen Chamberlain Papers*, AC52/32, Bruce to Amery, 5 May 1925.

35 *Ibid.*, AC52/82, Baldwin to Chamberlain, 27 September 1925.

36 Final Protocol of the Locarno Conference, 1925, *Parliamentary Papers*, Cmd 2525 of 1925.

37 Richardson, *The Evolution of British Disarmament Policy*, p. 42.

38 *DBFP*, Series IA, Vol. III, Sir W. Tyrrell (FO) to the Marquess of Crewe (Paris), No. 1758[C5473/5294/18], 28 June, 1927.

39 *Ibid.*, The Marquess of Crewe to Sir A. Chamberlain, No. 1497 [C5891/33/18], 8 July 1927.

40 CAB2/4, Minutes of 205th meeting of the CID, 17 November 1925, *Foreign Office Papers*, FO371/11066, W8909/9/98, Chamberlain to Cecil 18 September 1925; *ibid*. W9183/9/98, Minute by Chamberlain, 2 October 1925.

41 CAB2/4, Minutes of 205th Meeting of the CID, 17 November 1925.

42 *Ibid.*

43 CAB24/179, Cabinet Memoranda, CP165(26), Sub-Committee on the Reduction and Limitation of Armaments, 22 April 1926.

44 *Ibid.*

45 *Ibid.*

46 CAB24/189, Cabinet Memoranda, CP256(27), Memorandum by Alexander Cadogan, 26 October 1927.

47 CAB23/52, Cabinet Conclusions, 35(26)11, 2 June 1926.

48 *Ibid.*
49 CAB2/4, 213th Meeting of the CID, 1 June 1926.
50 *Ibid.*
51 *Ibid.*
52 *Ibid.*
53 See Richardson, *The Evolution of British Disarmament Policy.*
54 CAB24/189, Cabinet Memoranda, CP256(27), Memorandum by Alexander Cadogan, 26 October 1927.
55 *Ibid.*
56 See Richardson, *The Evolution of British Disarmament Policy*, p. 63.
57 CAB24/198, Cabinet Memoranda, CP301(28), Memorandum by Lord Eustace Percy, President of the Board of Education, 12 October 1928.
58 *Cecil Papers*, ADD51079, Cecil to Chamberlain, 10 April 1927.
59 *Austen Chamberlain Papers,* AC54/54, Bridgeman to Chamberlain, 3 July 1927.
60 See Richardson, *A History of Disarmament and Arms Control*, Chapter 9.
61 CAB4/16, CID Paper No. 808-B, Memorandum by the Naval Staff, 14 April 1927.
62 CAB23/54, Cabinet Conclusions, 34(27)3, 25 May 1927.
63 CAB4/16, CID Paper No. 815-B, Memorandum by the Secretary, 6 July 1927.
64 CAB23/54, Cabinet Conclusions, 37(27)10, 29 June 1927.
65 *Ibid.* Italics added.
66 *Ibid.*
67 Gibson to Kellogg, 30 June 1927, *FRUS*, 1927, Vol. 1 p. 65, cited in Richardson, *Evolution of British Disarmament Policy*, p. 124.
68 CAB23/54, Cabinet Conclusions, 38(27)5, 4 July 1927.
69 *Ibid.*
70 CAB27/350, Proceedings and Memoranda of Cabinet Committee on Further Limitation of Naval Armaments (LNA) (27) Series), 1st Meeting, 15 July 1927.
71 CAB21/321, Transcript of notes by Major Casey, Australian Liaison Officer, 12 June 1928.
72 *Ibid.*
73 *Cecil Papers*, ADD51104, Chamberlain to Geneva Delegation and Washington Embassy, 12 July 1927.
74 *Ibid.*
75 *Ibid.*, ADD51118, Minutes of the Third Conference of British Empire Delegations, 24 June 1927.
76 *Bridgeman Papers, Political Notes,* Vol. II, p. 143.
77 See B.J.C. McKercher, *The Second Baldwin Government and the United States, 1924–1929*, p. 66.
78 *Bridgeman Papers, loc. cit.*
79 *Baldwin Papers*, Vol. 130, Bridgeman to Baldwin, 9 July 1927.
80 *Ibid.*, 1 July 1927.
81 *Ibid.*, 11–12 July 1927.
82 *Bridgeman Papers, Political Notes*, Vol. II, p. 151.
83 *Cecil Papers*, ADD51118, Minutes of Third Conference of British Empire Delegation, 24 June 1927.
84 S. Roskill, *Naval Policy between the Wars,* p. 506.
85 *Ibid.*
86 CAB27/350, LNA (27), 1st Meeting, 14 July 1927.
87 *Ibid.* This question of 'equality of rights' rather than equality of numbers, was to arise again, with greater consequences, in relation to German demands during the 1932–4 World Disarmament Conference.

88 *Ibid.* 2nd Meeting, 18 July 1927.
89 *Ibid.*
90 Richardson, *Evolution of British Disarmament Policy*, p. 128.
91 CAB23/54, Cabinet Conclusions, 44(27)1, 26 July 1927.
92 *Ibid.*
93 CAB27/350, LNA (27), 3rd Meeting, 19 July 1927.
94 *Cecil Papers*, ADD51079, Cecil to Chamberlain, 9 April 1927.
95 CAB27/350, LNA(27)2, 23 July 1927.
96 CAB27/350, LNA(27), 3rd Meeting, 19 July 1927.
97 For more detailed analyses of the Coolidge Conference proposals and implications see Roskill, *Naval Policy between the Wars* and Richardson, *The Evolution of British Disarmament Policy*.
98 Cited in Roskill, *op. cit.*, p. 512.
99 *Cecil Papers*, ADD51104, First Lord to Cabinet and Admiralty, 28 July 1927.
100 *Ibid.*
101 *Ibid.*, Telegram from Cecil, 28 July 1927.
102 *Ibid.*, Chamberlain to First Lord, 29 July 1927.
103 Roskill, *op. cit.*, p. 513.
104 *Bridgeman Papers, Political Notes*, Vol. II, p. 157.
105 *Cecil Papers*, ADD51079, Cecil to Chamberlain, 17 July 1927.
106 *Ibid.*, 10 August 1927.
107 *Ibid.*, ADD51099, Cecil to Bridgeman, 22 November 1927.
108 *Ibid.*, ADD51104, Telegram to Embassies, 2 August 1927.
109 *Baldwin Papers*, Vol. 130, Howard to Baldwin, 3 August 1927.
110 *Ibid.*, Bridgeman to Baldwin, 21 June 1927.
111 McKercher, *op. cit.*, p. 59.
112 Roskill, *op. cit.*, p. 514.
113 McKercher, *op. cit.*, p. 71.
114 *Ibid.*, p. 69.
115 *Ibid.*, p. 70.
116 Richardson, *The Evolution of British Disarmament Policy*, p. 139.
117 Christopher Hall, *Britain, America and Arms Control, 1921–37*, p. 51.
118 S. de Madariaga, *Morning Without Noon*, p. 88.
119 *Cecil Papers*, ADD51104, Howard to Foreign Office, 18 July 1927.
120 CAB27/350, LNA(27), Minutes of 1st Meeting, 15 July 1927.
121 *Cecil Papers*, ADD51104, Telegram from First Lord to Cabinet, 1 August 1927.
122 CAB24/192, Cabinet Memoranda, CP189(28), Memorandum by the Chancellor of the Duchy of Lancaster, 16 June 1928.
123 *Ibid.*
124 *Ibid.*, CP190(28), Memorandum by the First Lord of the Admiralty, 11 May 1928.
125 *Ibid.*, CP16(28), Note of Conversation between Lord Cushendun and the French Ambassador, 24 January 1928.
126 *Ibid.*, CP184(28), Memorandum by the Secretary of State for Foreign Affairs, 9 June 1928.
127 *Ibid.*
128 CAB23/58, Cabinet Conclusions, 31(28)1, 6 June 1928.
129 *Austen Chamberlain Papers*, AC55/266, Chamberlain to Esmé Howard, 13 February 1928.
130 *Ibid.*, AC55/267, Howard to Chamberlain, 9 March 1928.
131 See Richardson, *Evolution of British Disarmament Policy*, p. 162.

132 CAB24/192, Cabinet Memoranda, CP190(28), Memorandum by the First Lord of the Admiralty, 11 May 1928.
133 *Ibid.*, CP191(28), Memorandum by the Chancellor of the Duchy of Lancaster, 16 May 1928.
134 *Ibid.*, CP192(28), covering Telegram No. 64, L.N. Chamberlain to Cushendun, 7 June 1928.
135 *Ibid.*, CP193(28) Memorandum by the Lord Privy Seal, 18 June 1928.
136 CAB24/197, Cabinet Memoranda, CP283(28), Mr Houghton to Lord Cushendun, 28 September 1928.
137 *Bridgeman Papers, Political Notes*, Vol. II, p. 161.
138 *MacDonald Papers*, PRO30/69/1753/1, diary entry 26 September 1928.
139 *Cecil Papers*, ADD51099, Cecil to H.A. St George Saunders, 28 November 1928.
140 CAB2/4, 213th Meeting of the Committee of Imperial Defence, 1 June 1926.

7 THE LABOUR GOVERNMENT, 1929–31

1 *MacDonald Papers*, PRO30/69/1753/1, diary entry 30 January 1929.
2 *Ibid.*, 4 June 1929.
3 Chamberlain to Ida and Hilda Chamberlain, 6 June 1929, cited in Carlton, *MacDonald versus Henderson*, p. 16.
4 Henry Winkler, *Arthur Henderson*, in G.A. Craig and F. Gilbert (eds) *The Diplomats 1919–39* (Vol. 2) p. 321.
5 *MacDonald Papers*, PRO30/69/1753/1, diary entry 9 June 1929.
6 *Ibid.*, 7 June 1929.
7 Parmoor, *A Retrospect*, p. 296. At this time Parmoor was 78 years old, and felt that he was too old to carry on effectively the work at Geneva. He felt that Henderson would continue to support the policies in which he himself believed.
8 CAB23/61, Cabinet Conclusions, 52(29)2, 11 December 1929.
9 Cecil, *A Great Experiment*, p. 200.
10 *Ibid.*, pp. 200–1.
11 B. Pimlot, *Hugh Dalton*, p. 184.
12 CAB16/63, CID Sub-Committee on Singapore (SP (25) Series), 1st Meeting, 16 January 1925.
13 CAB4/15, CID Paper No. 701-B, Memorandum by the Chiefs of Staff, 22 June 1926.
14 CAB16/63, CID Sub-Committee on Singapore (SP (25) Series), Paper No. 304-C (SD-3), October 1927.
15 CAB16/91, 1st Meeting of Singapore Sub-Committee of Chiefs of Staff, 7 February 1928.
16 CAB16/63, CID Sub-Committee on Singapore (SP (25) Series), Note by Hankey, 6 July 1928.
17 CAB21/335, CID Sub-Committee on the Development of the Singapore Naval Base, June 1930.
18 CAB2/4, 244th Meeting of the CID, 25 July 1929.
19 CAB4/18, CID Paper No. 955-B, 25 July 1929.
20 *Chamberlain Papers*, AC55/280, Howard to Chamberlain, 25 January 1929.
21 *Ibid.*
22 *Ibid.*, AC55/467, Chamberlain to Salisbury, 29 April 1929.
23 CAB24/28, Cabinet Memoranda, CP344(28), Memorandum by R.L. Craigie, Foreign Office, 14 November 1928.

24 *Ibid.*
25 FO371/13521, A4177/30/45, Memorandum by R. Lampson, Foreign Office, 12 June 1929.
26 *Ibid.*
27 FO371/13520, A4117/30/45, Memorandum by MacDonald, 17 June 1929.
28 *Ibid.*
29 FO371/13522, A5300/30/45, MacDonald to General Dawes, 6 August 1929.
30 FO371/13522, A5401/30/45, Extract from Army and Navy Journal, 13 August 1929.
31 FO371/13521, A5036/30/45, MacDonald to Dawes, 24 July 1929.
32 *Alexander Papers*, AVA 5/2/5, MacDonald to Alexander, 17 September 1929.
33 FO371/13552, A7087/3895/45, American newspaper editorials, 11 October 1929.
34 FO371/13552, A7034/3895/45, joint statement by Hoover and MacDonald, 10 October 1929.
35 FO371/13552, A7371/3895/45, Campbell to Henderson, 24 October 1929.
36 *The Times*, 16 January 1930, cited in Carlton, *op. cit.*, p. 121.
37 *Ibid.*, p. 122.
38 *MacDonald Papers*, PRO30/69/1753/1, diary entry 22 January 1930.
39 *Ibid.*, 27 January 1930.
40 CAB29/128, London Naval Conference 1930, Meetings of Members of British Delegation, 16 February 1930.
41 *Ibid.*
42 *Ibid.*
43 *Henderson Papers*, FO800/280, Tyrrell to Henderson, 28 March 1930.
44 *Ibid.*, Graham to Henderson, 21 March 1930.
45 *MacDonald Papers*, PRO30/69/1753/1, diary entry 17 March 1930.
46 *Ibid.*, 20 March 1930.
47 *Ibid.*, 25 March 1930.
48 FO371/14261, A2283/1/45, Foreign Office Minute, 18 March 1930.
49 *Ibid.*
50 *Ibid.*
51 *Henderson Papers*, FO800/280, Wigram to Henderson, 2 March 1931 and Tyrrell to Henderson, 3 March 1931.
52 CAB29/117, Draft Memorandum of the Cabinet Committee on the London Naval Conference.
53 *Ibid.*
54 *Ibid.*
55 See CAB29/128, Minutes of Meetings of Members of the British Delegation to the London Naval Conference, 28 February 1930.
56 *Ibid.*, 9 February 1930.
57 For a detailed account of these negotiations see C. Hall, *Britain, America and Arms Control, 1921–37*, pp. 95–6.
58 CAB29/128, Minutes of Meeting of Members of the British Delegation to the London Naval Conference, 28 February 1930.
59 CAB24/209, Cabinet Memoranda, CP12(30), Memorandum by the Treasury on Financial Aspects of the Naval Conference.
60 See, for example, Thomas Jones, *Whitehall Diary*, Vol. II, p. 231.
61 *MacDonald Papers*, PRO30/69/1753/1, diary entry 20 July 1930.
62 CAB24/209, Cabinet Memoranda CP12(30), Memorandum by the Treasury on Financial Aspects of the Naval Conference.

63 CAB27/392, Memoranda of the Cabinet Committee on the Optional Clause, Paper No. OC(29)8, 24 July 1929.
64 *Ibid.*, Paper No. OC(29)6, 22 July 1929.
65 See Carlton, *op. cit.*, pp. 73–4 .
66 FO371/14994, W9794/9586/98, Extract from the Verbatim Record of the Eleventh Ordinary Session of the Assembly of the League of Nations, 11 September 1930.
67 Henderson remained personally much more committed to French security, but was thwarted by MacDonald in the attempts he tried to make. When later asked what he felt to be the reason for the failure of the Disarmament Conference, he replied 'The failure to tackle security effectively before we started on disarmament' (Norman Angell, *After All*, p. 252). However, to meet French demands for security, as Lloyd George's Coalition had recognised, an *increase* in the British army might have been necessary. For Labour and the General Act see below p. 132.
68 Temperley's words to a German diplomat in Geneva, cited in Carlton, *op. cit.*, p. 94.
69 CAB4/20, CID Memoranda, Paper No. 1016-B, Report of the Sub-Committee on the Reduction and Limitation of Armaments, July 1930.
70 *Ibid.*
71 *Ibid.*
72 CAB2/4, Minutes of 250th Meeting of the CID, 29 September 1930.
73 *Ibid.*
74 *Ibid.*
75 CAB24/215, Cabinet Memoranda, CP339(30), Memorandum by the Air Staff, 14 October 1930.
76 *Ibid.*, CP340(30), Memorandum by the Air Staff, 14 October 1930.
77 CAB23/64, Cabinet Conclusions, 60(30)11, 15 October 1930.
78 *Ibid.*, 66(30)5, 6 November 1930.
79 *Ibid.*, 70(30)1, 26 November 1930.
80 Carlton, *op. cit.*, p. 96.
81 FO371/15703, W3526/47/98, Memorandum by Cadogan, February 1931. Interestingly, a marginal note beside these sentences suggested they be omitted.
82 Wheeler-Bennett, *The Pipe Dream of Peace*, p. 6.
83 There were, as will be shown in the following chapter, many other circumstances working against the success of real discussions, but as the Preparatory Commission's job was done, an arms agreement was now back in the hands of the Powers.
84 CAB4/20, CID Paper No. 1004-B, Memorandum setting out text of the General Act, 15 July 1930.
85 *Ibid.*, CID Paper No. 1013-B, Letter from Admiralty re: General Act for the Peaceful Settlement of International Disputes, 23 July 1930.
86 This was the same month in which the Credit Anstalt closed its doors; the financial crisis which was to undermine the Labour Government had begun.
87 CAB23/66, Cabinet Conclusions, 11(31)2, 4 February 1931.
88 *Ibid.*
89 CAB24/222, Cabinet Memoranda, CP195(31), Memorandum on The Disarmament Conference – The Three-Party Resolutions, 27 July 1931.
90 *Ibid.*
91 Hugh Dalton, *Call Back Yesterday – Memoirs 1887–1931*, p. 303.

8 THE NATIONAL GOVERNMENT, 1931–4

1 Now Viscount.
2 Created Viscount in 1932.
3 CAB23/69, Cabinet Conclusions, 48(31)6, 26 August 1931.
4 *Ibid.*, 86(31)6, 9 December 1931.
5 *Ibid.*, 90(31)4, 15 December 1931.
6 *Ibid.*
7 *Ibid.*
8 *Simon Papers*, FO800/285, Notes by Vansittart, 23 December 1931.
9 *Ibid.*, Memorandum by Selby, 6 December 1931.
10 *Ibid.*
11 *Ibid.*, Memorandum by Sargent, 9 December 1931.
12 *Ibid.*, Summary of Discussion on Disarmament Policy, 8 December 1931.
13 *Ibid.*
14 *Ibid.* The Foreign Office were ambivalent in their approach to the question of security; for example Allen Leeper (Head of the Western Department) maintains that Vansittart supported the idea of Britain making a 'bold initiative', whilst Leeper himself proposed a Continental Protocol of Mutual Assistance, but *without* British participation (*Leeper Papers*, LEEP 1/14, diary entries 25 December and 16 December 1931).
15 Marquess of Londonderry, *Wings of Destiny,* p. 56.
16 CAB23/70, Cabinet Conclusions, 3(32)3, 14 January 1932.
17 This contemporary abbreviation of the title of the conference will be used throughout the Chapter.
18 For recent analyses of the Conference see, for example, D. Richardson 'The Geneva Disarmament Conference 1932–34', in D. Richardson and G. Stone (eds) *Decisions and Diplomacy*, Chapter 3, Z. Steiner, 'The League of Nations and the Quest for Security', and M. Vaïsse, 'Security and Disarmament: Problems in the Development of the Disarmament Debates 1919–1934', both in R. Ahmann, A. M. Birke and M. Howard (eds) *The Quest for Stability: Problems of West European Security 1918–1957*. For the British position see D. Richardson and C.J. Kitching, 'Britain and the World Disarmament Conference', in P. Catterall and C.J. Morris (eds) *Britain and the Threat to Stability in Europe, 1918–45*.
19 F.S. Northedge, *The League of Nations: Its Life and Times 1920–1946*, p. 114.
20 CAB27/505, DC(M)(32), 1st Meeting of Ministerial Committee, 21 March 1932.
21 *Ibid.*
22 *Ibid.*
23 *Ibid.*
24 For a full analysis of the French position, see M. Vaïsse, *Securité d'abord.*
25 CAB27/505, DC(M)(32), 1st Meeting of Ministerial Committee, 21 March 1932.
26 On these points see Richardson 'The Geneva Disarmament Conference 1932–34', *loc. cit.*
27 Conversation among members of the American, British and German delegations, 26 April 1932, *FRUS, 1932*, Vol. 1, pp. 108–12. See also Temperley, *The Whispering Gallery of Eruope*, p. 203.
28 Gibson to Acting Secretary of State, 29 April 1932, *FRUS*, 1932, Vol. 1, pp. 112–14. Gibson was the principal American delegate to the Disarmament Conference.

29 E.W. Bennett, in *German Rearmament and the West, 1932–33*, maintains that Wheeler-Bennett's optimism stems from the fact that he obtained his information from German sources. Bennett's study includes a detailed analysis of the prospects of success of the Bessinge conversations from an American viewpoint.

30 Temperley, *op. cit.*, p. 204, Wheeler-Bennett, *The Pipe Dream of Peace*, p. 34.

31 Gibson to Stimson, 27 March 1932, *FRUS*, 1932, Vol. 1, pp. 54–9.

32 Bennett's interpretation of MacDonald's failure to pursue the matter is that, in fact, MacDonald's only reason for undertaking four-power talks was to 'guard against a Franco-German understanding in support of the French plan', a plan which, as MacDonald told one of Tardieu's associates, Britain considered unworkable. See, Bennett, *op. cit.*, pp. 150–1.

33 *MacDonald Papers*, PRO30/69/1753/1, diary entry 2 June 1934.

34 *Simon Papers*, FO800/286, MacDonald to Simon, 31 May 1932.

35 *Ibid.*, Hankey to MacDonald, 5 May 1932.

36 *Ibid.*, Londonderry to Simon, 12 May 1932.

37 CAB27/505, DC(M)(32), 2nd Meeting of Ministerial Committee, 5 April 1932.

38 *Simon Papers*, FO800/286, Londonderry to Simon, 12 May 1932.

39 *Ibid.*

40 *Leeper Papers*, LEEP 1/15, diary entry 13 April 1932.

41 CAB23/71, Cabinet Conclusions, 21(32)3, 2 May 1932.

42 *Ibid.*

43 *Ibid.*, 27(32)5, 11 May 1932.

44 As Allen Leeper pointed out, Britain had only five aeroplanes above this weight, so, in his words, 'it is all nothing' (*Leeper Papers*, LEEP 1/15, diary entry 6 May 1932). Leeper later noted that '[t]he King is furious over the suggested abolition of "his" air force. He is much worked on by Londonderry' (*Ibid.*, 8 June 1932).

45 CAB23/71, Cabinet Conclusions, 27(32)5, 11 May 1932.

46 *DBFP*, Ser. 2, Vol. III, Appendix V, p. 606.

47 *Ibid.*

48 *Ibid* .

49 Temperley, *op. cit.*, p. 211.

50 *Simon Papers*, FO800/287, Simon to Cabinet, 23 June 1932.

51 CAB23/71, Cabinet Conclusions, 38(32)2, 24 June 1932.

52 *Ibid.*

53 *Simon Papers*, FO800/287, Simon to Cabinet, 23 June 1932.

54 CAB23/71, Cabinet Conclusions, 38(32)2, 24 June 1932.

55 *Ibid.*

56 *Ibid.*

57 *Ibid.*, 39(32)1, 28 June 1932.

58 See R.C. Richardson, *The Problem of Disarmament in British Diplomacy, 1932–1934*, p. 63. To stimulate French opposition to the Hoover Plan, Britain entered into negotiations for a consultative pact with France which led to the Anglo-French Declaration of 13 July 1932. Behind the façade of the agreement to consult was a 'secret' interpretation, which attracted the French, by which MacDonald promised to consult with France prior to answering any German requests with regard to her 'liberation' from the Treaty of Versailles.

59 CAB23/71, Cabinet Conclusions, 39(32)1, 28 June 1932.

60 CAB23/72, Cabinet Conclusions, 41(32)4, 30 June 1932.

61 CAB23/71, Cabinet Conclusions, 39(32)1, 28 June 1932.

62 CAB23/72, Cabinet Conclusions, 57(32)1, 31 October 1932.

63 Paul-Boncour's plan relied heavily on the security aspect, advocating three concentric circles of security – or 'the three circles of hell' as Paul-Boncour himself referred to them (*Leeper Papers*, LEEP 4/1, Lecture on League of Nations given to Imperial Services College, 1932). The innermost circle contained the continental powers of Europe, the second comprised all the members of the League of Nations, and the outer one took in all the powers of the world. In the event of breach of the Kellogg Pact, the powers in the outermost circle would agree to prohibit economic or financial relations with the aggressor and refuse to accept any *de facto* situation brought about by such aggression. Those in the second circle would re-affirm their obligations under Article 16, and those in the innermost circle – those nearest to the seat of aggression – would participate in a mutual assistance pact, covering both political and military obligations. On the armaments side, there would be standardisation of national armies, and tanks and heavy mobile artillery would be abolished. For a more detailed analysis of the Paul-Boncour Plan see Richardson, *The Problem of Disarmament in British Diplomacy, 1932–1934*, pp. 93–5.

64 P.J. Noel-Baker, *The First World Disarmament Conference*, p. 105.

65 S. de Madariaga, *Morning Without Noon*, p. 253.

66 Temperley, *op. cit.*, p. 214.

67 *Ibid.*, p. 215.

68 Noel-Baker, *First World Disarmament Conference*, p. 110.

69 CAB23/72, Cabinet Conclusions, 49(32)1, 30 September 1932. Should the policy of securing the return of Germany to the Conference prove successful, Britain was still, in Allen Leeper's words, 'groping for a disarmament policy' – with Hankey advocating delay (*Leeper Papers*, LEEP 1/15, diary entry 5 September 1932).

70 *Ibid.*

71 *Ibid.*, 53(32)1, 19 October 1932.

72 *Ibid.*, 56(32)3, 31 October 1932.

73 *Ibid.*

74 *Ibid.*

75 *Ibid.*

76 The search for a solution went on in the Foreign Office in tandem with the Cabinet's search for a formula to bring Germany back into negotiations. See, for example, the *Cadogan, Avon* and *Leeper Papers* for discussions on Foreign Office efforts to produce a policy in the event of the Government's success in securing Germany's return.

77 *DBFP*, Ser. II, Vol. IV, No. 170.

78 *Ibid.*, No. 220.

79 CAB23/75, Cabinet Conclusions, 1(33)3, 19 January 1933.

80 *Ibid.*, 13(33)1, 1 March 1933.

81 *Cadogan Papers*, ACAD/1/1, diary entry 16 January 1933.

82 *Ibid.*, 25 January 1933.

83 *Ibid.*, 21 May 1933.

84 *Ibid.*, 30 January 1933.

85 It was not only his juniors who felt that way; as noted earlier, Cecil was sceptical about Simon's abilities. Simon's team at the Foreign Office were equally pessimistic about their chief's commitment to the conference: Allen Leeper commented that Simon gave him the impression that 'he doesn't want to do anything at Geneva but damp it down and rush off to be fourth man at [the Reparations Conference at] Lausanne' (*Leeper Papers*, LEEP 1/15, diary entry 10 June 1932). Simon apparently put much faith in the ability of the Lausanne

Conference to improve international relations to an extent which would make the Geneva Disarmament Conference unnecessary and irrelevant. (See, for example, *Simon Papers*, FO800/278, Memorandum by Simon, 10 June 1932.)

86 *Cadogan Papers*, ACAD/1/1, diary entry 30 January 1933.

87 *Ibid.*

88 *Ibid.*, 20 February 1933.

89 *Ibid.*, 21 February 1933.

90 *Avon Papers*, AP20/1/13, diary entry 1 March 1933.

91 CAB27/505, DC(M)(32), 12th Meeting, 2 March 1933. There is no actual record of Eden's memorandum in DC(M)(32), although it was clearly presented to the Committee members.

92 *Ibid.*

93 *Ibid.*, 14th Meeting, 5 March 1933.

94 *Ibid.*

95 *Ibid.*, 15th Meeting, 8 March 1933.

96 *Ibid.* Cunliffe-Lister maintained that while it would be 'quite indefensible to bomb Indians', if it came to a question of protecting the inviolability of the frontiers of India, then he thought there would be no difficulty. It was pointed out by Sir John Salmond that the leader of the Moslems in the Indian Assembly had already raised this question and had added that 'inevitably the persons who would be bombed by us would be the Moslems'!

97 *Ibid.* The Committee's conclusions on air reductions were that other powers should immediately reduce their forces to the level of those of the United Kingdom, a cut of one third in world air forces, and a limitation of the unladen weight of military aircraft. Londonderry registered his dissent from the above conclusions of the Committee.

98 CAB23/72, Cabinet Conclusions, 59(32)1, 8 November 1932.

99 *Ibid.*

100 CAB23/75, Cabinet Conclusions, 17(33)2, 13 March 1933.

101 *Ibid.*

102 CAB27/509, DC(M)(32)50.

103 CAB24/242, Cabinet Memoranda, CP159(33) Memorandum by Eden on His Majesty's Government and the Disarmament Conference, 15 June 1933.

104 CAB27/509, DC(M)(32)15.

105 CAB27/505, DC(M)(32), 17th Meeting, 19 June 1933.

106 *Avon Papers*, AP33/6, Cadogan to Eden, 6 March 1933.

107 *Ibid.*

108 *Ibid.*, AP20/1/13, diary entry 14 March 1933.

109 *Cadogan Papers*, ACAD1/1, diary entry 15 March 1933.

110 *Ibid.*, 13 March 1933.

111 For the text of the British Draft Convention, see Wheeler-Bennett, *The Disarmament Deadlock*, pp. 267–92. For a commentary see Richardson, *The Problem of Disarmament in British Diplomacy, 1932–1934*, pp. 122–3.

112 Temperley, *op. cit.*, p. 243.

113 Madariaga, *Morning Without Noon*, p. 275.

114 *Cadogan Papers*, ACAD1/1, diary entry 11 March 1933.

115 Quoted in Marquand, *Ramsay MacDonald*, p. 754. On his return from Rome, Simon again highlighted the real reason for presenting the MacDonald Plan to the Conference, informing the Cabinet that 'the Prime Minister had made a tremendous impression and had raised British prestige to the highest point. He was satisfied, therefore, that whatever was the ultimate fate of the Draft

Convention, the visit could not result in our discomfiture' (CAB23/75, Cabinet Conclusions, 20(33)10, 22 March 1933).

116 Wheeler-Bennett, *op. cit.*, p. 104. This was in spite of MacDonald's declaration in Cabinet in November 1932 that if he went to Geneva he did not wish merely to make a speech and then to return. 'To do any good it was necessary to follow up any statement that was made' (Cabinet Conclusions, CAB 23/72, 58(32)3, 2 November 1932).

117 CAB 23/75 Cabinet Conclusions, 33(33)4, 5 May 1933.

118 CAB 27/505, DC(M)(32), telegram to Eden, 12 May 1933.

119 For a full analysis of this point, see Richardson and Kitching, *op. cit.*, pp. 44–52.

120 CAB23/76, Cabinet Conclusions, 39(33)1, 9 June 1933.

121 CAB27/505, DC(M)(32), 17th meeting, 19 June 1933.

122 *Ibid.*, 18th Meeting, 25 July 1933.

123 *Ibid.*

124 *Documents Diplomatiques Français 1932–1938*, Ser. 1, Vol. 3, document no. 229.

125 See Richardson, *The Problem of Disarmament in British Diplomacy*, pp. 139–40.

126 CAB23/77, Cabinet Conclusions, 51(33)2, 20 September 1933.

127 *Ibid.*

128 *Ibid.*, 52(33)1, 9 October 1933.

129 CAB24/243, Cabinet Memoranda, CP228(33), Memorandum by Simon, 3 October 1933.

130 *Ibid.*

131 See, for example, *DBFP*, Ser. II, Vol. V, Nos 428 and 432.

132 CAB23/77, Cabinet Conclusions, 52(33)1, 9 October 1933.

133 CAB24/243, Cabinet Memoranda, CP237(33), 11 October 1933. The two major principles were '(1) that there must be preliminary period, (2) during that period there should be no rearmament of Germany'.

134 On this point see Richardson and Kitching, *op. cit.*, p. 51.

135 *DBFP*, Ser. II, Vol. V, Nos 485 and 489.

136 CAB24/245, Cabinet Memoranda, CP299(33) Annex I, 12 December 1933.

137 *Ibid.*

138 The Cabinet debated for a long time whether to take Hitler up on this point. If it went uncontested they feared he would use it for propaganda purposes. It was eventually decided that they should not be drawn into a polemic discussion.

139 The East Fulham by-election on 26 October had seen a Labour candidate, campaigning on a Peace platform, turn a minority of 14,000 votes into a majority of 5,000.

140 CAB23/77, Cabinet Conclusions, 69(33)3, 13 December 1933.

141 CAB24/245, Cabinet Memoranda, CP294(33), 8 December 1933.

142 *Ibid.*

143 *Ibid.*

144 *Ibid.*

145 *Ibid.*

146 See Richardson, *The Problem of Disarmament in British Diplomacy, 1932–1934*, pp. 189–90.

147 CAB23/78, Cabinet Conclusions, 9(34)2, 14 March 1934.

148 *Ibid.*, italics added.

149 *Ibid.*, 10(34)3, 19 March 1934.

150 *Ibid.*, 12(34)1, 22 March 1934.

151 *Ibid.*

152 This conclusions mirrors that arrived at by the Lloyd George Coalition in relation to Poincaré's demands for guarantees which would involve an increase in Britain's armed forces on a basis suitable to France rather than to Britain.

153 CAB23/78, Cabinet Conclusions, 12(34)1, 22 March 1934.

154 This is one of the few occasions on which the question of public opinion entered into the Cabinet's deliberations. Having convinced the general public, after the Great War, that only disarmament could prevent another such horror, little further attention was given to this area, public support being very much an underlying, but largely unspoken, consideration. It was not until the East Fulham by-election and the League of Nations Union Peace Ballot in the autumn of 1934 that the Cabinet was forced to take the strength of public opinion into much greater consideration.

155 CAB23/78, Cabinet Conclusions, 12(34)1, 22 March 1934.

156 *Ibid.*

157 CAB27/506, DC(M)(32), Vol. II, 34th Meeting, 27 March 1934.

158 *Ibid.*, 36th Meeting, 9 April 1934.

159 See Richardson, *The Problem of Disarmament in British Diplomacy, 1932–1934*, p. 197.

160 CAB23/79, Cabinet Conclusions, 20(34)2, 9 May 1934.

161 Avon, *The Eden Memoirs: Facing the Dictators*, p. 93.

162 See, for example, CAB23/77, Cabinet Conclusions, 51(33)2, 20 September 1933.

163 CAB23/76, Cabinet Conclusions, 39(33)1, 9 June 1933.

164 *Documents on German Foreign Policy, 1918–1945*, Ser. C, Vol. I, No. 94 For further elaboration on this point, see Richardson, 'The Geneva Disarmament Conference', *loc. cit.*.

165 *Avon Papers*, AP20/1/14, diary entry 30 May 1934.

166 *MacDonald Papers*, PRO69/1753/1, diary entry 2 November 1934.

167 *Cecil Papers*, ADD51081, MacDonald to Cecil, 5 March 1934.

9 CONCLUSION

1 See, for example, Sir Alexander Cadogan's assessment of the disarmament situation, Cabinet Memoranda, CP256(27) 27 October 1927, CAB24/189.

2 See, for example, Temperley, *The Whispering Gallery of Europe*, Chapter 13.

BIBLIOGRAPHY

British government archives – Public Record Office

Admiralty Papers (ADM1 and ADM181)
Arms Traffic Convention Committee (CAB16/59 and CAB27/274)
Cabinet Conclusions (CAB23)
Cabinet Papers (CAB24)
Chiefs of Staff Committee (CAB53)
Committee of Imperial Defence Memoranda (CAB2 and CAB29)
Committee of Imperial Defence Minutes (CAB4)
Committee of Imperial Defence Sub-Committees on the Singapore Naval Base (CAB16/63, CAB16/91, CAB21/335 and CAB27/236)
Compulsory Arbitration Committee (CAB27/330)
Disarmament Policy Committee (CAB27/361–3)
Foreign Office Papers (FO371)
Foreign Policy – Security Committee (CAB27/275)
Further Limitation of Naval Armaments Committee (CAB27/350)
Geneva Protocol Committee (CAB16/56)
Imperial Meetings (CAB32/2)
Interdepartmental Sub-Committee on Preparation for the Disarmament Conference (CAB16/104)
League of Nations Reports (PRO30/52)
London Naval Conference (CAB29/117 and CAB29/128)
Ministerial Committee DC(M)(32) (CAB27/505–7)
Naval Programme Committee (CAB27/273 and CAB27/355)
Optional Clause Committee (CAB27/392)
Reduction and Limitation of Armaments Committee (CAB16/61, CAB 16/71–4 and CAB16/98–100)
Reduction and Limitation of Armaments Policy Committee D.PC. (31) Committee (CAB27/448)
Reduction of Armaments – Protocol for Pacific Settlement of International Disputes (CAB16/56)
Registered Files (CAB21)
Three Party Committee (CAB16/102)
Washington Naval Conference (CAB30)

Various private papers (FO800 and CAB63) (See below)

207

Unpublished private papers

Earl Alexander of Hillsborough, Churchill Archive Centre, Cambridge
Earl of Avon, Birmingham University Library
Stanley Baldwin, Cambridge University Library
Earl of Balfour, British Museum and Public Record Office
William Bridgeman, Salop County Record Office
Sir Alexander Cadogan, Churchill Archive Centre, Cambridge
Viscount Cecil of Chelwood, British Museum
Sir Austen Chamberlain, Birmingham University Library
Neville Chamberlain, Birmingham University Library
Sir Eyre Crowe, Public Record Office
Baron Cushendun, Public Record Office
Sir Maurice Hankey, Churchill Archive Centre, Cambridge, and Public Record
    Office
Arthur Henderson, Public Record Office and Brotherton Library, Leeds University
Sir Samuel Hoare, Cambridge University Library
William Leach, Private possession of Richard Leach
Allen Leeper, Churchill Archive Centre, Cambridge
David Lloyd George, House of Lords Record Office
James Ramsay MacDonald, Public Record Office
Marquess of Reading, Brotherton Library, Leeds University
Sir John Simon, Brotherton Library, Leeds University
Lord Robert Vansittart, Churchill Archive Centre, Cambridge

Published documents and official sources

France

Ministère des Affaires Étrangères, *Documents Diplomatiques Français 1932–1939*,
    Series 1 (1932–5), Imprimerie Nationale, Paris, 1964 *et seq.* (Vols 1–4)

Germany

US Department of State, *Documents on German Foreign Policy, 1918–1945*, Series C
    (1933–7), Government Printing Office, Washington, 1957. *et seq.*

Great Britain

(eds), HMSO, 1947 *et seq.* Series IA and II, W.N. Medlicott, D. Dakin and M.E.
    Lambert (eds), London, HMSO, 1966 *et seq.*
House of Commons, *Parliamentary Debates*, Fifth Series, London, HMSO, 1909 *et seq.*
Parliamentary Papers

United States of America

Department of State, *Papers relating to the Foreign Relations of the United States, Diplomatic Papers*, Government Printing Office, 1957 *et seq.*

Memoirs, diaries and autobiographies

Amery, L.C.M.S. *The Forward View*, Bles, London, 1935
—— *The Leo Amery Diaries Vol. 1: 1896–1929*, J. Barnes and D. Nicholson (eds), Hutchinson, London, 1980
—— *The Empire at Bay — The Leo Amery Diaries 1929–1945*, J. Barnes and D. Nicholson (eds), Hutchinson, London, 1988.
—— *My Political Life*, Hutchinson, London, 1953–5 (3 vols)
Angell, Sir N. *After All*, Hamish Hamilton, London, 1951
Avon, Earl of *The Eden Memoirs: Facing the Dictators*, Cassell, London, 1962
Beatty, Admiral of the Fleet, Earl *The Beatty Papers: Selections from the Private and Official Correspondence and Papers of Admiral of the Fleet Earl Beatty, Volume II, 1916–1927*, Ranft, B. (ed.), Scolar Press, for the Navy Records Society, 1993
Cadogan, Sir A. *The Diaries of Sir Alexander Cadogan 1938–1945*, D. Dilks (ed.), Cassell, London, 1971
Cecil of Chelwood, Viscount *All the Way*, Hodder and Stoughton, London, 1949
—— *A Great Experiment*, Cape, London, 1941
—— *The Way of Peace*, Philip Allan, London, 1928
Chamberlain, Sir A. *Down the Years*, Cassell, London, 1935
—— *Peace in our Time*, Philip Allan, London, 1928
Churchill, W.S. *The Gathering Storm*, Cassell, London, 1964
Clemenceau, G. *Grandeur and Misery of Victory*, Harrap, London, 1930
Cooper, A.D. *Old Men Forget*, Hart-Davis, London, 1953
Croft, Lord H.P. *My Life of Strife*, Hutchinson, London, 1948
d'Abernon, Viscount *An Ambassador of Peace*, Hodder and Stoughton, London, 1929–30 (3 vols)
Dalton, E.H.J.N. *Call Back Yesterday – Memoirs 1887–1931*, Muller, London, 1953
—— *The Fateful Years, 1931–45*, London, 1957
—— *The Political Diaries of Hugh Dalton, 1918–40, 1945–60*, B. Pimlott (ed.), Cape, London, 1986
Davidson, J.C.C. *Memoirs of a Conservative*, R. R. James (ed.), Weidenfeld and Nicolson, London, 1969
Esher, Viscount *Journals and Letters of Reginald, Viscount Esher*, Ivor Nicholson and Watson, London, 1938
François-Poncet, A. *The Fateful Years: Memoirs of a French Ambassador in Berlin, 1931–1938*, Gollancz, London, 1949
Grey of Fallodon, Viscount *Twenty-Five Years*, Hodder and Stoughton, London, 1928 (3 vols)
Hamilton, M.A. *Remembering my Good Friends*, Cape, London, 1944
Hankey, M.P.A.H. *Diplomacy by Conference*, Ernest Benn, London, 1946
Hardinge, Lord *Old Diplomacy: The Reminiscences of Lord Hardinge of Penshurst*, John Murray, London, 1947

Harris, H.W. *Life So Far*, Cape, London, 1954

Headlam-Morley, Sir J. *A Memoir of the Paris Peace Conference 1919*, Methuen, London, 1972

Henderson, A. *Consolidating World Peace*, Clarendon Press, Oxford, 1931

Howard, Sir E.W. *Theatre of Life*, Hodder and Stoughton, London, 1936

Jones, T. *A Diary with Letters, 1931–1950*, Oxford University Press, London, 1954

—— *Whitehall Diary*, R.K. Middlemas (ed.), Oxford University Press, London, 1969 (3 vols)

Kirkpatrick, I. *The Inner Circle*, Macmillan, London, 1959

Liddell Hart, B.H. *Deterrent or Defence*, Stevens, London, 1960

—— *Memoirs*, Cassell, London, 1965 (2 vols)

Lloyd George, D. *The Truth about the Peace Treaties*, Gollancz, London, 1938 (2 vols)

—— *War Memoirs*, Ivor Nicholson and Watson, London, 1934

Londonderry, Marquess of *Wings of Destiny*, Macmillan, London, 1943

MacDonald, J.R. *Protocol or Pact*, Labour Party, London, 1925

Madariaga, S. de *Morning without Noon: Memoirs*, Saxon House, Farnborough, 1974

Nicolson, H. *Diaries and Letters, 1930–39*, Collins, London, 1969

Parmoor, Baron *A Retrospect*, Heinemann, London, 1936

Riddell, Lord *Lord Riddell's Intimate Diary of the Peace Conference and After, 1918–1923*, Gollancz, London, 1933

The Riddell Diaries 1908–1932, J.M. McEwan (ed.), 1986

Samuel, Viscount *Memoirs*, Cresset, London, 1945

Simon, Viscount *Retrospect*, Hutchinson, London, 1952

Temperley, A.C. *The Whispering Gallery of Europe*, Collins, London, 1938

Templewood, Viscount *Empire of the Air*, Collins, London, 1957

—— *Nine Troubled Years*, Collins, London, 1954

Thomas, J.H. *My Story*, Hutchinson, London, 1937

Vansittart, Sir R.G. *Lessons of My Life*, Hutchinson, London, 1943

—— *The Mist Procession*, Hutchinson, London, 1958

—— *Bones of Contention*, Hutchinson, London, no date

Wheeler-Bennett, J. W. *The Disarmament Deadlock*, George Routledge, London, 1934.

Biographies

Barros, J. *Office Without Power: Secretary-General Sir Eric Drummond 1919–1933*, Clarendon Press, Oxford, 1979

Birkenhead, Earl of *Halifax: The Life of Lord Halifax*, Hamish Hamilton, London, 1965

Blaxland, G. *J. H. Thomas: A Life for Unity*, Frederick Muller, London, 1964

Bowle, J. *Viscount Samuel*, Gollancz, London, 1957

Boyle, A. *Montagu Norman: A Biography*, Cassell, London, 1967

Campbell-Johnson, A. *Sir Anthony Eden*, Robert Hale, London, 1955

Colvin, I.G. *Vansittart in Office: an Historical Survey of the Origins of the Second World War Based on the Papers of Sir Robert Vansittart*, Gollancz, London, 1965

Cross, C. *Philip Snowden*, Barrie & Rockliff, London, 1966

Dutton, D. *Austen Chamberlain: Gentleman in Politics*, Ross Anderson Publications, Bolton, 1985

—— *Simon: A Political Biography of Sir John Simon*, Aurum Press, London, 1992

Feiling, Sir K.G. *The Life of Neville Chamberlain*, Macmillan, London, 1947

Gilbert, M. *Churchill: A Life*, BCA/Heinemann, London, 1992

—— *Winston S. Churchill* (Vol. 5/companion Vol. 5:1), Heinemann, London, 1976–9

Hamilton, M.A. *Arthur Henderson*, Heinemann, London, 1938

—— *Ramsay MacDonald*, Cape, London, 1929

Hyde, H.M. *Lord Reading: The Life of Rufus Isaacs, First Marquess of Reading*, Heinemann, London, 1967

James, R.R. *Anthony Eden*, Macmillan, London, 1987

—— *Churchill – A Study in Failure*, Weidenfeld, London, 1970

Jones, T. *Lloyd George*, Oxford University Press, London, 1951

Jenkins, E.A. *From Foundry to Foreign Office*, Grayson and Grayson, London, 1933

Jenkins, R. *Baldwin*, Collins, London, 1988

Mackay, R.F. *Balfour: Intellectual Statesman*, Oxford University Press, Oxford, 1985

Marquand, D. *Ramsay MacDonald*, Cape, London, 1977

Middlemas, R.K. and Barnes, A.J.L. *Baldwin: A Biography*, Weidenfeld and Nicolson, London, 1969

Nicholson, Sir H. *Curzon: The Last Phase*, Constable, London, 1934

Petrie, C. *The Life and Letters of the Right Hon. Sir Austen Chamberlain*, Cassell & Company, London, 1939–40 (2 vols)

Pimlott, B. *Hugh Dalton*, Macmillan, London, 1985

Rose, N. *Vansittart: Study of a Diplomat*, Heinemann, London, 1978

Roskill, S.W. *Admiral of the Fleet Earl Beatty*, Collins, London, 1980

—— *Hankey: Man of Secrets*, Collins, London, 1970–4 (3 vols)

Smuts, J.C. *Jan Christian Smuts*, Cassell, London, 1952

Taylor, A.J.P. (ed.) *Lloyd George: A Diary by Frances Stevenson*, Hutchinson, London, 1971

Wrench, J.E. *Geoffrey Dawson and our Times*, Hutchinson, London, 1955

Young, G.M. *Stanley Baldwin*, Hart-Davis, London, 1952

Young, K. *Arthur James Balfour*, G. Bell & Sons, London, 1963

Monographs and other special studies

Ahmann, R., Birke, A.M. and Howard, M. (eds) *The Quest for Stability: Problems of West European Security 1918–1957*, The German Historical Institute London, Oxford University Press, 1993

Angell, N. *The Great Illusion*, Heinemann, London, 1911

Barnett, C. *The Collapse of British Power*, Alan Sutton, Gloucester, 1987

Bennett, E.W. *German Rearmament and the West, 1932–1933*, Princeton University Press, Princeton, 1979

Bond, B. *British Military Policy between the Two World Wars*, Oxford University Press, London, 1980

Bull, H. *The Control of the Arms Race*, Weidenfeld and Nicolson, London, 1961

Carlton, D. *MacDonald versus Henderson: The Foreign Policy of the Second Labour Government*, Macmillan, London, 1970

Carr, E.H. *The Twenty Years' Crisis 1919–1939*, Macmillan, New York, 1966

Catterall, P. and Morris, C.J. (eds) *Britain and the Threat to Stability in Europe, 1918–45*, Leicester University Press, London, 1993

Chaput, R.A. *Disarmament in British Foreign Policy*, Allen and Unwin, London, 1935

Claude, Inis L., Jr *Swords into Plowshares*, University of London Press, London, 1965

Coates, W.P. *U.S.S.R. and Disarmament*, Anglo-Russian Parliamentary Committee, London, 1928

Craig, G.A. and Gilbert, F. *The Diplomats 1919–1939: Volume 2*, Atheneum, 1977

Dilks, D. *Retreat from Power – Studies in Britain's Foreign Policy of the Twentieth Century, Vol. 1*, Macmillan, London, 1981

Dockrill, M.L. and Goold, J.D. *Peace without Promise: Britain and the Peace Conferences, 1919–23*, Batsford Academic and Educational Ltd, London, 1981

Gathorne-Hardy, G.M. *A Short History of International Affairs 1920 to 1934*, Oxford University Press, London, 1934

Gilbert, M. *The Roots of Appeasement*, Weidenfeld and Nicolson, London, 1966

Goldstein, E. and Maurer, J. H. (eds) *The Washington Conference, 1921–22: Naval Rivalry, East Asian Stability and the Road to Pearl Harbour*, Frank Cass, Ilford, 1994

Hall, C. *Britain, America and Arms Control, 1921–37*, Macmillan, London, 1987

Henig, R.B. *The League of Nations*, Oliver and Boyd, Edinburgh, 1973

—— *The Origins of the Second World War*, Methuen and Co., London, 1985

Higham, R. *Armed Forces in Peacetime: Britain, 1918–1940, a Case Study*, Foulis, London, 1962

Howard, M.E. *The Continental Commitment*, Temple Smith, London, 1972

Jacobson, J. *Locarno Diplomacy*, Princeton University Press, Princeton, 1972

Jaffe, L.S. *The Decision to Disarm Germany*, Allen and Unwin, London, 1985

Jordan, W.M. *Great Britain, France and the German Problem, 1918–1939*, Oxford University Press, London, 1943

Kennedy, P.M. *The Realities Behind Diplomacy*, Allen and Unwin, London, 1981

—— *Strategy and Diplomacy*, Allen and Unwin, London, 1983

Kent, B. *The Spoils of War: The Politics, Economics and Diplomacy of Reparations, 1918–1932*, Clarendon Press, Oxford, 1991

Kitchen, M. *Europe between The Wars: A Political History*, Longman, London, 1988

Kissinger, H. *Diplomacy*, Simon and Schuster, London, 1995

Knight-Patteson, W.M. *Germany from Defeat to Conquest*, Allen and Unwin, London, 1945

Kyba, P. *Covenants without the Sword: Public Opinion and British Defence Policy 1931–1935*, Wilfrid Laurier University Press, Ontario, Canada, 1983

Lee, M. and Michalka, W. *German Foreign Policy 1917–1933: Continuity or Break?*, Berg, Leamington Spa, 1987

Lentin, A. *Guilt at Versailles: Lloyd George and the Pre-history of Appeasement*, Methuen, London, 1984

—— *Lloyd George, Woodrow Wilson and the Guilt of Germany*, Leicester University Press, Leicester, 1984

Loades, J. (ed.) *The Life and Times of David Lloyd George*, Headstart History, Bangor, 1991

MacDonald, J.R. *National Defence: A Study in Militarism*, The Office of The Herald, London, 1917

McIntyre, W.D. *The Rise and Fall of the Singapore Naval Base, 1919–1942*, Macmillan, London, 1979

McKercher, B.J.C. *Arms Limitation and Disarmament: Restraints on War, 1899–1939*, Praeger, Westport, Connecticut, 1992

—— *The Second Baldwin Government and the United States, 1924–1929*, Cambridge University Press/London School of Economics, London, 1984

McKercher, B.J.C. and Moss, D.J. (eds) *Shadow and Substance in British Foreign Policy*, University of Alberta Press, Edmonton, 1984

Madariaga, S. de *Disarmament*, Kennikat Press, Port Washington, 1967

Marks, S. *The Illusion of Peace: International Relations in Europe, 1918–1933*, Macmillan, London, 1976

Medlicott, W.N. *British Foreign Policy since Versailles, 1919–1963*, Methuen, London, 1968

Morgan, K.O. *Consensus and Disunity: The Lloyd George Coalition Government 1918–1922*, Clarendon Press, Oxford, 1979

Morgenthau, H.J. *Politics among Nations*, Alfred A Knopf, New York, 1984

Mowat, C.L. *Britain between the Wars, 1918–1940*, Methuen, London, 1955

Noel-Baker, P.J. *The Arms Race*, Calder, London, 1958

—— *Disarmament*, Pergamon Press, Oxford, 1979

—— *Disarmament and the Coolidge Conference*, Woolf, London, 1927

—— *The First World Disarmament Conference, 1932–33*, Pergamon Press, Oxford, 1979

—— *The Geneva Protocol for the Pacific Settlement of International Disputes*, King, London, 1925

Northedge, F.S. *The League of Nations: Its Life and Times 1920–1946*, Leicester University Press, Leicester, 1988 edn.

—— *The Troubled Giant*, Bell, London, 1966

O'Neill, R. and Schwartz, D.N. *Hedley Bull on Arms Control*, Macmillan, London, 1987

Orde, A. *Great Britain and International Security, 1920–1926*, Royal Historical Society, London, 1978

Peters, A.R. *Anthony Eden at the Foreign Office 1931–1938*, St Martin's Press, New York, 1986

Reynolds, P.A. *British Foreign Policy in the Inter-War Years*, Greenwood, Westport, Connecticut, 1974

Richardson, D. *The Evolution of British Disarmament Policy in the 1920s*, Pinter, London, 1989

—— *A History of Disarmament and Arms Control*, Routledge, London [forthcoming at time of publication]

Richardson, D. and Stone, G. (eds) *Decisions and Diplomacy: Essays in Twentieth-Century International History*, Routledge, London, 1995

Roskill, S.W. *Naval Policy between the Wars: The Period of Anglo-American Antagonism, 1919–1929*, Collins, London, 1968

Rostow, N. *Anglo-French Relations, 1934–36*, Macmillan, London, 1984

Taylor, A.J.P. *English History, 1914–1945*, Penguin, London, 1987

—— *The Origins of the Second World War*, Penguin, London, 1980

—— *The Trouble Makers: Dissent over Foreign Policy*, Panther Books, London, 1969

Vaïsse, M. *Sécurité d'abord*, Pedone, Paris, 1981

Vincent, Sir Graham *Stanley Baldwin and Rearmament, 1932–1938*, Unpublished typescript, Leeds University Library

Watt, D.C. *Personalities and Policies*, Longman, London, 1965

Wheeler-Bennett, J.W. *Disarmament and Security since Locarno, 1925–1931*, Allen and Unwin, London, 1932

—— *Information on the Reduction of Armaments*, Allen and Unwin, London, 1925

—— *Information on the Renunciation of War, 1927–1928*, Kennikat Press, New York, 1928

—— *The Pipe Dream of Peace*, Howard Fertig Inc., New York, 1971

Wheeler-Bennett, J.W. and Langermann F.E. *Information on the Problem of Security, (1917–1926)*, Allen and Unwin, London, 1927

Whittaker, D.J. *Fighter for Peace*, Sessions, York, 1989

Windrich, E. *British Labour's Foreign Policy*, Stanford University Press, Stanford, 1952

Articles

Carlton, D. 'Disarmament with Guarantees: Lord Cecil 1922–1927', *Disarmament and Arms Control*, 3, 2, Autumn 1965, pp. 143–64

Dockrill, M.L. 'Britain, the United States and France and the German Settlement, 1918–1920', in B. J.C. McKercher and D.J. Moss (eds), *Shadow and Substance in British Foreign Policy*, University of Alberta Press, Edmonton, 1984

Grun, G.A. 'Locarno: Idea and Reality', *International Affairs*, 31, 4, October 1955, pp. 477–85

Lentin, A. 'The Treaty that Never Was: Lloyd George and the Abortive Anglo-French Alliance of 1919' in J. Loades (ed.) *The Life and Times of David Lloyd George*, Headstart History, Bangor, 1991

Richardson, D. 'Process and Progress in Disarmament: some Lessons of History', in V. Harle and P. Sivonen (eds) *Europe in Transition*, Pinter Publishers, London, 1989

Richardson, D. and Kitching, C.J. 'Britain and the World Disarmament Conference', in P. Catterall and C.J. Morris (eds) *Britain and the Threat to Stability in Europe, 1918–45*, Leicester University Press, London, 1993

Sharp, A. 'Lloyd George and Foreign Policy, 1918–1922: The 'And Yet' Factor', in J. Loades, (ed.) *The Life and Times of David Lloyd George*, Headstart History, Bangor, 1991

Steiner, Z. 'The League of Nations and the Quest for Security', in R. Ahmann, A. M. Birke and M. Howard (eds) *The Quest for Stability: Problems of West European Security 1918–1957*, The German Historical Institute London, Oxford University Press, 1993

Towle, P. 'British Security and Disarmament Policy in Europe in the 1920s', in R. Ahmann, A. M. Birke and M. Howard (eds) *The Quest for Stability: Problems of*

West European Security 1918–1957, The German Historical Institute London, Oxford University Press, 1993

Theses

Richardson, R.C. *The Problem of Disarmament in British Diplomacy 1932–1934*, University of British Columbia, MA, 1969

Segal, E.B. *Sir John Simon and British Foreign Policy: The Diplomacy of Disarmament in the Early 1930s*, University of California, Ph.D., 1964

Shorney, D.J. *Britain and Disarmament 1916–1931*, Durham University, Ph.D., 1980

Underwood, J.J. *The Roots and Reality of British Disarmament Policy 1932–34*, University of Leeds, Ph.D., 1977

Wolf, B.R. *Viscount Cecil: A Reign of Peace through the League of Nations*, Purdue University, Ph.D., 1985

INDEX